This book provides an introduction to the positive theory of the budgetary process based on the theory of public choice. Although budgetary institutions are very diverse, both between and within countries, it is possible to identify key elements which are common to all forms of representative government. The author identifies these key elements as the supply of services by public agencies; demand for services by political bodies (cabinet, houses of parliament, etc.); negotiation between administrators of agencies and political bodies in an 'internal market'; and decision-making in the form of budgetary and substantive legislation. The book develops a step-by-step model which incorporates all these elements, a model which can be used to explain and predict budgetary decisions in existing institutions, as well as to analyse institutional change, including cost budgeting and various forms of privatization.

Budgetary decisions

Budgetary decisions

A public choice approach

Dirk-Jan Kraan

350.722
K89b

Published by the Press Syndicate of the University of Cambridge
The Pitt Building, Trumpington Street, Cambridge CB2 1RP
40 West 20th Street, New York, NY 10011-4211, USA
10 Stamford Road, Oakleigh, Melbourne 3166, Australia

First published 1996

Printed in Great Britain at the University Press, Cambridge

A catalogue record for this book is available from the British Library

Library of Congress cataloguing in publication data

Kraan, D.-J. (Dirk-Jan), 1947–
Budgetary decisions: a public choice approach / Dirk-Jan Kraan.
    p.   cm.
Includes bibliographical references.
ISBN 0 521 41871 2
1. Budget process. I. Title.
HJ2009.K7 1995
350.72'22 – dc20 95-833 CIP

ISBN 0 521 41871 2 hardback
ISBN 0 521 55867 0 paperback

JK

VN

Contents

Contents

Foreword

Public Choice should be a tool for improved management of the government. Dr Kraan has taken a major step in this direction by applying it to the actual process of budgeting. The book is not only a step forward in theory, it should be a major step towards making Public Choice a practical aid to a number of officials and politicians.

Speaking for myself, one of the more important aspects of this book is that it indicates that a lot of theoretical work which was actually developed to a large extent by Americans looking at the open American government also applies to European governments, although there things are less open. This is no surprise to me. I had always thought this was true, but I am delighted to have evidence instead of having to depend on my instincts. Here, again, Kraan has made a major step forward and pointed the way to what we hope will be considerable additional research.

There are also fairly sizeable theoretical improvements here. Relying on his experience, Kraan argues that the bureaucracy, in those areas where the differences among politicians are not too great, plays a constructive role. It tends to clarify and bring together the positions of the politicians, with the result that the endless cycling which may be regarded as the inevitable consequence of the Arrow theorem does not occur. In those cases where the differences among politicians are sizeable, Kraan follows a hint from the 'Calculus of Consent', arguing that as long as all of the proposals are for increasing the budget it is possible for log-rolling to lead to a definite outcome.

This book, then, is both of considerable scholarly importance, and a practical guide. I should say that my efforts to get earlier drafts of it read by American budget officials were mainly unsuccessful. This is not due to any inadequacy of the officials. Most of them are almost continuously engaged in what we call 'fire-fighting'. This simply means that they are heavily occupied with very short-range problems that have to be solved immediately. I presume the same is true in most European budgetary areas, with the result that the people in the field tend to be unable to do much reading of new material and depend on a gradually fading memory of what they learned in college.

It would seem to me that Kraan's book should first be introduced into public finance courses in universities as a combination of practical and theoretical approach to an important problem. But secondly, and I think even more important, it seems to me that a good many budgetary agencies would be well advised to work out a way for their serving officials actually to read it.

Gordon Tullock

Karl Eller Professor
of Economics and Political Science
University of Arizona

Preface

how-to

Public finance always was a normatively oriented subject of study. Modern textbooks about 'public economics' build on this tradition but intersperse exposition about normative themes with pieces of analysis about the actual course of decision-making. In that approach, the positive sections serve to add a flavour of pragmatism to the main arguments about 'motives for public intervention' and 'optimal allocation'. This Introduction moves the opposite way: it focuses on the positive theory of the budgetary process and adds some pieces of normative analysis by way of critical perspective. For those who are interested in positive analysis, this approach has the advantage that the relevant theoretical ideas can be developed systematically and in their natural order.

The positive economic theory of the budgetary process belongs, by method and subject, to the field of 'public choice theory'. This exposition builds particularly on two important themes of that field, namely the model of legislative demand and the model of agency supply. However, no prior knowledge of public choice theory is assumed; all relevant concepts and ideas are introduced and developed in the text. The only desirable prerequisite is an elementary knowledge of microeconomic theory.

This book is conceived as a systematic introduction to the positive theory of the budgetary process. As such, it aims to serve a double purpose: it should be suitable for use in a public finance or public economics course for economics students, possibly alongside a more normatively oriented textbook, and it should be useful to public sector economists who want to improve their knowledge of positive theory. Of course, the book should also be useful as a source of reference for public choice analysts. To them, the material covered will mostly be familiar, although there are some new ideas, especially in the sphere of bureaucratic behaviour and the role of institutions.

A large part of this book was written while I was working in the Directorate General of the Budget at the Ministry of Finance of the

Netherlands. This involved a considerable constraint on the precious time that is normally available for more relaxed activities, but there were also advantages. The job provided great inspiration for the ideas in the book, and the elaboration of the ideas in the book could often be used in the job. Budget bureaux typically exhibit a great common sense knowledge of the routines and mechanisms of public choice. Indeed, there exists no school where one can learn so much about the reality of political and administrative decision-making. It is, (of course,) the business of science to translate common sense knowledge into theory and, in so doing, to discover structures, connections and inferences that might otherwise remain obscure. However, without a sound basis in common sense knowledge ('intuition' as it is usually called by academics), theory construction becomes a sterile activity that is valueless from a practical as well as from a theoretical perspective.

I thank the colleagues in academia as well as in the Ministry who have read (parts of) the texts and provided comments. I want to name a few of them. Melvin Hinich long ago taught me the principles of game theory at Virginia Polytechnic Institutute, and has been a helpful and stimulating advisor ever since; he has provided many important ideas during the ongoing evolution of this book. Jo Ritzen gave many important suggestions, not only concerning the content of the arguments, but also concerning their presentation. Gordon Tullock was a stimulating critic in various stages of the preparation of the manuscript and, as ever, came up with many ideas. Christiaan Ruppert read some chapters and made useful comments concerning the structure of the volume. I am grateful for all these comments and emphasize, as usual, that none of the commentators is responsible for any remaining faults and errors. Furthermore, I thank Nathalie de Kievit for the perseverance and the meticulousness that she showed during the preparation of the typescript.

Finally, I wish to mention the great moral support by Leonoor and Oscar. They tolerated my seclusion from family life during uncountable evenings, weekends and holidays. Leonoor also gave great help preparing the typescript. Without her support and cheerful attitude this book would not have been written.

1 Introduction

Perspectives on budgetary decision-making

The subject of this book is the analysis of the budgetary process in representative government from the perspective of public choice theory. Since there is a large literature on the budgetary process as well as on public choice theory, it seems appropriate to start with some clarification about the place of the present volume within both areas of scholarly activity.

The budgetary process in representative government is a theme which is being studied from different theoretical perspectives, public choice theory being only one of them. Looking at the postwar literature, four main perspectives can be distinguished.

The first is the normative perspective. This has been characteristic of the mainstream public finance literature, as exemplified, for instance, by the seminal handbook by R.A. Musgrave (1959). The central concern in this literature has been the application of welfare theoretical principles to the budgetary decisions of government. Major new developments in this literature originated in revisions of welfare theory itself. One can think, for instance, of the generalization of the conditions for optimal allocation of public goods, as initiated by Samuelson (1954), and the development of a new approach to social welfare functions (so-called 'social choice theory'), as initiated by Arrow (1951).

Within the normative literature there is also a more practically oriented current, alongside the welfare theoretic branch. This is the area of financial management that gave rise to procedural innovations such as the Planning–Programming–Budget–System (PPBS), Management by Objectives (MBO) and Zero-Base-Budgeting (ZBB) in the USA, Programme Analysis and Review (PAR) and the Financial Management Initiative in the UK and the Reconsideration Procedure in the Netherlands. When Key in 1940 lamented 'the lack of a budgetary theory' concerning the question 'On what basis shall it be decided to allocate x dollars to activity A rather than

1

activity B?', he was probably referring to the aridity of ideas then prevailing in this practical sphere.[1] Since then, many ideas have been developed, described, implemented and abandoned again. A few have also been maintained, although it is not certain that present-day decision-makers are any better equipped to decide about the allocation of x dollars to activity A rather than activity B than they were in 1940. However this may be, the blame can no longer be put on the lack of ideas.

It is probably realistic to say that until quite recently the normative perspective, either in its welfare theoretical or in its financial management variant has been the dominant perspective in the literature about budgetary decision-making. The other three perspectives, including that of public choice theory, are based on a positive approach towards the budgetary process. The primary concern of these perspectives is the explanation and prediction, not the evaluation and improvement, of budgetary decisions. The distinction between the positive perspectives arises from their roots in different theoretical ideas, namely those of political systems theory, of organizational process theory and of microeconomic (more specifically, public choice) theory.

Political systems theory, as initiated by Easton (1953), has given rise to a research programme on budgetary decision-making which is known as 'output studies'. The central concern of this literature is the explanation of budgetary decisions, conceived as 'outputs' of the political system in the Eastonian sense, as a function of 'environment' and 'system characteristics'. Environmental factors relevant for budgetary decisions are, for instance, demographic conditions, unemployment and distribution of primary income. Systems characteristics are, for instance, interparty competition, voter turnout and distribution of seats in the legislature among the parties. The work that has been done in this research programme is largely empirical and focuses on the cross-sectional analysis of budgetary decisions of local governments. A central theme is the 'politics versus economics' controversy, in which some authors have concluded that politics is largely irrelevant for the outcomes of the budgetary process and others that it is a crucial factor alongside environmental (mainly economic) factors. The publications by Dye and Sharkansky are among the most influential in this area. The major criticism that has been raised against this perspective concerns the weak logical coherence of Eastonian systems theory. Since this theory lacks sufficient deductive structure to enable the analyst to reason from assumptions to inferences and hypotheses, it serves better as a 'language' for the systematic description of certain political phenomena than as a source of hypotheses that can be tested, and possibly falsified, in empirical work.

The organizational process perspective on budgetary decision-making was developed in the 1960s by Davis, Dempster and Wildavsky. This perspective has yielded a large and important literature that has increased our insights in the dynamics of the budgetary process and the motivations and strategies of decision-makers. It is seen by many authors as the principal alternative to the public choice perspective (and by some authors as the preferable alternative), although it will be argued below that both perspectives can also be seen as complementary.

In the organizational process literature, three aspects of the budgetary process are at the centre of interest:
1. Methods of problem-solving by individual decision-makers
2. Patterns of interaction among decision-makers
3. Actual outcomes (in monetary terms) of the various stages of the process, such as agency requests to the executive budget bureau or the minister of Finance, requests by the supreme executive authority to the legislature and final appropriations.

As far as methods of problem-solving are concerned, the organizational process perspective has its roots in the behavioural theory of decision-making as developed in the 1950s and 1960s by authors like Braybrooke, Cyert, Lindblom, March and Simon. Key concepts are 'bounded rationality' and 'disjointed incrementalism'. Budgetary decision-makers characterized by bounded rationality do not optimize the objective variables of the decision problem but 'satisfice' acceptable boundaries for those variables. To that end, they apply 'incremental' methods by focusing on a small number of policy alternatives that can be realized by small adjustments of the existing situation.

As far as patterns of interaction are concerned, the key concept is 'mutual adjustment'. According to Wildavsky (1964), the budgetary process is characterized by 'role differentiation' among decision-makers. This gives rise to such roles as 'guardian' and 'advocate', 'generalist' and 'specialist', 'decision-maker of first resort' and 'appeal court'. Actors hold 'partial views of the public interest' and 'take the base for granted' (the base is the existing funding level). It is essential that they be capable of making short-range, pragmatic, non-ideological compromises through mutual adjustment, because otherwise conflict breaks out and the process comes to a halt.

In organizational process theory, outcomes are a consequence of methods of problem-solving and patterns of interaction. There has been some confusion about the structure of the theory in this respect. Dempster and Wildavsky (1979) have stressed that their version of the theory – known as 'budgetary incrementalism' – is based upon assumptions about methods of problem-solving and patterns of interaction rather than about outcomes. From these assumptions, interesting and testable hypotheses about outcomes can be derived.

Davis, Dempster and Wildavsky have in particular explored some hypotheses about the request decisions of US federal agencies and about the appropriations decisions of the US Congress. According to these hypotheses, budgetary outcomes develop according to linear trends, with different growth parameters for different agencies. This growth pattern is due to the fact that the actors behave 'as if' they were using linear decision rules: agencies request each year a fixed, agency-specific percentual increase over last year's appropriation (the 'base') or over last year's request, and the political authorities subtract each year a fixed, agency-specific percentual margin from the requested increase (the 'basic incremental model', see Davis, Dempster and Wildavsky, 1966a, 1966b, 1971). The occurrence of occasional shifts in the growth parameters is acknowledged. In later work, these shifts are accounted for as consequences of a number of exogenous political and economic factors (the 'extended incremental model', see Davis, Dempster and Wildavsky, 1974; Wildavsky, 1974). In another version of organizational process theory, appropriations increases and decreases are dependent on the needs for the services that an agency supplies and, given a fixed revenue constraint, on the needs for the services of all other agencies (the 'trade-off model', see, for instance, Crecine, Kamlet, Mowery and Winer, 1981; Fisher and Kamlet, 1984; Kamlet and Mowery, 1987).

In general, it is characteristic of organizational process theory that the budgetary process is conceived of as a stable routine, that is fairly resistent to external shocks, and that adjusts itself only gradually to changes in environmental circumstances. Organizational process theory has little to say about outcomes that cannot be explained in this way.

The public choice perspective makes use of the conceptual and analytical apparatus of microeconomic theory and, more specifically, of public choice theory. Key concepts that can serve to illuminate the basic differences *vis-à-vis* the organizational process perspective are 'rationality', 'competence' and 'strategic interaction'.

Public choice theory is the microeconomic theory of government, and shares with other branches of microeconomic theory the assumption of individual rationality. According to this assumption decision-makers in government are capable of optimizing their choices in terms of their preferences. This does not mean that members of political authorities and administrators are always completely informed about the consequences of the choice alternatives, but it does imply that they are willing to use, and capable of using, available information to its full advantage, provided that the required effort is a sensible investment on its own account. It also implies that decision-makers can make up their minds to begin with, in other words that they are capable of ordering the potential consequences of the choice alternatives in terms of their individual preferences in a consistent way. In these respects, the assumption stands in contrast to the assumption of bounded rationality in organizational process theory.

Furthermore, in public choice theory, the set of choice alternatives available to each decision-maker is determined by the formal competences of the authorities to which they belong. These competences are described in legal rules which are part of the 'economic constitution' of government. In public choice theory, the decision-makers make optimal use of the competences granted to them in accordance with their preferences. The concept of 'competence' in public choice theory is comparable to that of 'role' in organizational process theory, but because of its definition in terms of legal rules, rather than of social expectations, it gives rise to a sharper delineation of the set of choice alternatives available to each decision-maker.

The concept of strategic interaction, finally, refers to the fact that in government decision-makers are usually cooperating in small groups, so that each individual vote has a noticeable effect on collective outcomes. Consequently, each actor is able to anticipate the reactions of other actors to her own choices. This characteristic implies that public choice theory has to rely strongly on game theory, which is the analytical apparatus for the study of interactive decision-making. The concept of strategic interaction plays a comparable role in public choice theory to that of mutual adjustment in organizational process theory, but it lacks the connotation of 'compromising' and does not exclude certain more aggressive strategies that are aimed at 'winning' a political or administrative struggle rather than at a smooth conduct of affairs.

Although there were some forerunners, public choice theory was developed primarily in the postwar period. In this period, it gradually extended its scope to all types of decision-making in all types of governments. As far as the budgetary process in representative government is concerned, two models are particularly relevant: (1) the model of legislative demand, and (2) the model of agency supply.

According to the model of legislative demand, the budgetary decisions of a political committee depend upon the individual demand for publicly provided services by each politician in the committee, on the voting and agenda rules for the committee, and upon the nature of the prevailing bargaining and coalition-building process. In a representative democracy, demand by the individual politician is supposed to be related to demand by the citizenry, but the nature of this relation can be modelled in different ways. In general, individual demand by an elected politician is assumed to be related to the preferences, tax prices of the services and incomes of electoral supporters as well as of the politician herself.

Whereas the model of legislative demand focuses on political demand under the condition of given tax prices for publicly provided services, the model of agency supply focuses on tax prices for publicly provided services under the condition of given political demand. According to the latter model, tax prices are set by bureaucrats who hold authority over public production units. They are dependent on the production cost of the services, on the demand for the services by politicians, on the structure of the internal market in which the bureaucrats sell the services to the politicians, and on the objectives of the bureaucrats. As far as market structure is concerned, relevant aspects are the bilateral monopoly character of the market and the information available to the bureaucrats about political preferences, and to the politicians about real production costs. As far as the objectives of bureaucrats are concerned, relevant aspects are the interests that they may have in providing protection to their clients in the private sector, and the opportunities to provide such protection arising from the nature of the services.

The differences between the public choice and organizational process perspectives lead to three mutually connected consequences. First, in the public choice perspective the emphasis is on the micro- level of analysis, in the organizational process perspective it is on the macro-level. In spite of the assurance by Wildavsky *et al.* that their version of organizational process theory is based on assumptions about problem-solving and patterns of interaction with respect to individual decision-makers, the link between between micro and macro remains weak. This is already apparent from the fact that organization process models often make use of ad hoc variables concerning the politicial system or the political orientation of incumbent political parties, with little foundation in theoretical ideas. Conversely, the public choice perspective has much more to say about budgetary decisions at the level of separate political and administrative officers and bodies than about final outcomes of the budgetary process. In other words, the link between micro and macro is weak in the public choice perspective as well, but here the important ideas and empirical results have to be sought at the micro- rather than at the macro-level. In this respect, one is reminded of the distinction between the macroeconomic and micro-economic theories of market behaviour as it existed in the heyday of Keynesianism: there also the micro-foundations of macro-theories were weak, non-existent or non-economic (in the sense of not being based on rational individual behaviour), and micro-theories had little to say about aggregate outcomes such as price levels, growth or employment. Only since the upsurge of neoclassical macroeconomics in the 1970s did attention begin to be be paid to the systematic (re)construction of macroeconomic theory on the basis of microeconomic assumptions. In the area of budgetary behaviour, attempts in that direction have only recently begun to be made.

Eventually, this may lead to a certain degree of integration of both perspectives.

Secondly, there is a different orientation of empirical work. As far as outcomes are concerned, organizational process research is largely concerned with data about decisions of administrative and political authorities, such as request estimates from agencies and final appropriations by the legislature. These data are used to test hypotheses either by cross-sectional or by time-series analysis. Public choice research usually requires less aggregated output data, for instance about the votes of individual members of a political body or the production costs of a particular service. Furthermore, public choice research often makes use of experimental data about bargaining processes. Such data have to be obtained from simulation experiments which are carried out under carefully controlled conditions, often in a laboratory setting. Another current of empirical public choice research is concerned with the objectives and preferences of elected officials and administrators of public agencies. This work is directed at the testing of the crucial assumptions about objective functions in public choice models.

Thirdly, the policy relevance of the public choice perspective is usually more straightforward than that of the organizational process perspective. This difference is due to the crucial role that decision rules play in public choice theory. One can think of the notion of 'competence' which is modelled as a condition on the set of choice alternatives of a political or administrative actor, and on the voting and agenda rules which are modelled as important determinants of decisions in committees. If outcomes are determined by decision rules, outcomes can be changed by changing the rules. This simple implication explains how the public choice perspective has given rise to a normative branch of its own. This branch has recently become known as 'constitutional economics', and is growing into a field of scientific inquiry in its own right. The policy relevance of organizational process theory is less straightforward. Because this theory leans strongly on assumptions about human behaviour of a fundamental psychological nature (methods of problem-solving, patterns of interaction), there is no easy connection to a more policy oriented approach. Although individual authors have sometimes ventured into the sphere of policy advice – think, for instance, of Wildavsky's (1980) pleas for a constitutional restriction on the deficit for the US federal government – the general attitude of the scholars in this field seems to be rather detached and more directed at understanding than at policy advice.

It has to be added to this observation that on closer examination the policy relevance of the public choice perspective is more problematic than might be thought at first sight. In this respect, there has been a gradual shift of methodological position. Whereas the traditional public finance analyst is willing to offer policy advice on concrete budgetary decisions on the basis of welfare theoretical criteria, the public choice analyst considers such advice as pointless because it supposes that there is some 'benevolent despot' in government who is willing to listen to such advice. Indeed, it is the main thrust of public choice theory that in concrete political systems, be they representative government or less democratic forms, such omnipotent, benevolent actors are not around, and that it is therefore necessary to study the competences and motivations of real decision-makers. However, if this approach subsequently leads to policy advice about the constitutional structure of the political system, the more radically minded public choice analyst will object that such advice in turn presupposes the presence of some 'benevolent constitutioner', which does not seem entirely realistic either.

There is much to say about this discussion, but it is not necessary to do so here. The position taken in this volume is that normative analysis makes sense, and is necessary at the level of regular budgetary policy (what are optimal budgetary decisions?) as well as of constitutional policy (what are optimal budgetary institutions, that is decision rules that produce optimal budgetary decisions?). However, the results of these kinds of analysis cannot directly be translated into policy advice, but should rather be used as a yardstick for the evaluation of proposals. In this respect, the approach pursued is in agreement with the radical public choice position that policy advice does not makes sense, at either the level of budgetary choice or at the level of constitutional choice, if it runs counter to the interests of the decision-makers. However, it is acknowledged that the constitutional economists are right in that there is usually more convergence among the interests of the decision-makers at the level of constitutional choice than at the level of budgetary choice, and therefore less distance between what is normatively desirable and what is practically feasible.[2] This volume will largely be concerned with the positive analysis of the budgetary process, but in order to emphasize the inherent policy relevance of the public choice perspective I shall feel free to insert considerations of a more normative nature, and I shall conclude with a chapter (chapter 8) about some concrete 'constitutional' proposals for improvements in the sphere of financial management and the organization of public production that are currently being discussed and implemented in many governments of the western world.

What kind of public choice theory?

After what has been said about the place of the public choice perspective in the budgetary literature, some remarks about the place of budgetary decision-making in the public choice literature are now in order.

This volume will focus on the models of legislative demand and agency supply as the basic public choice models on budgetary decision-making in representative government. However, even apart from the fields of non-democratic government and direct democracy, there are also other kinds of decision-making in representative government and, accordingly, other models in public choice theory. In order to get a better view of the specific nature and relevance of the models mentioned, it is helpful to take a step back and take a look at the structure of representative government as a whole.

It is characteristic of representative government that there are at least two, and usually three, levels of political decision-making – by the electorate, by the representative assembly (Parliament, Congress, City Council, etc.) and, usually, by the supreme executive authority (Cabinet, President, Governor, Mayor, etc.). Only in the so-called 'conventional system' of representative government, which exists in some countries at the level of local government, is an autonomous executive authority substituted by an appointed board or administrator (for instance, a 'city manager') under the direct hierarchical control of the representative assembly.[3] Alongside the political branch of government there is an administrative branch, which takes care of the production of public services. It typically consists of a number of separate agencies. These agencies may fall under hierarchical control of the supreme executive authority or the representative assembly, but may also enjoy a large degree of autonomy, depending on the structure of the administrative branch in each specific government. Finally, in some governments, there is a judicial branch, which typically consists of a number of independent courts and justices.

The competences of the political, administrative and judicial authorities are defined in the constitution. In the case of central government, some competence rules can be found in the legal document that is known under that name, but in general the legal concept, which is defined by procedural criteria, differs from the substantive concept, which is defined by political and economic criteria. The latter concept is the 'economic constitution', as referred to above. Apart from competence rules, the economic constitution contains participation and procedural rules. The participation rules describe the composition and conditions of access to the political, administrative and judicial authorities (including the rules for access to the electorate), and the procedural rules describe the way in which the collective decisions of the political, administrative and judicial authorities are derived from the (individual) votes of their members (including the electoral systems used for decisions by the electorate about the appointment of members of the representative assembly).

The competences attributed to the political, administrative and judicial authorities of a representative government are of various types. In connection with the budgetary process, two types are particularly important, namely those concerning budgetary and administrative decisions.

Budgetary decisions concern the authorization of financial flows into and out of governmental funds, including taxation. In a representative government, budgetary competence is mainly vested in the legislature. Accordingly, budgetary decisions are made by (the chambers of) the representative assembly, subject to approval or veto by the supreme executive authority. Usually, there is also a constitutional provision which requires the supreme executive authority to submit a proposal for an integrated annual budget to the legislature, even in governments where legislative proposals do not normally originate with the supreme executive authority, such as the US federal government.

Administrative decisions concern the production of services in public agencies. One must think on the one hand of the multitude of managerial decisions required to organize and run a production process (internal administrative decisions), and on the other of the decisions concerning the economic characteristics (quantities, qualities, prices) of the services to be produced, and the production factors and intermediate products to be used (external administrative decisions). Administrative competence of this kind is attributed to the administrators of public agencies, and can be delegated to hierarchically subordinate officials.

Public choice theory aims at the development of empirically relevant models for the exercise of all types of competences by all types of political, administrative and judicial authorities. Some kinds of decision-making have clearly been studied more intensively than others. The model of legislative demand applies to the budgetary decisions by the (chambers and committees of the) representative assembly and the supreme executive authority, and the model of agency supply applies to the external administrative decisions by the administrators of public agencies. These models are important because they are concerned with crucial elements of the budgetary process which, moreover, can be identified in every form of representative government.

It should be noted, though, that in most governments the budgetary process consists of more than single-shot decisions by representative assemblies, executive authorities and administrators of public agencies. Typically, this process consists of many phases, each of which is ruled by a quite complicated set of decision rules. Furthermore, even within the general category of representative government, these rules differ substantially between governments. It is well known, for instance, that in the US federal government the bargaining processes between both Houses of Congress and between each House and the President are of paramount importance. Within Congress, there is a strict division of competences among various kinds of committees involved in budgetary matters (authorizing committees, appropriations committees, financial committees and budget committees), which gives rise to bargaining processes between the committees. For none of these processes is there a close analogue in European parliamentary systems, such as those of the UK and the Netherlands. In the latter governments, on the other hand, the Cabinet is an influential decision-making body, which has no close analogue in the American system. The models of legislative demand and agency supply are concerned with only some phases of the budgetary process. These models are therefore not enough to explain or predict budgetary outcomes in any actual government. For the latter purpose, one would need a system-specific model that would cover all relevant phases of decision-making in the particular government under investigation. It is not the aim of the present volume to develop such a model. The aim is rather the exploration of models for elements of the budgetary process that are common to all forms of representative government.

Design of the volume

The present volume will treat the models of legislative demand and agency supply in a way that emphasizes the common conceptual apparatus and assumptions of both models. This makes it possible to present also an integrated model that treats demand as well as supply, and that focuses on the working of the 'internal market' for public services.

Chapter 2 provides an economic characterization of the budgetary process in representative government and identifies the particular phases of that process to which the models apply. Chapters 3–5 are concerned with the systematic development of the models of legislative demand and agency supply. Chapter 3 treats an elementary model of public demand by a single politician for public services available at a constant tax price. Chapter 4 presents the basic model of agency supply, which applies to a single bureaucrat, who decides about the tax price of a service to be sold to a single politician. Chapter 5 presents the basic legislative demand model, which applies to a committee of politicians with different preferences that decides about the demand for public services available at constant tax prices. For this purpose the chapter introduces the required elements of game theory. Readers who have some acquaintance with public choice theory will find many familiar themes in these chapters, but also some new ideas.

Chapters 6 and 7 build on the basic models and present some integrated models. Chapter 6 treats a model which applies to a number of bureaucrats, each of whom decides about the tax price of a service that she sells to a committee of politicians. This model makes it possible to examine interaction between politicians, between bureaucrats, and between politicians on the one hand and bureaucrats on the other. The resulting model does not in general induce a stable outcome and supports the hypothesis that the bargaining skills of the actors are a primary determinant of budgetary outcomes. This is a familiar hypothesis from public choice models of political decision-making. However, although this hypothesis has not been refuted in any general sense by empirical work, the trend in public choice analysis during the 1980s has still been to search for stability-enhancing mechanisms. Especially among empirically oriented scholars, there is a strong suspicion that under many institutional conditions the adage that 'anything can happen' does not apply. Chapter 7 treats some particular institutions in the sphere of formal or informal 'agenda rules' for political committees that might contribute to stability, and discusses the limitations to the impact of these rules that follow from the basic assumptions of the legislative demand model. This chapter also looks at some normative properties of agenda rules from a welfare theoretic point of view.

Chapter 8 provides some ideas about institutional reform, and concludes with a short reconsideration of the public choice perspective in view of the results attained.

As far as the style of argument is concerned, the usual dilemma of how to combine readability with a necessary mimimum of logical rigour is solved in the following way. The main text presents the argument almost entirely in verbal format. The models will also be formulated in symbolic notation, but the working of each model is suggested in outline by use of graphical illustrations. Numerical examples, as well as some proofs, are provided in the mathematical appendix. Hopefully this compromise will help to attract and retain the interest of readers with a practically oriented interest in budgetary matters who are emphatically included in the purported audience of the volume.

Guide to the literature
Some well-known studies of the budgetary process from the perspective of political systems theory ('output studies') are Dye, *Politics, Economics and the Public: Policy Outcomes in the American States* (1966) and Sharkansky, *Spending in the American States* (1968). A survey of the literature on the basis of this perspective is provided by Boyne, 'Theory, methodology and results in political science: the case of output studies' (1985). Some studies in the area of the behavioural theory of decision-making that have inspired the organizational process perspective on budgetary decision-making, are Braybrook and Lindblom, *A Strategy of Decision* (1963); Cyert and March, *Behavioural Theory of the Firm* (1963); Lindblom 'The

science of muddling through' (1959), *The Intelligence of Democracy: Decision-making Through Mutual Adjustment* (1965), *The Policy-making process* (1968); March and Simon, *Organizations* (1958); and Simon, *Administrative Behaviour: A Study of Decision-making Processes in Administrative Organization* (1945), *Models of Man* (1957), 'Theories of decision-making in economics and behavioral science' (1959), *The New Science of Management Decision* (1960). The organizational process perspective on budgetary decision-making was in the first place developed in Wildavsky, *The Politics of the Budgetary Process* (1964). See also the sequel to this seminal study, *The New Politics of the Budgetary Process* (1988), which takes account of the development of budgetary practice in the USA since the 1964 edition. Empirical results in support of incremental models were reported in Davis, Dempster and Wildavsky, 'A theory of the budgetary process' (1966a), 'On the process of budgeting: an empirical study of Congressional appropriations' (1966b), and 'On the process of budgeting II: an empirical study of Congressional appropriations' (1971). A reply to critical comments on some of these results is given in Dempster and Wildavsky, 'On change: or, there is no magic size of an increment' (1979). Empirical results in support of the 'extended incremental model' were reported in Davis, Dempster and Wildavsky, 'Towards a predictive theory of government expenditure: US domestic appropriations' (1974) and Wildavsky, *Budgeting: A Comparative Theory of Budgetary Processes* (1975). Trade-off models have been developed and tested in Russet, 'Who pays for defense?' (1969); Crecine, Kamlet, Mowery and Winer, 'The role of the US Office of Management and Budget in executive branch budgetary decision-making' (1981); Domke, Eichenberg and Kelleher, 'The illusion of choice: defense and welfare in advanced industrial democracies' (1983); Auten, Bozeman and Cline, 'A sequential model of Congressional appropriations' (1984); Fisher and Kamlet, 'Explaining presidential priorities: the competing aspirations level of macro-budgetary decision-making' (1984); Kamlet and Mowery, 'Influences on executive and Congressional budgetary priorities 1955–1981' (1987); and Kamlet, Mowery and Su, 'Upsetting national priorities: the Reagan Administration's budgetary strategy' (1988).

Comparisons of the organizational process and public choice perspectives on the budgetary process that conclude in favour of the former are Thompson and Williams, 'A horse race around a Mobius strip: a review and test of utility maximizing and organizational process models of public expenditure decisions' (1979) and Downs and Larkey, 'Theorizing about public expenditure decision-making: (as) if wishes were horses' (1979). An interesting contribution about the relation between micro- and macrobehaviour from a more general perspective is Schelling, *Micromotives and Macro Behavior* (1978). A certain degree of integration of both perspectives can be found in papers that attempt to discover a public choice explanation for macro-budgetary regularities that have been found in organizational process research. Examples are Kiewiet and McCubbins, 'Appropriations decisions as a bilateral bargaining game between President and Congress' (1985a) and 'Congressional appropriations and the electoral connection' (1985b).

The sensibility of normative reasoning about budgetary decisions within a given constitutional structure was originally put in question by Buchanan. Key papers in this respect are Buchanan, 'Positive economics, welfare economics and political economy' (1959), 'Politics, policy and the Pigovian margins' (1962) and 'Toward analysis of closed behavioral systems' (1972). The 'constitutional' approach to policy reform was developed in Buchanan, 'Constitutional economics' (1987) and 'The achievements and limits of public choice in diagnosing government failure and in offering bases for constructive reform' (1983). See also Buchanan (ed.), *Explorations into Constitutional Economics* (1989).

2 The structure of the budgetary process

Demand and supply in the public sector

Market economies are characterized by the public protection of private property rights. In such economies, goods can be alienated only on the basis of mutual agreement between proprietors. Usually such alienation involves exchange between suppliers and demanders, where suppliers are households that want to sell certain economic goods at a certain price and demanders are households that want to purchase certain economic goods at a certain price. The exchange decision is a contract that specifies quantities and sums of money to be transferred. The term 'market mechanism' is commonly used to denote the rule that relates the result of a contract or a set of contracts to the characteristics of demand and supply.

However, many households in market economies consist of more than a single individual. As far as the private sector is concerned, one can think of business corporations, families, foundations and associations. As far as the public sector is concerned, one can think of governments and incorporated public agencies. Since such a collective houshold can own property, it needs a mechanism of internal coordination in order to express its demand or supply in markets.

The term 'budget mechanism' is commonly used to denote the rule that relates the characteristics of demand or supply by a collective houshold to the preferences of its members. Note that the budget mechanism is not an alternative for the market mechanism, but rather a necessary complement to it for the case a household comprises more than a single individual.

In order to coordinate its members, a collective houshold needs decision rules that specify how binding collective decisions are to be made. For this purpose, these rules must not only indicate how collective decisions are to be derived from sets of individual decisions (for instance, by establishing an 'absolute majority'), but also whose individual decisions have to be taken

15

into account to begin with. In the latter area, two classes of actors must be identified:
1. Those whose individual decisions carry a certain weight in the counting procedure specified by the decision rule
2. Those whose individual decisions do not enter the counting procedure at all, although they are bound by the result.

The members of the former class make up the decision-making body or 'authority'.

Participation in collective decision-making can be wide or narrow. A referendum is an example of a decision in which the entire electorate participates. Most decision-making competences in governments, however, are attributed to relatively small bodies (ranging from two to perhaps 600 members) or to single officers. Whether participation is wide or narrow, if we want to explain collective decisions, we have to look at the underlying individual decisions and to study the working of decision rules.

Individual decisions as contributions to collective decisions are known as 'votes'.[1] It must be emphasized at the outset that a 'vote' in this sense is a theoretical concept that should not be identified with the practical act of issuing a vote. Incidentally, voting takes place by raising hands, or standing up, or by pronouncing 'yeas' and 'nays', but by far the largest part of votes is expressed by silent acquiescence when the chairman of a body states a conclusion.

A decision rule of particular interest is the one that reduces participation to the absolute minimum of a single officer. The decisions of the officers who decide by this rule, regardless of whether it concerns the President of the United States or a humble civil servant, are collective decisions, although they are taken by single persons.

Until the beginning of the 1970s government was mainly conceived in economic literature as a consumption household. This conception eliminated the need for a separate theory of public supply. Public economics basically consisted of a theory of public demand revelation in external markets.[2] This view was challenged by Niskanen's seminal 1971 study on the economic theory of bureaucracy (Niskanen, 1971). In that book, a model of public decision-making was developed that treated public agencies as separate economic households engaged in selling services to political committees, representing the consumers. This approach amounted to the conceptual breaking up of the governmental household into a number of production households on the one hand and a consumption household on the other. Niskanen's view implied the existence within government of internal markets where 'bureaux' were selling services to political 'sponsors'.

Niskanen's view does not lead to a theory of collective decision-making.

Essentially, his proposed theory of bureaucracy is concerned with market decision-making. By conceiving public agencies as separate economic households, Niskanen had, as it were, transformed hierarchical relations between authorities of the same household into contractual relations between authorities of different households. This conception enabled Niskanen to apply a known microeconomic theory (that of discriminating monopoly in private sector markets) to the transactions in the internal markets of government and to shed a new light on some important aspects of the allocative and distributive process within the public sector.

Budgetary decisions

The term 'budgetary decision' will be used in this volume to denote a collective decision by a competent authority of a government that authorizes expenditures from public funds or revenues to public funds. If a government takes part in a capitalistic economic system there are four kinds of budgetary decisions:
1. The purchase and sale of production factors and products from and to other housholds
2. Subsidies and regulatory levies, such as pollution fees, on goods traded by other households
3. (Money-)transfers to other households
4. Taxes charged to private households, including earmarked taxes, such as social insurance contributions, and non-regulatory price levies on goods traded by private households, such as sales taxes and taxes on value added.

In order to gain an insight in the nature of these kinds of decisions, it is helpful to make use of a flow chart of public expenditure and revenue, as shown in figure 2.1.

Figure 2.1 shows a single government indicated by the large rectangle in the middle of the chart. Markets 1–6 are indicated by ellipses. In accordance with the traditional view – as opposed to the Niskanean view – the government is provisionally conceived as a single integrated household. Hence the smaller rectangles A and B within the large rectangle can temporarily be ignored. This assumption will be dropped in the next section.

The arrows in figure 2.1 show the course of the money flows into and out of the government. Commodities flow in the opposite directions. The chart is set up in such way that the markets above the middle of the figure (markets 1, 2 and 6) determine 'what' is being produced in the economic system. The decisions concerned are called 'allocation'. The chart also shows 'for whom' products are being produced. The decisions concerned

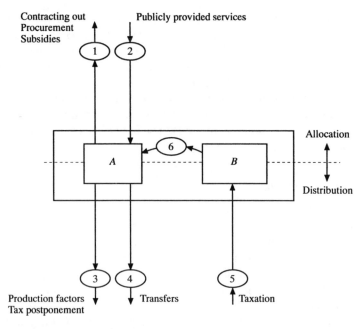

Figure 2.1 Flow chart of public expenditure and revenue

are taken in the markets below the middle of the figure (markets 3, 4 and 5) and are called 'distribution' (of income). In a capitalistic system, markets apparently fulfil an allocative as well as a distributive function.

Figure 2.1 shows two external allocative markets. Market 1 is the market where the government purchases products from the private production sector. One can think of procurement (for instance, office equipment) but also of the 'contracting out' by government of such goods as road construction or weapon systems. The private production sector is supposed to consist not only of profit-making firms but also of other private households that produce for the market and are accordingly counted as business households in standard statistical accounts: private hospitals, museums, homes for the elderly, etc. (the private non-profit sector). Market 2 concerns the products that government sells to other private and public households for money (charges, fees). One can think of postal services, public transportation, public education, etc.

Markets 3, 4 and 5 are the distributive markets. In market 3 the government purchases production factors (capital and labour) from other households (as far as capital is concerned, one should think of banks, pension funds, etc.). Capital borrowing should be conceived of in this connection as a commodity flow and interest payment as the reciprocal money flow. Furthermore, the commodity and money flows through market 3 should be considered as net flows, so that they include capital lending by government to the private sector and received interest.

The government not only borrows for productive purposes but also to supplement income from taxation ('consumptive credit'). In this case, the distributive transaction in market 3 has to be interpreted as the purchase of a 'good of tax postponement' (rather than of a production factor).[3]

Distribution of income is not exclusively dependent on the sale of factors of production for money. In the first place, there is 'redistribution', effected by money flows among private households (not indicated in the chart because the government is not involved) and by money flows from the government to other private and public households (market 4). One can think, for instance, of social security benefits. In the case of redistribution the offsetting commodity flow should be conceived of as the immaterial good of poverty prevention or, more generally, availability of an equitable income in certain groups of households. Income redistribution via market 4 includes revenue-sharing systems through which a government contributes to the revenues of another government. Since in the case of redistribution the money flow between households must originate in transactions to which both the granting and receiving party agree, it seems appropriate to consider redistributional transfers as market transactions.

In the second place, there is taxation, which is the main source of government income (market 5). Taxation leads to money flows from the private production and consumption sectors to the public sector.

Whereas the distribution of income resulting from the transactions in market 3 are known as primary distribution, the distribution resulting from the transactions in markets 4 and 5 is known as secondary distribution.[4]

The question arises whether the tax flows can be supposed to originate in market transactions. In the case of transfers in the opposite direction (from the public to the private sector), this is fairly evident. The case of taxes, however, is less obvious.

For a correct interpretation of these tax flows it is necessary to keep in mind that an individual relates to a government – whether a central or a local government – in two fundamentally different ways, first, as a member of certain private households[5] that happen to be in the sphere of influence of the government concerned, and secondly as a citizen, or member, of that government. In the latter case she is bound by the collective decisions of the governmental authorities, in which she may or may not participate herself. In the former case, on the other hand, she stands to the government in a contract relation. This is obvious in the case where a private household purchases from the government (public transport, etc.) or sells to the government (office equipment, labour, capital, etc.). It is less so in the case of the special type of 'contract' that obliges the payment of taxes (the 'fiscal contract').

In this respect, it is helpful to compare taxes with contribution fees of a private association. Although it is true that the magnitude of such fees is determined by the competent authorities of the association, anybody who does not want to pay them can avoid doing so by withdrawing from the association. Similarly, fiscal obligations can be interpreted as originating in a bilateral contract of association between a public and a private household. For local governments such as municipalities or special purpose corporations such as school districts, this interpretation seems natural. Association with such governments is mainly performed by choice of residence. In the case of the central government, the foundation of the fiscal obligation in a bilateral contract of association seems a little artificial; emigration is no serious alternative for the overwhelming majority of private households in most central governments. In this respect, it is important that the voluntariness which characterizes market decision-making in general is not a purely factual concept. Indeed, from the factual point of view one could query the voluntary nature of many kinds of private contracts: think of labour contracts, house-renting contracts, etc. But then, actual voluntary behaviour is not essential in this respect. What is essential is the conceptual distinction between on the one hand the actual necessity for private households to be in the sphere of influence of a government, including the necessity to enter a fiscal contract, and, on the other, the legal obligation of subjects to obey the decisions of governmental authorities.

A related aspect of taxation concerns the question of why tax payments should be considered as bilateral transactions. In this respect, it is important to distinguish between, on the one hand, the specific services that are available free of charge to subjects after the conclusion of the fiscal contract and, on the other, the right of members of private households to become subjects and to receive the entire bundle of unspecified services that is acquired by the conclusion of the contract. Only the latter right can be seen as the reciprocal of the tax payment. The provision of free services after the contract has become operative is an entirely internal affair within the public household. For this reason, free services are supposed to be consumed by the public household itself. This does not only apply to services for which pricing is technically impossible, like national defence or foreign development aid, but also to services for which pricing is theoretically possible but not applied in practice, like free public education or free highroads (tolls are technically possible).

The presented definition of a budgetary decision covers all kinds of incoming and outgoing money flows into and out of the government, as shown in figure 2.1 by the middle rectangle. The outgoing flows via markets 1 and 3 and the incoming flow via market 2 refer to the purchase and sale of production factors and products. The incoming flow via market 5 refers to the tax flow: mainly income and payroll taxes, corporate taxes and taxes on sales and value added. The outgoing flow via market 4 refers to transfers to the private consumption sector.

It remains to be seen how the last mentioned incoming and outgoing money flows, namely those of subsidies and regulatory levies on goods traded by the private sector, should be interpreted. Levies in this sense include pollution fees and excise duties (alcohol, tobacco, etc.). How have these flows been dealt with in figure 2.1?

Subsidies flow from government to the private production sector. They are attached to concrete units of product. The sale of a subsidized product by a private production household can thus be conceived as a sale to two buyers simultaneously. The private purchasing household and government both pay a part of the price. As far as the government is concerned, the sale can be seen as a transaction in market 1. Comparable to subsidies are sales of services by public agencies below cost price in market 2. In this case, a part of the cost price is paid by a public contribution in narrow sense (a public contribution to the price of a good other than a subsidy), which leads to a lower market price.

Such contributions are even conceivable with respect to the payment of taxes (market 5). Since taxes are prices for service bundles, the size of the public contribution can in this case be identified as the difference between some kind of normatively optimal tax price (for instance, the so-called 'Lindahl tax price') and the actual tax price.

Regulatory levies can be seen as the mirror image of subsidies. In this case, the private production or consumption household purchases as it were a 'licence to buy' from government simultaneously with the good that it purchases from another private household. As far as the government is concerned, this sale can be seen as a transaction in market 2 in figure 2.1.

With this, the identification of all kinds of budgetary decisions is completed. As it turns out, the definition covers all money flows entering and leaving the government. This means that the 'budget', as the complete set of budgetary decisions for a certain year, completely describes the external financial transactions of government (all transactions in markets 1–5).

Budgetary decisions as transactions in internal markets

The question now arises what can be learned from the Niskanean view of government for the explanation of budgetary decisions. Assume that public agencies can be considered as separate households that are producing services which are either sold directly to the private sector or to politicians who are representing the citizens. This assumption would lead to an adjustment of the chart of the economic system as indicated by the small rectangles A and B in figure 2.1.

The question may be asked in what respect this assumption would lead to a different economic interpretation of budgetary decisions than would result from the traditional assumption that a government is a single, integrated household. What can we know about decision-making in the internal market? Niskanen's basic idea is very simple in this respect: insofar as decisions with respect to the transactions of public agencies in external markets are formally taken by political authorities, these decisions might as well be considered to concern transactions in the internal market. To see this, note that apart from saving and dissaving – which require separate authorization – the balance of all money flows into and out of agencies from and to external markets must necessarily equal the money flow via the internal market. In other words, by deciding formally about the external expenditures and revenues of agencies, the political authorities materially decide about the money flows into the agencies via the internal market – that is, about their own expenditures for the services delivered by the agencies.[6]

The change of perspective involved in the Niskanean view of the governmental organization is fundamental. By the somewhat abstract way its basic idea has been expressed above it might seem that its value is mainly theoretical. This is not the case. The Niskanean view of government is first and foremost inspired by practical experience. Participants tend to perceive the budgetary process as an annual market where public agencies in a very real sense are trying to 'sell' their services to political authorities. This involves marketing strategies, clientele building, public relations, and so forth.

Nevertheless, it should be firmly kept in mind that from the formal point of view there is always the important difference that budgetary decisions do not involve the services flowing through the internal market but only those that are externally sold or purchased. Expenditure and revenue estimates are tied to the descriptions of commodities acquired from and delivered to private households ('civil service salaries', 'subsidies for orchestras', 'educational fees', 'material expenses', etc.). Public budgets are therefore necessarily 'input oriented'. This characteristic is not a curable defect of a public budget, as has sometimes been alleged, but rather an essential feature of it. However, from the specific point of view of the political authorities that have to decide about the money flows into the agencies, this formal aspect of the budget is a serious obstacle to control. The more autonomous an agency is, and the less it can be controlled by hierarchy alone, the more interest the political authorities will have in controlling it via the budget. For that purpose, output data for public agencies are essential.

Although output data for public agencies are not included in the budget, the question arises whether they can be derived from the budget, in a similar way as the financial means flowing into the agencies via the internal market can be derived from it. It turns out that this is not the case. Whereas the money flow is closed within the government as a whole, so that it is possible to derive the internal flow into the agencies from the external flows entering and leaving them, value is added to commodities in the public agencies, so that it is not possible to derive the internal service flow leaving the agencies from the external flows leaving and entering them. Whereas by inspection of the budget it is possible to judge whether government as a whole is buying 'value for money' from the private sector, it is not possible to judge in this way whether the political authorities are buying 'value for money' from public agencies. The latter is possible only if the agencies provide separate data about the services produced for internal consumption.

This explains the emergence of a variety of practices involving the addition of data about internally supplied services (output data) as an appendix to the budget. Practices of this kind are known as 'performance budgeting'.

The competence rules of the budgetary process

Every model of the budgetary process has to be based upon assumptions about decision rules. The following two questions have in particular to be dealt with: (1) which authorities are taking demand and supply decisions in internal and external markets according to the prevailing competence rules, and (2) which procedural rules apply to the generation of these decisions. In the remaining part of this chapter an attempt is made to answer these questions for the main variants of representative democracy.

Since we want to focus on key characteristics, it seems sensible to start with a broad description of the stages and phases of the budgetary process that are common to the main forms of representative government.

Budgetary decision-making is a cyclical process. Usually, the budget authorizes expenditures and revenues for one year. Consequently, the cycles succeed one another with an interlude of one year. Since the duration of every cycle is at least three years, there is a large overlap between subsequent cycles. If everything happens on time, the first stage of the cycle, namely that of budget preparation, has been completed at the beginning of the fiscal year. After the beginning of the fiscal year two more stages follow, namely those of budget execution and auditing.

The distinction between budget preparation on the one hand and execution and auditing on the other has to do with the necessity recognized by every but the most simple household to plan expenditures and revenues in advance. Without such planning there would be a continuous need to adjust revenue decisions to expenditures decisions and vice versa, in order to keep the household solvent. In order to avoid such ad hoc decision-making, the budgetary process is split up in an annual authorization process, which results in decisions with respect to legitimate future transactions, and an actual spending and revenue-raising process, consisting of these transactions themselves. The authorization process is called 'budget preparation', the spending and revenue-raising process 'budget execution'. In order to secure consistency between both processes, a further stage of 'auditing' is added, in which the legitimacy of realized transactions is retrospectively controlled on the basis of prevailing authorizations. Since for the purpose of modelling the distinction between authorization and execution is immaterial, this study focuses on decision-making only in the preparatory stage.

The general character of the competence rules in the preparatory stage, depends upon the participation rule for the supreme executive authority. In this respect, three major variants of representative government must be recognized. The crucial distinctions with respect to budgetary decision-making are indicated in table 2.1.

In both the presidential and the parliamentary system the supreme executive authority has its own constitutional competences. These competences include the right to submit budgetary proposals for legislative consideration, and the right to approve or disapprove (veto) the ensuing legislation. The stage of budget preparation can therefore be partitioned into two substages in these systems, namely those of executive budget preparation and legislative budget preparation, both of which lead to 'budgetary decisions' in the sense of the definition presented on p. 17. Only in the situation where the supreme executive authority lacks the right of approval or of veto with respect to budgetary and substantive legislation will budget preparation consist of only one stage. Under such circumstances, it makes no sense to assume that this authority, for instance the 'City manager', is taking 'budgetary decisions'. This situation is characteristic of the 'conventional system' which is mainly applied in local government.

Within the stage of executive budget preparation, the following six phases can usually be identified:
1. An extrapolation and target-setting exercise on the part of the executive budget bureau, sometimes followed by a round of preliminary political decision-making about targets or ceilings by the supreme executive authority

Table 2.1. *Major variants of representative government*

Constitutional system	Supreme executive authority[a]	Participation rule for the supreme executive authority	Executive approval of legislation
Parliamentary system	Cabinet,[b] Executive council, etc.	Rule of parliamentary confidence	Required
Presidential system	President, Governor, Mayor, etc.	Election by the electorate (directly or indirectly)	Required
Conventional system	City manager, etc.	Nomination by representative assembly	Not required

[a]In some forms of representative democracy no supreme executive authority exists. Instead, separate executive competences are attributed to a number of elected officers. This arrangement can, for instance, be found in some cities in the USA. Budgetary requests are submitted directly to the legislature under this arrangement. A central executive budget is lacking. This system, that may be considered as a fourth principal variant of representative democracy, will not be further considered.
[b]In the parliamentary system, the executive competence at the level of central government may formally be vested in a (non-elected) President or King 'under ministerial responsibility'. In practice under this arrangement, the executive competence is wielded by the Cabinet.

2. Submission of request estimates by the administrators of agencies
3. Investigation of request estimates by the budget bureau
4. Negotiations between the separate agencies and the budget bureau
5. Decision-making by the supreme executive authority about the remaining points of difference
6. Submission of the executive budget to the legislature, and related proposals to change substantive law.

Legislative budget preparation is less uniform than executive budget preparation. An important factor in this respect is the constitutional position of the supreme executive authority. In the parliamentary system, that authority consists of a collective body, for instance the cabinet, whose members are dependent on the confidence of parliament for their continuation in office. In the presidential system the executive authority consists of a single officer who is elected periodically by the electorate (or an electoral college).

In general, the representative assembly has greater impact upon the budget in the presidential than in the parliamentary system. The cause of this difference is not that in the presidential system the competences of the supreme executive authority with respect to legislation are more restricted than in the parliamentary system. In particular, the veto right which is usual in the presidential system is equivalent to the right of approval which is usual in the parliamentary system. The difference rather originates in the rule of confidence, which is a distinctive characteristic of the parliamentary system. Contrary to what is often supposed, the rule of confidence largely works in favour of the executive authority. The members of that body can make use of the fact that their continuation in office is dependent on the confidence of the representative assembly by attaching their political fate to the implementation of particular policies, regardless of whether such policies belong to their formal competence. The British Cabinet, for instance, treats all budgetary legislation as a matter of confidence, so that all potential amendments on executive bills are suppressed. Although in a parliamentary system parliament is certainly entitled to abandon confidence on account of budgetary matters, such action would often, and in a two party-system virtually always, amount to political suicide by the incumbent party. Under such circumstances, the influence of parliament on budgetary matters is often dependent on persuasion and informal pressure behind the scenes rather than on formal competence.

In the presidential system, on the other hand, the veto threat is often the only means by which the executive authority can influence the legislative process. In budgetary matters, the efficacy of the veto competence is dependent on the possibility of a so-called 'line item veto'. If this possibility is lacking, only entire laws can be vetoed. Often the consequences of such a decision are so grave that the veto threat lacks sufficient credibility to be effective.

Under the circumstances mentioned, the legislative process tends to be better developed in presidential than in parliamentary systems. Some phases of legislative budget preparation are lacking in parliamentary systems, or exist only in a rudimentary form. With this proviso, the legislative stage can be divided in the following phases:

1. An extrapolation and target-setting exercise on the part of the legislative budget bureau or staff unit, sometimes followed by a round of preliminary decision-making about targets or ceilings for broad expenditure and revenue categories by the representative assembly[7]
2. An investigation of the executive budget and related proposals to change fiscal and substantive law in standing committees;[8] hearings of agency administrators
3. Development of legislative proposals (in the parliamentary system,

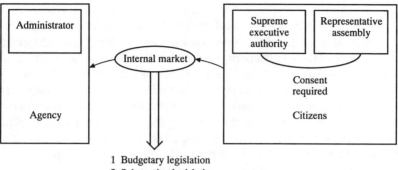

1 Budgetary legislation
2 Substantive legislation

Figure 2.2 Basic competence rules of the budgetary process in the parliamentary and presidential system

   amendments on the executive proposals) in the standing committees
4. Consideration of the committee proposals in the representative assembly; submission of amendments; decision-making by the representative assembly
5. In the case of a bicameral assembly, steps 1–4 are repeated – possibly in a rudimentary form – in the other House; if the other House has the right of initiative or amendment, a mediation phase and an additional round of decision-making may be necessary in order to attain the agreement of both Houses
6. The legislative budget and related fiscal and substantive bills are returned for approval to the supreme executive authority.

   In view of these procedures, the competence rules of executive and legislative budget preparation can be schematized as indicated in figure 2.2.

   The scheme amounts to an operationalization of some of the theoretical concepts that were introduced in the preceding sections. It indicates that decisions about public demand are taken by the representative assembly and the supreme executive authority on behalf of citizens, and that decisions about public supply are taken by administrators on behalf of agencies. The empirical plausibility of the scheme is obviously open to discussion, and some considerations in support of the proposed operationalizations are therefore in order.

   First, the question arises which officers must be considered as administrators of agencies, in the sense of suppliers of public services. According to Niskanen, the officer who decides about supply is the 'senior official of a bureau with a separate, identifiable budget'. In Niskanen's analysis this official is supposed to deal directly with the Appropriations Committees of the US Congress. Although Niskanen is not explicit in this respect, it seems probable that he was mainly thinking of the secretaries of departments and directors of bureaux and offices of the US federal government. However, in European parliamentary systems the position of ministers is rather different from that in the US federal government. First, as far as the budgetary process is concerned, they not only bear administrative, but also (ultimate) political responsibility. Indeed, as members of cabinet, ministers decide themselves about the executive budget. Secondly, in these systems ministers are usually prominent members of their parties. Often they are also elected members of parliament, even if there are rules that oblige them to resign from parliament within a certain period after nomination. Consequently, their motivation is generally more political than bureaucratic. In this light, it seems hardly compatible with the assumptions of the Niskanean model to consider ministers in parliamentary systems primarily as administrators who bear the responsibility for public supply.

A more appropriate way of applying the model to these systems could be to consider the top officers of the permanent civil service as the administrators who bear this responsibility. However, this raises a question with respect to the autonomy of agency administrators *vis-à-vis* the political authorities that the model assumes. In the UK and the Netherlands there has been a movement in the direction of greater autonomy for executive agencies, but this is a relatively recent development. On the other hand in most West European countries, including the UK and the Netherlands, there exists a variety of executive public agencies that exhibit a large degree of autonomy by virtue of special statutes, alongside departmental divisions. In the UK, some of these agencies are known as 'quangos' (quasi-autonomous non-governmental organizations). One can also think of public enterprises and foundations. In Sweden, and to a certain degree in Denmark, there is a long tradition of separating execution from policy-making as a matter of principle. In those countries, execution is organized in independent public agencies and withdrawn from political intervention in general. It appears, then, that officers of public agencies can hold different degrees of autonomy depending on the competences attributed or delegated to them in particular cases. The scheme assumes, in accordance with the Niskanen criterion, that budget-holding officers can be considered as administrators of public agencies. It will be argued in chapter 4, however, that in order to build an empirically relevant model it is necessary to make a further distinction among agency administrators. In particular, it will be proposed that the supply behaviour of an officer who is subject to effective hierarchical control has to be analysed by a different type of model than the supply behaviour of a more autonomous officer.

A second aspect of the scheme presented that needs some comment concerns the role of administrators during legislative budget preparation. Various observers of the legislative budgetary process have noted that the discussions with the representative assembly and its committees are a delicate affair for the responsible administrators. On the one hand they must secure the interests of their agencies, on the other they are formally bound to their agreements with the supreme executive authority as recorded in the executive budget. The extent to which administrators can afford to advocate the interests of their own agencies after having voiced some formal support for the executive budget varies according to political culture, personal reputation and specific circumstances. In general, however, it may be assumed that experienced administrators have little trouble in revealing the salutary policies that could be implemented if more money were furnished than asked for in the executive budget.[9]

Thirdly, it is indicated in the scheme that budgetary decisions are not only taken in the form of acts commonly designated as 'budgetary legislation' (appropriation acts and annual authorization acts with respect to revenues and borrowing).[10] This follows from the fact that the presented definition of budgetary decision is based on material criteria.

There are two main differences between the formal and the material concept of the budget. The first difference is that in spite of the so-called 'universality principle', which has been a basic principle of public finance since the times of the French Revolution, 'off-budget expenditure' exists in most governments. The major sources of off-budget expenditure are tax expenditures, contributory expenditures and loans.

Tax expenditures are not authorized by appropriation acts but by fiscal legislation in the form of exemptions; for the purpose of empirical analysis, they should be considered as normal expenditures.

Contributory expenditures are funded by fees, charges or earmarked taxes such as social insurance premiums. In many governments considerable efforts have been made in recent years to (re-)integrate contributory expenditures into the regular appropriations process. Nevertheless, substantial financial flows of this kind often remain withdrawn from budgetary control. For the purpose of empirical analysis, the substantive laws that authorize such expenditures should be considered as budgetary decisions.

Loans are treated in various ways. Direct loans from government to the private sector are often authorized through regular appropriations but sometimes are not.[11] Usually, public guarantees on loans provided by private financial institutions are not authorized by appropriations either.[12] Loans and guarantees on loans should for the purpose of empirical analysis be considered as normal expenditures, and the substantive laws and decrees that authorize these expenditures as budgetary decisions.

The second difference between the formal and the material concept of the budget is that substantive legislation may fully determine subsequent budgetary legislation. Expenditures that are effectively authorized by prior substantive legislation are known as 'back-door expenditures'. Back-door spending should be distinguished from off-budget spending. Back-door expenditure is reflected in the (expenditure side of the) formal budget, off-budget expenditure is not. The main forms of back-door expenditure are entitlement legislation and substantive legislation that establishes contract authority (the authority to incur obligations concerning future expenditures). In some governments, certain expenditures on the basis of entitlement legislation need not even be appropriated on an annual basis. In the US federal government, for instance, a substantial part of entitlement spending is exempted from the annual appropriation requirement. In view of the fact that in these cases the material decisions are taken in the process of substantive legislation rather than in that of budgetary legislation in the formal sense, it is appropriate to consider the substantive laws in question as the true 'budgetary decisions' in the sense of the definition presented.

The procedural rules of the budgetary process

The competence rules surveyed so far show that political authorities sometimes consist of single officers and sometimes of collective bodies. The question that must be dealt with now is how these authorities decide about transactions in internal markets.

It is useful to make a distinction between two types of procedural rules, namely voting rules and agenda rules. Voting rules define a collective decision on the basis of one or more sets of individual decisions known as votes. The votes may be nominal (a single choice from a pair or set of alternatives), ordinal (a ranking of alternatives according to preference), or cardinal (a numerical evaluation). If a single proposal must be selected from a set of more than two alternatives by pairwise nominal votes, more than one round of voting is required. In that case, the alternatives must subsequently be paired against each other and the voting rule must specify the order of voting (so-called binary agenda procedures). Agenda rules select the proposals that committee members can put forward against a given status quo proposal (the proposal to refrain from a new decision). The selection is made from the universe of proposals that political authorities can potentially approve according to the prevailing competence rules.

The voting rules in use by political authorities are remarkably uniform throughout the western world. Authorities consisting of single officers use the obvious rule that the individual decision of the officer automatically becomes the collective decision. Authorities consisting of collective bodies decide by absolute majority rule. Tie-breaking rules may differ. Often the chairman casts the decisive vote. If there are more than two alternatives, binary agenda procedures are used and the order of voting is determined by (some variant of) 'Robert's rules of order' (Robert, 1893).

As far as agenda rules are concerned, the situation is more complicated. Many kinds of formal and informal agenda rules are in use, and not all of them are easily observable. It will appear that under many circumstances modelling is simplified by assuming restrictive agenda rules. Such assumptions might eliminate theoretical problems that are induced by less restrictive rules. From a methodological point of view, however, it seems desirable to start the analysis from a minimum of agenda structure and not to take refuge too easily in assumptions that are more or less begging the entire question of explanation and prediction of outcomes.

The least restrictive agenda rule is that of the so-called 'open agenda' procedure. This rule implies that every member of a collective body is entitled to put any proposal on the agenda at any time, and that all proposals are voted against the status quo proposal in the order in which they are proposed. The open agenda procedure is a theoretical minimum; each more specific assumption has to be justified, both factually (in the sense that it exists) and normatively (in the sense that its existence is explainable).

An important aspect of agenda rules is the definition of the status quo proposal employed. As far as budgetary decisions are concerned two possibilities arise: (1) the 'current law budget', which is the budget authorized by the last approved budgetary or substantive law, and (2) the 'current services budget', which is the budget that follows from continuation of prevailing output levels (output levels funded by budgetary or substantive law at the time of decision-making), accounting for future real and inflationary cost increases and for changes in the number of eligible consumers. The current law budget is zero after expiration of prevailing authorizations and therefore a quite impracticable status quo proposal. In many governments, provisions have therefore been made in order to secure that the current services budget shall prevail if new budgetary authorizations have not been approved in time (so that the status quo proposal is the current services budget).

It is one of the strong features of the public choice approach to the analysis of budgetary decision-making that it does not appeal too rapidly to institutional aspects of the process that are neither easily observable nor explainable in themselves as a rational outcome of a hypothetical process of constitutional choice. Why should members of collective bodies acquiesce in the existence of agenda rules that systematically discriminate against them? And how do such rules arise in the first place?

The approach taken in this volume is that first the open agenda assumption will be explored for all political authorities consisting of collective bodies (chapters 5 and 6). Only after the explanatory capacity of that assumption has been considered, will assumptions be added about more restrictive agenda rules (chapter 7). In this approach, it seems preferable to discuss the empirical plausibility of the more restrictive agenda assumptions as they are introduced.

Guide to the literature

The analysis of public decision-making on the basis of a positive rather than normative theory of political demand is a cornerstone of the public choice approach, as it was developed in the 1950s and 1960s by Buchanan, Downs, Olson and Tullock. This type of analysis can be found in the classical works such as Downs, *An Economic Theory of Democracy* (1957); Buchanan and Tullock, *The Calculus of Consent* (1962); and Olson, *The Logic of Collective Action* (1965). The theory of bureaucratic supply originates in Niskanen, *Bureaucracy and Representative Government* (1971).

Institutional aspects of the budgetary process in particular governments, including 'competence rules', are usually described in books that treat the budgetary process from the perspective of public administration. This literature is very large. It may suffice to name a few especially important or useful works with respect to four countries, namely the USA, the UK, France and the Netherlands. For the USA, see Berman, *The Office of Management and Budget and the Presidency 1921–1979* (1979); Leloup, *The Fiscal Congress: Legislative Control of the Budget* (1980); Lynch, *Public Budgeting in America* (1979); Mills and Palmer (eds.), *Federal Budget Policy in the 1980s* (1984); Schick, *Money and Congress* (1980); Sharkansky, *The Politics of Taxing and Spending* (1969); Wander, Herbert and Copeland (eds.), *Congressional Budgeting* (1984); Wildavsky, *The New Politics of the Budgetary Process* (1988); White and Wildavsky, *The Deficit and the Public Interest. The Search for Responsible Budgeting in the 1980s* (1989). For the UK, see Heclo and Wildavsky, *The Private Government of Public Money* (1974); Robinson, *Parliament and Public Spending* (1980). For France, see Lord, *The French Budgetary Process* (1973). For the Netherlands, see Drees, *Nederlandse Overheidsuitgaven* (1985); Koopmans and Wellink, *Overheidsfinanciën* (1971); Toirkens, *Schijn en Werkelijkheid van het Bezuinigingsbeleid* (1988).

3 Demand in the public sector

Public and private goods

An important building block for the theory of legislative demand is the distinction between 'public goods' and 'private goods'. The term 'public good' will be used in this book for an economic good that can, and does, benefit everybody. This is the definition which is known as the 'polar case of a pure Samuelsonian public good'.[1] A pure public good in this sense has two outstanding characteristics. The first is the supply characteristic known as 'non-rivalry' among consumers. It implies that at given costs of supply, an additional consumer does not affect the benefits of existing consumers (the good 'can benefit everybody'). The second is the demand characteristic of 'universal demand'. A good can qualify as a public good, only if it actually figures in everybody's utility function (the good 'does benefit everybody'). This definition stands in opposition to the one of a pure private good: an economic good that can, and does, benefit only a single person.

In view of the important consequences of the distinction between public and private goods, it seems useful to review the concept of a Samuelsonian public good. It is also useful to consider some intermediate cases.

First, it must be emphasized that the concept of 'public good' as defined here has nothing to do with government. Public goods are provided privately and publicly. Conversely, governments are providing public and private goods. Of course, there are certain reasons why public goods, according to certain normative criteria, may be provided more efficiently in the public than in the private sector, but there are also circumstances under which the opposite will be the case. Similarly, for that matter, there are circumstances under which private goods may be provided more efficiently in one or the other sector.

Secondly, the concept of 'public good' as defined here does not presuppose the possibility of exclusion of potential consumers. Public goods may be 'excludable' in the sense that consumers can be required to pay a price before they are admitted to consumption, or they may not. Well-known examples of the latter are national defence and foreign development aid. There is a relation between the possibility of exclusion and the mode of provision, in that excludability offers better opportunities for efficient provision in the private sector than non-excludability. Neither in this respect, however, is there a straightforward relation, in the sense that excludable public goods are, or should always be, provided in the private sector and non-excludable public goods in the public sector.

It has often been observed that there are various intermediate cases. These cases are of two kinds. One has to do with the criterion of non-rivalry of consumption; the other with the criterion of universal demand.

A first important intermediate case is that of goods with limited capacity. This concerns the supply characteristic of non-rival consumption: such goods can only be provided to additional consumers without affecting the benefits of existing consumers until the capacity limit is reached. After that point, additional consumers cause either a cost increase for the producer as a consequence of capacity adjustment or a benefit decrease for the consumer as a consequence of impaired quality or congestion. Goods of this kind are very common, and have often been treated as private goods in the economic literature. Indeed, in the Anglo-Saxon branch of the literature, the concept of 'public good' hardly existed before the appearance of Samuelson's papers in the 1950s (1954, 1955, 1958). In accordance with the traditional Pigovian approach, the services delivered to individual consumers by a fixed facility were treated as private goods characterized by decreasing marginal and average costs. If the fixed facility is inexhaustible, the total cost function of such services is a step function whereby the first consumer bears the entire cost of the facility and each subsequent consumer bears no costs. However, many fixed facilities are not completely inexhaustible, so that the total costs of capacity make an upward step at every point where a capacity limit is attained and the fixed facility has to be adjusted. Examples are roads, trains, parks, museums, etc.

As the Samuelsonian analysis has shown, it is important to recognize the special case of decreasing costs, originating in the presence of public goods. Marginal and average costs of such goods are decreasing only when the services available to separate consumers are conceived as separate units. When the services available to separate consumers are conceived as the same unit, 'enjoyed in common by all', such goods need by no means exhibit decreasing costs. An additional road need not be cheaper than an existing road, but an additional passenger on an existing road is much cheaper than the first passenger on that road. A public good is characterized, as it were, by a double quantity dimension: its capacity, which determines the maximal number of persons it can benefit, apart from externalities, and its scale, which determines the degree to which it benefits each individual beneficiary. In public transport, for instance, the number of carriages of a train and the frequency of rides during peak hours belong to capacity, but the number of stations in the line network and the frequency of rides during low hours, belong to scale. In the case of pure public goods, the marginal and average cost of capacity functions are decreasing throughout, but the marginal and average cost of scale functions will usually have the normal convex shape (decreasing at low outputs and increasing at high outputs).

Since the seminal paper by Tiebout (1956), in which the intermediate case of limited capacity public goods was described and analysed, the goods in question have been known as 'local public goods'. This name is somewhat misleading, because local public goods need by no means be located in a small area. Telecommunication networks and the services of the Supreme Court are instances of the contrary situation.

A second intermediate case is that of 'unequal benefit shares'. This case is conceptually identical to that of private goods with 'externalities in consumption'. It is already apparent that from the perspective of the demander, public goods can be conceived of as bundles of private goods. From this perspective public goods are a special kind of 'joint products' or 'jointly supplied' services (in the Marshallian sense: sheep yield wool and meat). It is well known that joint products are in general characterized by the fact that additional consumers of one kind of product do not affect the benefits of another kind. Usually, however, each kind of product is consumed by many people, so that there is rivalry among the consumers of the same kind of product. Joint products must therefore in general be seen as private goods from the perspective of supply. Only in the special case of public goods is there a separate kind of product for each beneficiary, so that there is no rivalry among any pair of beneficiaries.

Usually, the kinds of private products that flow from a given public good differ between beneficiaries. Buchanan has spoken in this connection about public goods that provide different quantities of 'homogeneous quality consumption units' to different beneficiaries (a fire station that is closer to someone's home than to somebody else's home and thus gives to the former person a 0.0005 probability that his property will suffer fire damage and to the latter person a 0.0007 probability: Buchanan, 1968). In the case of negative externalities certain people are even exposed to effects that they perceive as 'private bads'.[2] Of course, different beneficiaries often put different values upon a public good available to them, but in the case of 'unequal benefit shares' the reason for such deviating evaluation would not consist in differences of a subjective nature (differences in tastes or income), but rather in the nature of the public good itself (for instance, its location).

Denzau and Mackay (1976) have further elaborated the concept of benefit shares by introducing a parameter of 'publicness'. This parameter, say α_i, serves to transform units of collective supply into units of individual demand. So, for instance, $x_{1i} = \alpha_i x_1$, where x_{1i} represents the quantity of public good 1 available to actor i and x_1 the quantity produced. The parameter α_i satisfies: $0 \leq \alpha_i \leq 1$; furthermore $\sum_{i=1}^{i=|M|} \alpha_i = 1$ if good 1 is a pure private good wherein $|M|$ is the number of beneficiaries and $\alpha_i = 1$ for every $i = 1,2\ldots,|M|$, if good 1 is a pure public good. Although the unified treatment of public provision according to this approach has a certain analytical appeal, it is not adopted here for two reasons.

In the first place, the distinction between objective and subjective factors entering the evaluation of a publicly provided service is usually hard to operationalize. The benefits that a public good offers to separate individuals are almost never identical. This is not only true for a fire station that may be near to, or far from, somebody's home, but even for such typical public goods as national defence, which for a person who lives in a 'sensitive area' (an Englishman in the Falkland Islands) might have a quite different meaning than for an average citizen. One wonders how different 'benefit shares' and different 'evaluations of equal benefit shares' could be distinguished in such cases. This point has also been emphasized by Samuelson (1969a), in a reaction to comments about his definition of a public good. In this connection, the author proposed to bring the entire case of private goods with externalities in consumption under the public good category. On the same occasion he expressed regret about his earlier admission of the 'polarity' of the public good concept, and suggested that the 'pure private good' rather than the public good should be considered as the knife-edge polar case, against which reality should be judged. This would imply that almost every empirically relevant type of publicly provided service should be considered as a public good. In accordance with this argument, the case of unequal benefit shares will be treated in the present volume as an intermediate case in the area of demand rather than in that of supply characteristics.

In the second place, the variable benefit-share approach will not be adopted – and neither, for that matter, will Samuelson's proposal to treat all publicly provided services as public goods – for a pragmatic reason. It turns out that a rough dichotomy is handy in practice for purposes of positive as well as normative analysis. It seems preferable therefore to maintain the traditional terminology. Accordingly, the term 'private good' will be used in this book in all instances of private goods in demand with only moderate externalities and the term 'public good' for all instances of public goods in demand generating more or less evenly distributed benefits, apart from externalities.

Table 3.1. *Supply and demand characteristics of economic goods*

Supply characteristics
a Pure public good in supply (no rivalry among any pair of consumers)
b Local public good (rivalry among every pair of consumers after capacity limit is reached)
c Jointly supplied private goods (no rivalry among any pair of consumers of different kinds of goods)
d Pure private goods in supply (rivalry among every pair of consumers)

Demand characteristics
a Pure public good in demand (evenly distributed benefits among all)
b Group good (evenly distributed benefits among a limited number of persons, apart from externalities)
c Private good with externalities (one person receives most of the benefits)
d Pure private good in demand (one person receives all of the benefits)

A third intermediate case is that of so-called 'group goods'. This concerns a demand characteristic: a group good is a public good that benefits only a limited group of persons, apart from externalities. On the one hand, a group good resembles a public good, because within the group of beneficiaries the distribution of benefits is relatively even. On the other hand, some people do not benefit at all, or benefit only from externalities. In one sense, all public goods are group goods because public goods that benefit everybody hardly exist. For the purpose of empirical analysis, however, it is important that there are also many public goods that benefit only a limited group of citizens of a given government.

Group goods are often local public goods, but not necessarily so. Examples of group goods that are pure public goods from the perspective of supply characteristics are defence (pacifists do not benefit), television broadcasts (many people do not look) and lighthouses (many people never board a ship). On the other hand, local public goods are by definition group goods (a good that can benefit everybody, does not necessarily benefit everybody, but a good that cannot benefit everybody, necessarily does not benefit everybody).

The preceding survey of supply and demand characteristics of various kinds of goods is summarized in table 3.1.

Objectives of politicians

In order to model the demand behaviour of political authorities, assumptions have to be made about the preferences of their members for publicly provided services. The question arises as to what can be said about these preferences, and more particularly how these preferences relate to the preferences of citizens.

In the literature about the legislative demand model, reasoning often starts from the assumption that politicians have preferences for publicly provided goods, and the question of how the preferences of politicians are formed is considered as something for a different area of investigation, namely electoral theory. This approach is not entirely satisfactory. Since in electoral theory it is often assumed that politicians are interested in electoral success, rather than in policy outcomes, it suggests a cleavage between the objectives of politicians in the areas of legislative and electoral behaviour. Such a cleavage is problematic because, even if it is assumed that electoral voting is largely prospective rather than retrospective, that is to say determined by the platforms of the candidates with respect to future policy decisions rather than by the positions taken by them with respect to past policy decisions, it is still implausible that politicians would entirely ignore the platforms on which they were elected, as soon as elections were over. Such behaviour would surely create a credibility problem at the next election! In this light, it seems preferable to build a model of legislative demand on the basis of an assumption about the preferences of politicians which is at least compatible with plausible ideas about political behaviour in elections.

Looking at the public choice literature about elections, two basic views about the motivation of politicians can be distinguished. In the first view, the objective of politicians is electoral success in the sense of the absolute number of votes or the relative share of the votes (plurality). In the second view, the objective of politicians is the implementation of preferred policies. The first view is the dominant one. It has it roots in the work of Downs (1957), and has inspired most of the subsequent work on the spatial theory of electoral competition as developed by Tullock (1967b) and Davis, Hinich and Ordeshook (1970).

The second view is often associated with the work of Wittman (1973, 1977, 1983, 1990), but it can also be traced in the earlier public choice literature. The contributions by Buchanan (1967), Wagner (1976) and Goetz (1977) on 'fiscal illusion' are particularly relevant in this respect, and that work has its roots in turn in the Italian tradition in public finance.[3] Buchanan noted that in contrast to the Anglo-Saxon public finance litarature, the Italian literature had a long tradition of positive, as opposed to normative, analysis. In this tradition, a distinction was made between democratic systems in which politicians have to win elections in order to implement policies, and 'ruling class' systems in which they do not. In models of ruling class systems politicians are free to pursue preferred policies, which amount to the generation of maximal tax receipts in order to pay for expenditures that benefit the ruling class. Fiscal illusion plays a role in the ruling class model because there are certain checks on the tax ability of government, which may originate in the possibility of revolt among the dominated classes or in certain competences of an elected assembly with respect to new taxation. The politicians of the ruling class therefore have an interest in manipulation of the tax structure in such a way that the burden on individual citizens seems smaller than it really is. Buchanan has noted that in this respect the differences between democratic and ruling class systems are relative. Although in a democracy politicians can only implement policies if they are elected or enjoy the confidence of elected assemblies, they have a certain ability to misrepresent the burden of taxation in a similar way as conceived by the classical Italian authors. Moreover, Buchanan reminded us of the fact that fiscal illusion is also possible on the expenditure side of the budget, and that this offers an opportunity to politicians to authorize expenditures in favour of private interests in such a way that the benefits to society as a whole seem larger than they really are.

The point of departure of Wittman is somewhat different. According to Wittman, the electoral process is characterized by uncertainty on the part of the electors as well as on the part of the politicians. The electors are uncertain about the policy positions of the politicians and the politicians are uncertain about the preferences of the electors. Accordingly, the choice of a policy position (electoral platform) by politicians is inherently determined by probabilistic considerations. This implies that the politician has an opportunity to trade off the probability of winning the election against the proximity of the policy position to be adopted by way of electoral strategy (the strategic policy position) to the policy position preferred by herself. Wittman's approach differs from that of Buchanan in that it does not need intentional fiscal illusion in order to create freedom for politicians to pursue preferred policies, because there is lack of information on the part of electors and politicians anyway. However, both approaches concur in that they leave room for policy preferences as an important determinant of political behaviour.

Wittman has also observed that even apart from incomplete information on the part of electors and/or politicians, there is an opportunity to trade off electoral success against the proximity of strategic to preferred policy position if elections take place according to a system of proportional representation. In that case, party leaders who are not exclusively interested in the size of the parliamentary party can sacrifice seats in order to shorten the distance between the strategic and the preferred policy position.

It might seem that this distinction between the two basic views of political motivation is rather fundamental. This would indeed be the case if it were interpreted in the sense that politicians consider policy as a means to winning elections according to one view, and winning as a means to policy implementation according to the other, as suggested by Wittman (1983). However, on closer inspection this interpretion makes too much of the distinction. The crucial point is that if: (1) there is complete information on the part of electors about the policy positions of politicians and on the part of politicians about the preferences of electors, and (2) elections take place according to a first-past-the-post system (no proportional representation), and (3) there exists a policy position that is an electoral equilibrium in the sense that a politician maximizes electoral votes or plurality by adopting it, then there is no inconsistency between the objectives of electoral success and implementation of preferred policies. The compatibility of both propositions follows from the fact that under the conditions mentioned every deviation of the strategic policy position from the electoral equilibrium leads to certain electoral defeat. There is therefore no trade-off between the probability of winning and the proximity of strategic to preferred policy position. Consequently, the politician who maximizes votes or plurality will choose exactly the same strategic policy position as the politician who seeks the implementation of preferred policies. Since most of the models of electoral competition that specify the objective function of politicians as the maximization of votes or plurality satisfy the conditions mentioned, these models are mostly consistent with the view that the motivation of politicians is ultimately founded in policy preferences. According to this argument, the pursuit of electoral success can be considered in these models as an instrumental objective in relation to the ultimate objective of preferred policy implementation, to the same extent as in models that specify the objective function of politicians explicitly in the latter way.

A contrast between both views on political motivation may arise only if one or more of the conditions mentioned is not satisfied. Buchanan and Wittman have particularly pointed to the possibility of incomplete information on the part of electors and/or politicians, and Wittman has pointed to the possibility of proportional representation. Furthermore, Wittman has identified a number of empirically testable consequences that under incomplete information and in systems of proportional representation follow from the different assumptions. He reasons that in those cases the assumption of preferred policy implementation, in contrast to the assumption of vote or plurality maximization, supports the following hypotheses for two-candidate elections:[4] (1) the strategic policy positions of politicians do not converge, (2) the strategic policy positions of politicians on an issue may diverge from the electoral equilibrium, even in the same direction, (3) the size of the deviation of the strategic policy position of a politician on an issue from the electoral equilibrium will be larger to the extent that there is a stronger electoral bias in her favour caused by incumbency, coat-tail effects (support by a popular recently elected politician), larger party registration, success on another issue, charges of corruption against the opponent, or general popularity, and (4) the size of the deviation of the strategic policy position of a politician on an issue from the electoral equilibrium will be larger to the extent that the elasticity of electoral response (the quotient of the relative changes of vote plurality and strategic policy position) is smaller.

Wittman (1983) mentions many empirical studies in support of each of these hypotheses. Although these studies have not been conducted in order to test inferences from specific assumptions about political motivation, the combined evidence seems to offer strong support to the view that politicians seek the implementation of preferred policies and are not exclusively interested in electoral success. Studies by Ginsburg (1976) and Page (1978), which show persistent differences in policy stands of Democratic and Republican candidates in presidential elections in the USA over prolonged periods of time, and studies by Sullivan and Uslaner (1978) for the USA and Robertson (1976) for the UK, which show that candidates can afford to choose more extreme strategic policy positions to the extent that they enjoy a higher probability of winning for other reasons, are particularly noteworthy. This evidence supports the hypotheses (1) and (3) already mentioned. Furthermore, in a survey of the literature on the effects of the electoral competitiveness, Fiorina (1973) concludes that the thesis that more competitive districts induce more moderate strategic policy positions by the candidates is so well accepted that it has become part of the 'corpus of knowledge'. This evidence supports hypotheses (3) and (4), because more competitiveness implies less bias (a more equal probability of winning) as well as a higher elasticity of response (fewer votes may change the outcome).

Although the evidence in support of the assumption of preferred policy implementation is rather convincing, one caveat is in order. Hypotheses (1) and (2) (non-convergence and deviation from equilibrium) only discriminate unequivocally between the alternative assumptions about political motivation if the impact of policy preferences is due to uncertainty on the part of electors and/or politicians, or to an electoral system of proportional representation. However, it may also be the case that there is no electoral equilibrium. The literature on electoral theory suggests that this might happen in particular if the electorate is sharply divided over a number of essentially different issues. In such a situation, the density function that represents the distribution of the electorate over the more-dimensional policy space is multimodal (has many local tops), and the chance is high that there is no equilibrium position. A democratic system that has to work under such conditions can easily evolve into an 'interest group democracy'. In such a system, electoral strategy is a question of coalition-building, and for that purpose candidates will in general choose non-central policy positions. Since there is no equilibrium, an interest group democracy offers ample opportunities for politicians to pursue individual policy interests.[5] What a vote or plurality maximizing politician will do in an interest group democracy is hard to say. She, too, has to build a coalition of minorities, and will therefore choose an eccentric strategic policy position; but in what respect(s) this position will deviate from the position of the politician who is motivated by policy preferences can be answered only on the basis of specific models for each of those cases.

In view of the empirical evidence, the models to be treated in this volume will use the assumption that the ultimate objective of politicians is the implementation of preferred policies. As already indicated, this assumption is consistent with most of the work that uses the assumption of vote or plurality maximization if the latter is interpreted as a merely instrumental objective. An additional consideration is that this assumption may solve the problem of the cleavage between political objectives in the electoral and legislative areas mentioned at the beginning of this section. However, this solution gives rise to another problem. If it is assumed that politicians seek the approval of the same preferred policies in both the electoral and legislative areas, then the question arises as to what role remains for the strategic policy positions (electoral platforms) of the politicians in elections.

In the spatial theory of electoral competition it is usually assumed that the electors vote for the strategic rather than for the preferred policy positions of the candidates, but if the electors know that the latter deviate from the former and that the candidates, after being elected, will further pursue their preferred policies in the legislative domain, it seems quite implausible that they will still vote for the strategic policy positions. This difficulty can be avoided by assuming that the politician acts in the legislative domain on the basis of her strategic policy position in the electoral domain. This would imply that she would relinquish her policy preferences in the legislative domain and that she would be content with the impact these preferences might have had upon her strategic policy position in the electoral domain. This solution is barely satisfactory, however. It still implies a kind of cleavage between both domains of political behaviour, in that the politician acts on the basis of different preferences in each domain. Moreover, from an empirical point of view it seems more plausible that individual policy preferences play a larger role in the legislative than in the electoral domain than the other way around.

A better solution is to assume that electors do indeed not vote for strategic policy positions, but rather for estimated preferred policy positions. This need not imply that electoral platforms do not play any role in elections whatsoever. These platforms are important for the electors for the very reason that they are affected by individual policy preferences, and hence give an indication of the true preferences of the candidates and the kind of deals that the candidate is willing to conclude in the legislative area, once she is elected. Of course, this argument has profound consequences for electoral theory. This need not concern us here, however. For the present it suffices to conclude that preferred policy implementation is an assumption for the motivation of politicians in the area of legislative behaviour that is compatible with reasoning about political motivation in other areas of political behaviour. Furthermore, this argument implies that there is a certain relation between the preferences of an elected politician and the preferences of her electoral supporters, so that the politician can be considered as 'representative' for a part of the electorate.

A partial approach to the public demand for public goods

It should be mentioned at the outset that the theory of public demand, as presented here, differs in an essential way from the standard theory of private demand. Whereas the standard theory is concerned with individual preferences which automatically affect actual economic events, namely the allocation and distribution of economic goods, the theory of public demand is concerned with individual preferences, which may or may not affect actual economic events, depending on the result of negotiations with suppliers and the subsequent voting process among fellow demanders. This crucial difference has two consequences for the analysis of demand behaviour:

1. In the private sector, there is usually competition at the demand side and/or the supply side of the market. Therefore prices are set by the market, or by the supplier or by the demander. In the first case, both suppliers and demanders are price-takers, in the second case, the demanders are price-takers, in the third case the suppliers are price-takers. In the public sector, there is neither competition at the demand side nor at the supply side of the internal market. Prices rather follow from a negotiation process that focuses on budgets for discrete packages of services. In order to analyse this process, demand theory must be developed in terms of total rather than marginal values.
2. In the private sector, actors can swiftly adjust to changing circumstances by individual action: therefore demand theory is largely devoted to the properties of optimal situations from the individual perspective. In the public sector, actors often find themselves in non-optimal positions

without being able to adjust by individual action; demand theory has therefore to focus on the properties of suboptimal rather than optimal situations from the individual perspective.

The present chapter treats the demand behaviour of an individual member of a political authority. This actor will be called a 'politician'. The politician is considered as representative for a part of the citizenry, regardless of whether she is elected or appointed.[6] Let us first consider the voting behaviour of the politician with respect to a single public good under the assumption that all other service levels are held constant (hence the 'partial' character of the model).

This situation can be described by the following model.

Model I

$$\max u_\theta(x_1, m_\theta) \tag{1}$$

$$p_{\theta 1} x_1 + m_\theta = g_\theta. \tag{2}$$

The politician is called theta: θ.

There is one variable quantity of a public good: x_1. This variable will be called the 'output' variable. The public good will provisionally be considered as a pure public good. The politician evaluates the public good in terms of a private numeraire good: m_θ. One can think of this good as money available for private expenditure, or as 'net private income'.

Expression (1) describes the objective of the politician in terms of an ordinal utility function. It is assumed to be monotonically increasing, continuous and quasiconcave.[7] Equation (2) describes the income constraint of the politician for a given time period; g_θ denotes gross (before-tax) private income; $p_{\theta 1}$ denotes the tax price of the public good to the politician, which can provisionally be conceived as the cost price (c_1) times the individual tax share (τ_θ). So: $p_{\theta 1} = \tau_\theta c_1$.

The central ideas to be introduced in the context of this model are those of the Preference Function, the Total Evaluation Function and the Budget Output Function. All three functions are evaluation functions that express the appreciation of the politician for packages of publicly provided services. Whereas the Preference Function measures her appreciation in terms of utility, the Total Evaluation Function and the Budget Output Function measure it in money, or 'willingness to pay'.

Figure 3.1b illustrates the Preference Function (PF) by use of an ordinary indifference diagram. At output q_1 the utility of θ is indicated in figure 3.1a by the indifference curve that intersects the income constraint at that output. Clearly the politician is in a suboptimal position at that output

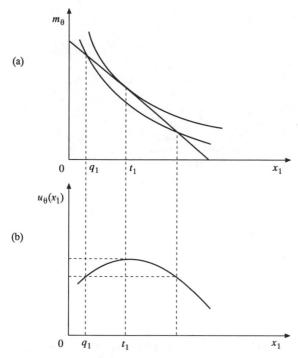

Figure 3.1 The Preference Function in a demand model for one public good

from her individual perspective. Her optimal position is at output t_1, where a higher indifference curve touches the budget constraint.

The PF is an example of a constrained utility function. It measures utility along the income constraint. It differs from the unconstrained utility function in various respects. At this point, it is important to note that is is not monotonically increasing, but that it has a top. This implies that whereas the politician is 'unsatiable' in the unconstrained situation, she has a finite optimal output in the constrained situation. The point in the output space that indicates this output is called the politician's 'ideal point' (t_1 in figure 3.1).

In contrast to the PF, the Total Evaluation Function (TEF) is not a utility function. Rather, it measures the appreciation of the politician for public outputs in money. A complication in this respect is that in general the marginal utility of money is not constant, so that the value of a given public output to the politician (her individual 'benefit') may vary according to net private income available for other purposes.

For the case of model I the TEF is illustrated in figure 3.2. Figure 3.2a

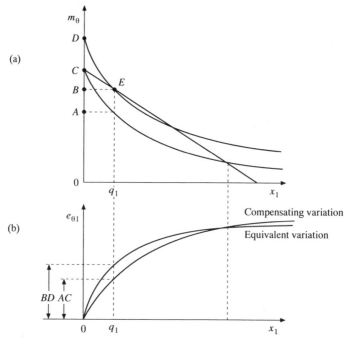

(a)

(b)

Figure 3.2 The Total Evaluation Function in a demand model for one public good

makes clear that the amount of money the politician is willing to pay for alternative output levels of the public good, given the income constraint, can be read off from the indifference diagram as intervals of the m_θ axis. Figure 3.2a shows, for instance, that she is willing to contribute a sum indicated by the axis interval AC for output q_1. Figure 3.2b pictures the relation between the output levels that can be funded given the income constraint and the corresponding axis intervals in a separate diagram. The value of the TEF of θ for service 1 is denoted by $e_{\theta 1}$. Figure 3.2 makes clear that the concept of total value that is employed by the TEF can be operationalized in two different ways. In this respect, it is akin to the concept of consumer's surplus.

It is well known that consumer's surplus can be measured in different ways, dependent on the treatment of income effects. In the presence of income effects there is a difference between, on the one hand, the amount of money a consumer in an initial situation is willing to pay for a move to a second situation if that move is actually taking place and, on the other hand, the amount of money a consumer must receive in order to be indemnified if that move is not actually taking place. The same holds true for total value as measured by the TEF.

Figure 3.2 illustrates both measures of consumer's surplus and total value as line segments of the m_θ coordinate for a move from initial situation C, where the public good is not provided, to a second situation E, where the output provided is q_1. The maximum amount of money the politician is willing to pay in exchange for this output is indicated by AC. This payment brings her back on her original indifference curve after the public good has actually become available. It can be divided into BC, which is the sum to be paid for the given output q_1 of the public good, and AB which is the consumer's surplus resulting from this output. However, when she has to be indemnified when the move to E is not actually taking place, the situation is different. In that case, the payment to be made in order to bring her on the indifference curve she would have arrived upon if the public good had become available is indicated by BD. It can be divided into the sum to be saved, indicated by BC, and the missed consumer's surplus, indicated by CD. Only in the 'Marshallian' case of zero income elasticity are both consumer's surpluses equal. Otherwise, the missed consumer's surplus resulting from the non-occurring increase in public good provision is larger than the actual consumer's surplus resulting from the occurring increase, due to the fact that, *ceteris paribus*, the marginal rate of substitution of money for public goods is larger in the former case.

The definition of the TEF given above, chooses for one of these measures of total value, namely for the one that corresponds to the Hicksean concept of 'quantity compensating variation' as distinguished from that of 'quantity equivalent variation' (Hicks 1943, 1956). 'Compensating variation' refers to willingness to pay (need to be paid) for the realization of a move, equivalent variation to willingness to pay (need to be paid) for the cancellation of a move. In the present case, the move is a quantity change from zero to some positive output. If a good is normal – not inferior – total value in the sense of equivalent variation will be larger than total value in the sense of compensating variation for all outputs that are smaller than some break-even output which is larger than the optimal output. This is due to the fact that if the politician can acquire subsequent units of a good at a tax price that is lower than their marginal value she will end up with a larger net private income available for other purposes than if she is required to pay the marginal value for each subsequent unit. Accordingly, in the former situation she is richer and, if the good is normal, the value of the same output is larger to her than it is in the latter situation. However, if the politician can only acquire a very large output at a given tax price per unit, such that the 'consumer's deficit' on the higher than optimal part of the output exceeds the consumer's surplus on the lower than optimal part, then she is better off by paying the marginal value for each subsequent unit. This implies that at those high outputs total value in the sense of compensating variation exceeds total value in the sense of equivalent variation. Figure 3.2 shows that at some higher than optimal output both TEF curves are crossing.

The idea of measuring total value by compensating variation finds its rationale in empirical relevance. In the negotiation process in the internal market agency administrators may be interested in extracting the largest possible part of the potential consumer's surplus from the political authorities. The measure of compensating variation indicates the maximum amount of money that can be extracted by strategic price-setting for a given change in output (realization of a move). This is the measure that is needed in the analysis of the negotiation process.

It must be emphasized that in spite of the fact that the TEF fulfills a similar role in the analysis of public demand as the Individual Demand Function (IDF) in the analysis of private demand, the TEF remains an entirely different concept. Before turning to the Budget Output Function, it may be useful to review the differences.

A first difference regards the type of relation that both functions express. Whereas the IDF measures quantity as a function of price, the TEF measures value as a function of quantity. This difference can probably be exposed most clearly by introducing an intermediate concept, namely that of the Marginal Evaluation Function (MEF). The MEF resembles the IDF more than the TEF, in that it is also a marginal function. In particular, the MEF measures the price that a consumer is willing to pay for the last unit of a given quantity.

Figure 3.3 illustrates the difference between the MEF and the IDF for the case of model I, by use of an indifference diagram. Figure 3.3b shows the (ordinary or 'Marshallian') IDF as well as a demand function that compensates for income effects based on initial situation q_1: the Compensated Individual Demand Function (CIDF).

Figure 3.3c shows two variants of the MEF. The vertical coordinate indicates 'marginal value' in the sense of the MEF (denoted by $e'_{\theta 1}$). Whereas in the MEF quantity is the independent variable, in the demand function it is the dependent variable (although it is usually measured at the vertical coordinate). The distinction between the two variants of the MEF is based upon the treatment of income effects.

Just like the IDF, the MEF is dependent on prices that have been paid for inframarginal units. The (ordinary) MEF assumes, similarly to the (ordinary) IDF, that the price paid for inframarginal units is equal to the price of the marginal unit. This implies that the MEF measures the slope of subsequent indifference curves along a linear income constraint. The MEF illustrated in figure 3.3c is based on price OA/OB in figure 3.3a. However,

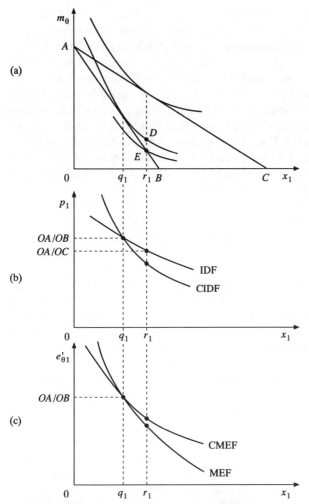

Figure 3.3 The Marginal Evaluation Function and the Individual Demand Function in a demand model for one public good

changes of output along a linear budget constraint induce income effects. This is so because such changes imply that the price the consumer pays or receives for subsequent units is larger or smaller than the marginal value of those units to her. This implies that she will end up with a different amount of money available for other purposes than in the case where she pays the marginal value for each subsequent unit. Consequently, marginal value (the value of the marginal unit to her) will be different as well.

Analogous to the IDF, the MEF can be compensated for such income effects. In the case of figure 3.3, for instance, a move from output q_1 to output r_1 would require a positive sum indicated by DE (in figure 3.3a) to compensate for the income effect (to keep the consumer on the same indifference curve). This implies that the resulting function expresses marginal value if, starting from a given initial situation, the price paid or received for subsequent units equals their marginal value. Hicks has called this function the 'Compensated Marginal (E)valuation Function' (CMEF) (Hicks, 1956). Just as the CIDF, the CMEF is dependent on the initial situation.

Note that if the good is normal (not inferior), and if the initial situation is at the optimal output (q_1 at price OA/OB), the value of the MEF is smaller than that of the CMEF in the entire output domain, due to negative income effects if output is either decreased or increased. If, on the other hand, the initial output is not optimal, there will be an interval in the output domain in which the MEF exceeds the CMEF. This interval will coincide with the interval in which the indifference curve through the point that indicates the initial situation is located below the income constraint. If, starting from such an initial situation, output moves into this interval, positive income effects will affect the ordinary MEF because prices paid (received) for subsequent units will lag behind (exceed) marginal value. Accordingly, net private income will shrink more slowly (grow more rapidly) and marginal value (the value of the marginal unit to the consumer) will be higher.

Since both the CIDF and the CMEF measure the slope of the indifference curve through the point that indicates the initial situation, both functions are identical. In contrast, the MEF does not coincide with either of the individual demand functions. Only in the Marshallian case does the MEF coincide with the IDF and, for that matter, with the CMEF and the CIDF as well.

Whereas the MEF and the CMEF account for the evaluation of non-optimal situations, they do not yet account for the evaluation of discrete alternatives. For the latter need, the TEF purports to provide. This constitutes the second major difference from the individual demand function. In particular, the TEF is the definite integral of the CMEF for initial situation zero, from zero to the argument output. Denoting the TEF by $e_{\theta 1}(x_1)$ and the CMEF for initial situation zero by $e'_{\theta 1}(x_1)|(0)$:

$$e_{\theta 1}(x_1) = \int_0^{x^1} e'_{\theta 1}(x_1)|(0)\,dx_1.$$

The fact that the TEF is cleared for income effects means that this function measures the budget that the politician is willing to pay if perfect price discrimination is applied over all inframarginal units between zero and the argument output, so that in this entire interval all consumer's surplus is eliminated. This means that the TEF measures the maximal amount of money the politician is willing to pay for a given output. Clearly, this is the measure which is needed in the analysis of the negotiation process in the internal markets of the public sector.

An important aspect of the TEF is that – in contrast to the MEF – it is not dependent on the shape of the income constraint. This implies that the TEF provides for a monetary measure of output which is independent of tax price. On the other hand, the TEF is not a utility function like the PF. Therefore higher TEF values may not be identified with higher utilities. Indeed, politicians may very well prefer outputs with lower TEF values above those with higher ones, depending on the utility they derive from the remaining net private income available for other purposes.

In the mathematical appendix (pp. 211–13) the relations between MEF, CMEF, TEF and several other notions from the theory of private demand such as the IDF and CIDF are illustrated by a numerical example.

A final note about the TEF concerns its status from a methodological point of view. In this respect, the TEF fulfils a role that is analogous to that of the IDF in the standard theory of private demand. Like indifference fields and income constraints, both functions are theoretical concepts that are not meant to be subjected to empirical testing. However, as the IDF is providing the theoretical foundation for the market demand function, which can be estimated empirically and used for forecasting purposes, the TEF is providing the theoretical foundation for the Budget Output Function. The latter function must also be considered as an empirical concept.

The Budget Output Function (BOF) indicates the maximal amount of money – 'budget' – that a politician as a member of a political authority is willing to pay for a given output of a good.[8] The BOF is based on the supposition on the part of the politician that her share of the price of the public good remains constant when output is changed. This implies that it can be derived from the TEF through division by the tax share of the politician:

$$b_{\theta 1} = e_{\theta 1}/\tau_\theta.$$

The BOF and the TEF from which it is derived are illustrated in figure 3.4 for a tax share of 1/3. It should be emphasized that although the methodological status of the BOF is comparable to that of the market demand function, the nature of both functions is fundamentally different. Whereas the market demand function is an aggregate function, in the sense

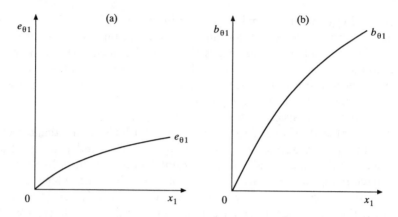

Figure 3.4 The Total Evaluation Function and the Budget Output Function in a demand model for one public good

that it is built up from the IDFs of numerous consumers, the BOF remains a function that characterizes the demand behaviour of an individual politician.

The BOF expresses total benefits for the citizenry, but remains an individual function. It expresses, in other words, an individual view on what government ought to be willing to pay. It would obviously also be possible to define a function that would indicate the sum of the TEFs of all citizens: a kind of 'collective total evaluation function'. Since in the public sector consumers do not decide for themselves, such a function would lack empirical content. For the same reason, the famous 'vertical summation' of individual demand curves, which Samuelson has introduced to derive the optimality conditions for public allocation, lacks empirical content. As Samuelson (1955) has emphasized, there is no practicable procedural rule that is capable of producing optimal collective decisions about the purchase of public goods on the basis of individual decisions. If, on the other hand, we are interested in the positive theory of collective decision-making, it turns out that the BOF is an important tool of analysis.

A general approach to the public demand for public goods

Let us now consider the voting behaviour of a politician in a committee that purchases two public goods in an internal market.

It has often been recognized in the literature that collective decision-making about the purchase of public goods can in principle be organized in two different ways. One is the way of tax price adjustment. Thereby the individual tax share of each consumer is gradually altered until a position is attained in which all consumers agree about the output of the public good to be purchased. By using an adequate voting procedure, and in the absence of collusion among groups of politicians, this position can theoretically be found.[9] This is the optimal position defined by the seminal papers of Samuelson on the pure theory of public goods (1954, 1955, 1958), and the corresponding tax shares yield the so-called 'Lindahl prices'.

In practice, this solution has little relevance to budgetary decision-making in government. Decisions about expenditures are usually made completely separately from decisions about taxation. The voting procedures necessary to find the Lindahl optimum are also quite impracticable.[10] Therefore in most real governments the decision-making process proceeds entirely via the expenditure side of the budget, namely via bargaining and voting. As it turns out, this process proceeds in a fundamentally different way if more than a single service is involved than if only a single service is being decided upon. The difference originates in the much wider opportunities that the formation of coalitions offers in the former case. In particular, politicians can exchange concessions about different services, so-called 'coordinated voting'. In order to study the decision-making process under this condition, the notions of the PF, TEF and BOF need to be generalized. This will be done in two steps. First we shall consider a model with two public goods, then a model with an arbitrary number of public goods.

Model II

$$\max u_\theta(x_1, x_2, m_\theta) \tag{1}$$

$$p_{\theta 1} x_1 + p_{\theta 2} x_2 + m_\theta = g_\theta. \tag{2}$$

Model II includes outputs of two pure public goods: x_1 and x_2. Equation (1) describes political preferences, (2) the income constraint. The second public good, like the first, is available at a constant tax price. Again, the utility function is supposed to be monotonically increasing, continuous and quasi-concave. In this model a PF, a TEF and a BOF can also be derived.

Figure 3.5 illustrates the three-dimensional output space of model II in perspective. ABC is the plane which indicates the income constraint. The vertical coordinate measures the numeraire good (net private income). The surface DEF is the convex three-dimensional indifference surface defined by a given output combination, for instance (q_1, q_2).

As in model I, the PF is a constrained utility function. For the two-dimensional case the PF of the politician will have the shape of a single-peaked utility mountain. It will have its top at the politician's ideal point (point (t_1, t_2) in figure 3.5).

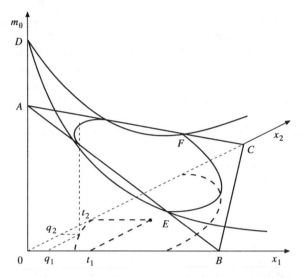

Figure 3.5 An indifference surface in a demand model for two public goods

The TEF surface is the shifted mirror image of the indifference surface through point A (not shown in figure 3.5), with the horizontal plane that intersects the m_θ axis in point A as the plane of symmetry. In model II, the TEF is a bivariate function.

The BOF in model II is straightforward. Just as in model I, it is the TEF divided by the politician's tax share.

Again, the argument is summarized with the help of a numerical example in the mathematical appendix (p. 216–22).

We may now proceed to the completely general case which is described by model III. Model III treats the demand behaviour of an individual politician in a political authority that purchases n public goods.

Model III

$$\max u_\theta(x_1, x_2, \ldots x_n, m_\theta) \tag{1}$$

$$p_{\theta 1} x_1 + p_{\theta 2} x_2 + \ldots + p_{\theta n} x_n + m_\theta = g_\theta. \tag{2}$$

In the case of model III, the budget can be used to purchase n different public goods.

Again, the political maximand is supposed to be monotonously increasing, continuous and quasi-concave. All of the n public goods are available at a constant tax price. The shapes of the politician's resulting multivariate PF, TEF and BOF are straightforward, and need no further explanation.

Public demand for private and group goods

In this section, the analysis will be extended to the public demand for private and group goods. The first step involves the introduction of a single private or group good as a possible destination of public expenditure. For this purpose, we shall make use again of model I.

Model I

$$\max u_\theta(x_1, m_\theta) \tag{1}$$

$$p_{\theta 1} x_1 + m_\theta = g_\theta. \tag{2}$$

Let us now suppose that the output variable x_1 refers to a private good in demand, with or without externalities, or a group good.

As far as private goods are concerned, we may think of a good that is purchased by a political authority and subsequently distributed free of charge among the citizens, for instance an educational service or a medical service, but also of a good that is partially paid for by private households and partially by a subsidy or public contribution in the narrow sense,[11] for instance housing, public transportation, a cultural service, etc.

A complicating factor with respect to subsidies is the structure of the external market concerned (market 1 in figure 2.1). Usually the government takes the position of a price-setting monopsonist with respect to the services it purchases through subsidies. Under this condition, output decisions are mostly taken via the public funding share per unit of output (a given funding share induces a certain output). However, even if output is decided via the public funding share per unit, the output variable x_1 has to be interpreted as the total number of publicly funded units per consumer, and not as the public funding share per unit of output.

Note also that in general private goods remain private, even if they are partially funded by public means. Admittedly, public contributions and subsidies often come into existence by virtue of positive externalities (external effects of production or consumption that benefit persons other than the producer or consumer), but it would be a fallacy of normative reasoning to identify the publicly funded part of a private good with its externalities. In the course of the analysis it will appear rather that the publicly funded part of the price of private goods may well exceed the benefits from externalities.

The same reasoning applies to transfers and discriminatory tax reductions. In these cases, the transfers or tax reductions must be seen as the price that the political authority pays for availability of an equitable income in a certain private household. This good may be supposed to have relatively strong externalities, but again there is no guarantee that actual expenditures will not exceed the total benefits from the externalities.

If a private good in demand or a group good is also a private good in supply or a local public good, the relation between cost price and tax price is not only dependent upon the tax share of the politician and her electoral supporters, but also upon the number of (eligible[12]) consumers and upon the capacity of each good. Since the capacity per unit of a pure private good in supply is one consumer by definition, a separate unit has to be produced for every consumer. The total number to be produced per unit of output provided to each consumer will in that case equal the number of consumers. The capacity per unit of a local public good is larger than one consumer, but often smaller than the entire citizenry. The total number of goods to be produced per unit provided to each consumer will in that case equal the number of consumers divided by the capacity per unit.

The number of (eligible) consumers and the capacity per unit exert a strong influence upon the tax price of a private good in supply or a local public good. Given a number of consumers of h, a capacity per unit of k, $k < h$, a tax share of τ_θ and a constant cost price of c_1, the tax price per unit of output is: $(h/k)\tau_\theta c_1$. This sum will equal the cost price if: $(h/k)\tau_\theta = 1$, that is, if: $\tau_\theta = k/h$. For a citizen with an average tax share, this condition will be satisfied if the service is a pure private good in supply and if it is provided to all citizens (if the number of citizens is $|M|, k/h = 1/|M| = \tau_\theta$).

Since publicly provided private goods are usually not provided to all citizens, cost prices will typically exceed tax prices. In particular, individual tax prices will lag behind cost prices to the extent that the number of consumers is smaller. In the extreme case that a private good is provided to a single citizen, the individual tax price will be τ_θ times the cost price. In practice, the public mode of provision then amounts to *gratis* provision. If a private good is provided to half of the citizenry (for instance primary education), the individual tax price amounts to one half of the cost price. In general, to the extent that the number of consumers of a private good is smaller, the public mode of provision will be more profitable to the consumers in comparison to the private mode.

A similar reasoning applies to local public goods. For these goods, the cost price will exceed the tax price of a citizen to the extent that the number of consumers is smaller and the capacity of the local public good is larger. This is the case because to the extent that either condition applies, the number of units that have to be produced per unit of output provided to each consumer is smaller. This implies that to the same extent the tax price of a citizen with a given tax share will be smaller.[13]

Let us now turn to the PF, the TEF and the BOF for private and group goods. Assume first, that the politician and her electoral supporters belong to the consumers of the good; in other words, the good figures in her utility function and she does not only benefit from externalities. In that case, all three functions are exactly equal to those for pure public goods. Figures 3.1, 3.2 and 3.4 are illustrative of the derivation of these functions under this condition. We have seen that if a private good in demand or a group good is also a private good in supply or a local public good, the number of (eligible) consumers and the capacity per unit will have a strong influence upon the politician's tax price. The values of both the TEF and the BOF will therefore be larger to the extent that the number of consumers is smaller and the capacity per unit is larger.

The PF, the TEF and the BOF take a different shape as soon as goods are introduced which are not consumed by the politician and her electoral supporters. In order to examine this possibility it has to be supposed that the output variable of model I refers to such a good. An obvious question is whether under this condition the output variable enters the politician's utility function at all. The answer is that it may do so in the case of externalities. If externalities are absent, x_1 vanishes from the politician's utility function, but in practice many private and group goods purchased by political authorities have externalities.[14]

From the perspective of empirical analysis it is important how an externality influences the voting behaviour of a politician who is not a consumer of the service concerned. In this respect, two types of externalities have to be distinguished: the one that does, and the one that does not induce a positive consumer's surplus over certain output intervals for a politician who is not a consumer of the private or group good concerned.

Figure 3.6 shows the indifference field of a politician in the cases that a private or group good induces no externality (figure 3.6a), that it induces an externality of the first type (figure 3.6b), and that it induces an externality of the second type (figure 3.6c).

As appears from figure 3.6, only the case of a pure private good in demand is characterized by horizontal indifference curves throughout the output domain. Note that indifference field shown in figure 3.6a implies a utility function which is weakly but not strictly quasi-concave.

In the case of an externality of type I, the politician values positive output levels positively, although her optimal output level is zero. In other words, she is not willing to finance any positive output level entirely by public

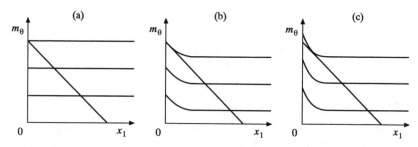

Figure 3.6 Indifference fields of a politician who does not benefit or who is a beneficiary of an externality in a demand model for one private or group good

means, that is to say without any private contribution by the consumers, although her welfare increases when the good is purchased. Examples of goods exhibiting this type of externalities are cultural services (theatre, museums, etc.), higher education, public transport. In the case of an externality of type II, the politician's optimal output level is positive. She is willing to finance low output levels entirely by public means, even if the consumers are not able or willing to contribute by private means. Examples are social insurance, medical care, basic education. Since externalities of type I are not relevant for the purpose of positive analysis, the term 'externality' will henceforth be used exclusively with respect to type II externalities.[15]

It can easily be seen that in the absence of externalities, the PF of a politician who is not a consumer is monotonically decreasing. This is the case because such a politician has to pay a tax price for services that are not benefiting her. Furthermore, the value of the politician's TEF and BOF will be zero throughout in this case. When, on the other hand, the good has a positive external effect upon the politician, her PF will have a top close to the origin and her TEF and BOF will have a small but positive value throughout the output domain.

A general approach to the public provision of private and group goods can be pursued with the aid of model II.

Model II

$$\max u_\theta(x_1, x_2, m_\theta) \tag{1}$$

$$p_{\theta 1} x_1 + p_{\theta 2} x_2 + m_\theta = g_\theta. \tag{2}$$

In order to allow conclusions about the empirically relevant case that a politician does not benefit from all publicly provided services, it will first be supposed that the first good benefits the politician but that the second does

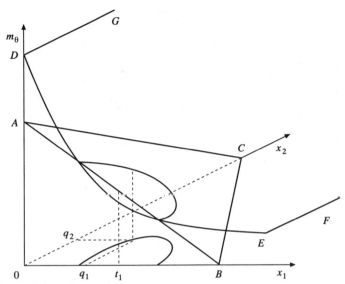

Fɪɢure 3.7 An indifference surface in a demand model for two private goods or group-goods if the politician benefits from one good

not. Figure 3.7 illustrates the three-dimensional output space of model II for this case.

ABC is the plane which indicates the income constraint. Its angle with the ground plane depends on tax prices, and hence on the number of (eligible) consumers and the capacity of each good. The vertical coordinate measures the numeraire good (net private income). The surface *DEFG* is the convex three-dimensional indifference surface defined by a given output combination; for instance (q_1, q_2). Figure 3.7 illustrates the case of a private or group good without external effect upon the politician. Consequently, the indifference surface exhibits a cylindrical shape (the curve of intersection with a plane given by a constant output of the second good, will not vary with that output). If the second good induced an externality – either of type I or type II – the indifference surface would bend upward close to the plane characterized by $x_2 = 0$.

The PF will have again the shape of a single peaked utility mountain. Its top will be at the politician's ideal point, which lies upon the x_1 axis (point $(t_1, 0)$ in figure 3.7).

The surface of the TEF is the mirror image of the indifference surface through point *A* (not shown in figure 3.7) with the horizontal plane that intersects the m_θ axis in point *A* as the plane of symmetry. The BOF can be derived from the TEF in the same way as in previous models through

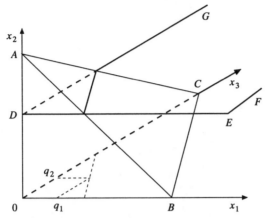

Figure 3.8 An indifference surface in a demand model for two private or group goods if the politician benefits from neither good

division by the tax share. The argument is summarized again with the help of a numerical example in the mathematical appendix (pp. 222–4).

It can also be supposed that the politician does not benefit from either of the publicly provided services. Figure 3.8 illustrates the three-dimensional output space of model II for that case. The plane $DEFG$ is the indifference surface defined by a given output combination, for instance (q_1,q_2). Figure 3.8 illustrates the case of private or group goods without external effects upon the politician. Consequently, the indifference surface is the plane perpendicular to the coordinate that measures the numeraire good. If a good induced an externality – either of type I or II – the indifference surface would bend upward at low output levels of that good.

The PF will have the shape of single-peaked utility mountain. Its top will be located at the politician's ideal point, which lies in the origin. Since the indifference surface through point A is a plane perpendicular to the coordinate that measures the numeraire good, the value of the TEF and the BOF will be zero throughout their domain.

Finally, the completely general case has to be considered. For this purpose, we can make use of model III and suppose that the goods figuring in this model can be of any kind.

Model III is repeated below in vector notation. The vector $\bar{x}$ is of dimensionality n and stands for any combination of outputs. The vector $\bar{p}_\theta$ is of equal dimensionality and stands for the tax prices of the publicly provided services to the politician.

Model III

$$\max u_\theta(\bar{x}, m_\theta) \tag{1}$$

$$\bar{p}_\theta.\bar{x} + m_\theta = g_\theta. \tag{2}$$

For this completely general model it is shown in the mathematical appendix (p. 224–8) that the PF is quasi-concave and hence unimodal ('single-peaked'). This property will be needed in later chapters.

Guide to the literature

The concept of a public good originated in the continental literature, especially in the works of Lindahl, Mazzola, Sax and Wicksell. The most relevant passages from these works are reprinted in Musgrave and Peacock (eds.), *Classics in the Theory of Public Finance* (1967). Public goods appeared in the Anglo-Saxon literature in Bowen, 'The interpretation of voting in the allocation of economic resources' (1943) and, subsequently, in the seminal papers by Samuelson, 'The pure theory of public expenditure' (1954), 'Diagrammatic exposition of a theory of public expenditure' (1955) and 'Aspects of public expenditure theories' (1958). In Musgrave's influential handbook, *The Theory of Public Finance* (1959), the term 'social good' is used for something akin to the Samuelsonian public good (Musgrave used 'public good' for a good provided by government). However, Musgrave's (early) concept of a social good differs from the Samuelsonian public good in that it is not only based on the criterion of non-rivalry in consumption, but also on that of non-excludability. This was made explicit in Musgrave, 'Provision for social goods' (1969). Later Musgrave recognized that both characteristics are independent sources of market failure and noted that it had become customary to reserve the term 'social good' for the case of non-rivalry in consumption only (Musgrave and Musgrave, *Public Finance in Theory and Practice*, 1973, p. 54). At present, excludable public goods are commonly referred to as 'club goods'.

The concept of a local public good was first recognized by Tiebout, 'The pure theory of local expenditure' (1956). It was elaborated in Bergstrom and Goodman, 'The price and income elasticities of demand for public goods' (1973), and Borcherding and Deacon, 'The demand for the services of non-federal governments' (1972), and was subsequently used extensively in empirical work.

The relationship between public goods and jointly supplied private goods was firstly explored by Head, 'Public goods and public policy' (1962). Head criticized the emphasis laid by Samuelson and Musgrave on demand characteristics. See also Head, 'The theory of public goods' (1968). Both papers are reprinted in Head, *Public Goods and Public Welfare* (1974). The distinction between pure public goods in supply and jointly supplied private goods was further elaborated and clarified in Buchanan, 'Joint supply, externality and optimality' (1966); Mishan, 'The relationship between joint products, collective goods and external effects' (1969); and Samuelson, 'Contrast between welfare conditions for joint supply and for public goods' (1969b). The idea of 'variable benefit shares' was proposed in Buchanan, *The Demand and Supply of Public Goods* (1968), and elaborated in Denzau and Mackay,

'Benefit shares and majority voting' (1976). Samuelson, 'Pure theory of public expenditure and taxation' (1969a), argues that the case of unequal individual consumption shares of a public good is indistinguishable from that of unequal benefits from equal consumption shares, and can therefore be omitted. For a systematic treatment of the normative and positive theories of externalities, group goods, local public goods and club goods, see Cornes and Sandler, *The Theory of Externalities, Public Goods and Club Goods* (1986).

Since the reintroduction of the concept of a public good in the economic literature by Samuelson, there have been critical comments on the implied attribution of the benefits of such a good to individual consumers. Examples are Margolis, 'A comment on the pure theory of public expenditure' (1955), which was an immediate reaction to Samuelson's first paper and the more recent paper, Malkin and Wildavsky, 'Why the traditional distinction between public and private goods should be abandoned' (1991). The contents of these papers are more relevant for normative (welfare theoretic) arguments concerning public goods than for empirical ones. The same is true for Meerman, 'Are public goods public goods?' (1980), which states that most traditional public goods – defence, general administration, law enforcement, etc. – do not figure in utility functions of citizens because they are intermediate rather than final services. Apart from the merits of this argument, it would solely imply that for the purpose of empirical analysis, these goods should be considered as group goods which are valued exclusively by private sector producers, rather than as pure public goods.

According to the dominant view in the public choice literature, the objective function of politicians is maximization of electoral votes or plurality. This view originates in the work of Downs, *An Economic Theory of Democracy* (1957). The view that politicians seek the implementation of preferred policies has roots in the work of Buchanan and others on fiscal illusion, for instance in Buchanan, *Public Finance in Democratic Process* (1967). A theory of electoral competition on the basis of the latter view has been stated and developed by Wittman, 'Parties as utility maximizers' (1973), 'Candidates with policy preferences: a dynamic model' (1977), 'Candidate motivation: a synthesis of alternative theories' (1983) and 'Spatial strategies when candidates have policy preferences' (1990).

The modern theory of public demand starts with two books by Buchanan in the late 1960s, *Public Finance in Democratic Process* (1967) and *The Demand and Supply of Public Goods* (1968). The former focuses on the relationship between tax regimes and demand, the latter on the relationship between the demand for separate services under a given tax regime. In a similar spirit is Tullock, *Private Wants, Public Means* (1970a) from the same period. An econometric approach to the estimation of tax shares is provided in Denzau and Mackay, 'Tax systems and tax shares' (1985). Important results concerning the relation between demand and the progressiveness of the tax system are reported in Barzel and Deacon, 'Voting behavior, efficiency and equity' (1975). Lovell explored the relationship between the structure of individual utility functions, tax prices and the distribution of ideal points in an output space for a single service, 'The collective allocation of commodities in a democratic society' (1975). These results were generalized by Kenny, 'The collective allocation of commodities in a democratic society: a generalization' (1978). Empirical studies about the individual demand for publicly provided goods are Barr and Davis, 'An elementary political and economic theory of the expenditures of local governments' (1966) and the papers by Borcherding and Deacon (1972) and Bergstrom and Goodman (1973) mentioned above.

After the initial treatment in Buchanan, *The Demand and Supply of Public Goods* (1968), the general approach to public demand was further explored by Browning, 'The diagrammatic analysis of multiple consumption externalities' (1974) and 'Collective choice and general fund financing' (1975). Advanced, set theoretic treatments can be found in Denzau and Parks, 'A problem with public sector preferences' (1977) and 'Deriving public sector preferences' (1979). The public demand for private goods was explored by Spann, 'Collective consumption of private goods' (1974).

4 Supply in the public sector

The economic theory of bureaucracy

In the western world a large part of the publicly provided services is produced by public agencies. Although there are considerable differences between governments, public production is everywhere a common phenomenon. It is useful to emphasize this fact at the outset of this chapter, because it is neither a logical necessity nor an intended result of policy design. Furthermore, it has not always prevailed in the past. Even such 'typically public' tasks as tax collection and national defence have in earlier times been contracted out to private persons and organizations. The great expansion of the public production sector is a development of the twentieth century, and more particularly of the latter half of that century. It is, of course, tempting to presume a relationship between this development and the expansion of the public consumption sector which has taken place in the same period; it seems as if the political authorities have shown a systematic preference for public suppliers over private ones. Whether this is true or not, and if true, whether there have been good reasons for it, can be answered only on the basis of careful positive analysis. The present chapter reviews the work in this area, and presents the basic model of agency supply.

The first attempt to theorize about production in large, state-like organizations dates back to the 1930s and is due to the German sociologist Weber (1921, 1948). To this end Weber introduced the term 'bureau'. He defined a bureau as an organization which: (a) is large, (b) makes use of employees who are dependent on the organization for their private income, (c) appoints, retains and promotes its employees on the basis of role performance, (d) is structured hierarchically, (e) is not owned by its employees and (f) performs complex administrative tasks by delegation of functionally specialized tasks to its employees. It should be noted that Weber's definition does not specifically refer to a public organization. Weber's interest focuses on the processes of internal coordination and control, which he perceived as essentially similar in large private and public organizations. Furthermore, in his view, these processes were basically effective and efficient in comparison to older forms of organization (hereditary office, guilds) in the public as well as in the private sector of the economy.

In the 1940s a radically different view was exposed by the Austrian economist von Mises (1944). Von Mises emphasized the crucial difference between (public) bureaux and (private) firms, which in his view hinged on the necessity to sell products in a market as a source of revenue. According to von Mises production in (public) bureaux is inherently inefficient because the incentives that guarantee efficiency in (private) firms are lacking. These incentives are the profit motive and competition. Both incentives can exist only if an organization is dependent on revenue from the sale of its products. Remarkably, von Mises' argument does not result in the recommendation to separate public consumption from production and to transfer production to the private sector, but rather in the thesis that state intervention must be severely limited. This thesis cannot be deduced from the inefficiency of public production only. However, in von Mises' view it follows from the additional consideration that because of the lack of an appropriate demand-revealing mechanism, public consumption cannot be organized efficiently either.

Weber and von Mises can be considered as the founding fathers of the theory of bureaucracy. When their contributions are compared, it becomes apparent that von Mises saw more clearly than Weber that large production organizations may fulfil quite different roles in the economic system. In spite of certain common characteristics, as mentioned in Weber's definition of a bureau, such organizations may also diverge widely in their external behaviour towards customers. However, neither Weber nor von Mises paid much attention to the internal behaviour of separate actors within the bureaucratic organization. That is to say, neither of them came to the point of stating a truly economic theory of bureaucracy, which is founded upon assumptions about rational individual behaviour. The latter was accomplished in two books of the mid-1960s, Tullock (1965) and Downs (1967).

The point of departure of Tullock's analysis is the behaviour of the individual bureaucrat. In accordance with the usual economic methodology, Tullock assumes that the bureaucrat is a rational actor who pursues her individual interest. In Tullock's view, the bureaucrat is motivated by the objective of rising in the hierarchy. 'Rising' implies an increase in the number of subordinates and a larger impact on the output of the organization. Moreover, rising is usually attended by an increase in personal income and in the perquisites of office. Tullock examines the consequences of this assumption for the actions of the bureaucrat in response to various environments that are characteristic of the governmental organization.

Downs' approach resembles that of Tullock in many respects. He, too, starts from assumptions about rational individual behaviour and focuses on organizations that produce an output that is not sold in external markets. However, Downs makes more specific assumptions about bureaucratic motivation. He distinguishes between motives in the sphere of self-interest and motives in the sphere of altruism. Among the former he counts the desire for power, money income, prestige, convenience and security, among the latter the desire to serve the public interest. Subsequently, Downs distinguishes between five types of bureaucrats. Two types are wholly self-interested, namely the climber, who is mainly motivated by power, income and prestige; and the conserver, who is mainly motivated by security and convenience. Three types are characterized by motives in the sphere of self-interest as well as altruism. These so-called 'mixed motive' types are the zealot, who is exclusively committed to a very specific policy goal; the statesman, who is committed to a very broad policy goal; and the advocate who takes an intermediate position. On the basis of this typology of bureaucrats, Downs develops a large set of hypotheses concerning the life cycle of bureaux, internal characteristics common to all bureaux, the behaviour of individual bureaucrats of the various types and the patterns of communications, control, and change within bureaux. Many of these hypotheses have to do with the composition of the workforce of a bureau in terms of the various types of bureaucrats.

Although the books by Tullock and Downs can be considered as the starting point of the economic theory of bureaucracy in the proper sense, they do not lead to a truly deductive theory, for two reasons. In the first place neither Tullock nor Downs makes a clear distinction between production and consumption in the public sector. In their view, every political decision concerns production and consumption simultaneously; in this respect, they do not deviate from the traditional view of government as a single economic household. According to both authors, each government is characterized by a hierarchical structure with a 'sovereign' at its top. The sovereign can be a single individual, a group, or a whole electorate; there is no distinction between politicians and bureaucrats in this view. Characteristically, in Tullock's book every offical is called a 'politician', down to the humblest civil servant.

In the second place, Tullock and Downs do not arrive at an explicit, deductive theory because they do not make precise assumptions about the relation between bureaucratic/political competences and objectives. As far as competences are concerned it is necessary to specify explicitly the types of decisions that bureaucrats or politicians can make. As far as objectives are concerned, it is necessary to specify utility functions with specific arguments that are related to the choice alternatives. The first book in which this was done was Niskanen (1971).

The basic structure of the Niskanean model has already been mentioned in chapter 2. The distinction between the public consumption household on the one hand and the public production household(s) on the other is essential. The consumption household, called 'the sponsor', buys services from the production household, called 'the bureau', in an internal market of the government. The authority that decides for the sponsor about demand is a (committee of) politician(s), the authority that decides for a bureau about supply is a bureaucrat. Budgetary decisions can be seen as the transactions by which the bureaucrats sell their services to the politicians. The Niskanean model will be the point of departure for the development of the model of agency supply in this chapter. It will appear however, that the original Niskanean model has to be amended in order to improve its explanatory and predictive power. The amendments will concern (a) the structure of the internal market and (b) the objectives of bureaucrats.

The structure of the internal market

Soon after the publication of the (1971) study by Niskanen in which the idea of the analytical distinction between bureaux and sponsors was developed, various discussions concerning the structure of the resulting internal market arose. The key assumption by Niskanen in this respect was that:

The sponsoring organization is usually dependent on a specific bureau to supply a given service, and the bureau usually does not have a comparable alternative source of financing. In the jargon of economics, the relation between the bureau and its sponsors is that of a 'bilateral monopoly'. (Niskanen, 1971, p. 24)

It is well known that models of bilateral monopoly require additional assumptions about bargaining behaviour in order to generate determinate results. In this respect several variants of the Niskanean model have been proposed and explored in the literature. Some of these will now be reviewed.

The variants of the Niskanean model can most easily be exposed with the help of a cost–benefit diagram. Figure 4.1 confronts the benefits of a service to a politician, as measured by the Budget Output Function (BOF) of that actor, with the cost of the service to the bureaucrat, as measured by the Total Cost Function (TCF) of that actor. The BOF is indicated in the figure 4.1 by $b_{\theta 1}$, the TCF by c_1. The TCF is based on the usual assumption that there are some fixed costs in the production process and that marginal costs

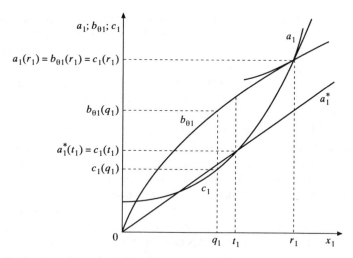

Figure 4.1 Costs and benefits of a publicly provided good

are constant or increasing in the long run. With respect to production, there is no need to make a difference between private and public goods; as far as public goods are concerned, output should in this connection be interpreted in the sense of 'scale' and not in that of 'capacity'.

In view of the lack of competition on both sides of the internal market, the bureaucrat is not only a simple monopolist, in the sense that she can raise supply price above marginal costs, but also a discriminating monopolist, in the sense that she can charge different prices for identical units of output. In Niskanen's words:

A bureau offers a promised set of activities and the expected output(s) of these activities for a budget. The primary difference between the exchange relation of a bureau and that of a market organization is that a bureau offers a total output in exchange for a budget, whereas a market organization offers units of output at a price. The bureau's characteristic 'package' offer of a promised output for a budget has important implications for the behavior of bureaus: under many conditions it gives a bureau the same type of bargaining power as a profit-seeking monopoly that discriminates among customers or that presents the market with an all-or-nothing choice. (Niskanen, 1971, p. 25)

Whether or not the bureaucrat will actually raise price above marginal costs depends upon the objectives motivating her behaviour. In this respect, it is important that in the public sector producer's surplus cannot be taken home in the form of monetary 'profit'. In the original version of his model, Niskanen assumed that under this condition the bureaucrat will maximize the budget rather than producer's surplus. The specification of the bureaucratic maximand will be taken up in the next section, but for the purpose of the present discussion the Niskanean maximand may be used as an example. Let us therefore see what the consequences of bureaucratic budget maximization are under the cost–benefit conditions illustrated in figure 4.1.

Note, first, that if the politician is assumed to be completely passive, an all-or-nothing offer by a budget maximizing bureaucrat of output r_1 at a budget $b_{\theta 1}(r_1)$ is accepted by the politician. This outcome is dependent on the supposition that the politician does not respond to a bureaucratic offer with an offer of her own. The bureaucrat, in other words, is making the final (decisive) offer, possibly after negotiations in which the politician has been making offers as well. The party who is making the final offer will henceforth be called the 'dominant party' in the bilateral monopoly.[1] The outcome of the budget–output combination $(b_{\theta 1}(r_1), r_1)$ thus represents the outcome of the bargaining process when the bureaucrat is: (a) capable of making all-or-nothing offers, (b) independent, and (c) dominant with complete information. The plausibility of each of these assumptions has been called in question; this has led to additional variants of the bilateral monopoly model wich will now be considered.

All-or-nothing offers

The idea that a bureaucrat could confront a politician with an all-or-nothing offer seems scarcely realistic. It appears, however, that the result of the analysis is not dependent on the assumption of all-or-nothing offers. This was already recognized by Niskanen in his original study, where he remarks:

Bureaus do not, in fact, present their sponsors with an all-or-nothing choice. But the offer of a total output for a budget, under many conditions, gives them the same type of bargaining power. (Niskanen, 1971, p. 25 n.)

At another place Niskanen explains:

In effect, a bureau's supply function is identical to the sponsor's demand function up to the point of equilibrium output. (Niskanen, 1971, p. 63)

Although the wording of the latter statement is somewhat unfortunate – the function indicating the supply price for the marginal unit is better not called a supply function if that price differs from the prices of inframarginal units – the purport is clear enough: the bureaucrat can be required to present proposals for alternative budget–output combinations. Whereas the bureaucrat is still able to manipulate the universe of alternatives available to the politician by fixing a price-tag of her own choice to each potential output level, according to the present assumption she is no longer in a position to reduce the universe of alternatives by removing potential output levels from it altogether. An all-or-nothing offer implies that the universe of alternatives is effectively reduced to two alternatives;[2] the present assumption implies that it corresponds to a complete, albeit manipulated, total cost function. This function can be called the 'Apparent Budgetary Cost Function' (ABCF), because it describes the 'apparent costs' of public production, that is to say the costs that are revealed by the bureaucrat during the bargaining process. They consist partially of real (minimal) costs and partially of producer's surplus.

This elaboration of the Niskanean model does not lead to different results than the extreme assumption that the bureaucrat confronts a completely passive politician with an all-or-nothing choice. This is also illustrated in figure 4.1. The curve indicated by a_1 shows the shape of the ABCF that induces a budget maximizing decision by the politician. Similarly to the TCF, the ABCF is a convex function. At outputs smaller than r_1, the slope of the ABCF curve is smaller than that of the BOF curve, at outputs larger than r_1, it is larger than that of the BOF curve; furthermore, the value of the ABCF exceeds that of the TCF at every output, so that apparent costs will always cover real (minimal) costs. In terms of Pigovian monopoly theory, this kinked shape of the ABCF implies that the bureaucrat engages in price discrimination of the second degree.[3]

The kinked ABCF represents a well-known bureaucratic strategy. This strategy amounts to the claim, made by the bureaucrat during budgetary negotations, that an increase of output to the level preferred by the bureaucrat costs little money, but that a further increase beyound that level is very expensive. Once the output level preferred by the bureaucrat is attained, the strategy amounts to the claim that a decrease of output hardly saves money or, what amounts to the same thing, that a given budgetary cut necessitates a very large decrease of output, and that an increase of output is very expensive or, what amounts to the same thing, that a given budgetary increment yields merely a small increase of output.

The assumption that bureaucrats are obliged to reveal a complete ABCF seems more realistic than the alternative that all-or-nothing offers suffice. The question arises, however, whether the former assumption is realistic enough. Since it does not diminish the capacity of the bureaucrat to apply price discrimination of the second degree, the idea has arisen that further constraints on the shape of the ABCF are necessary. An interesting assumption in this respect was advanced by Miller and Moe (1983). According to these authors, politicians in their dealings with bureaucrats often make use of the rule of thumb that services can be produced at constant costs per unit. This rule implies that they require the bureaucrat to reveal a linear ABCF through the origin. Such an ABCF is illustrated in figure 4.1 by the line indicated by a_1*. This variant amounts to the idea that bureaucrats, although monopolists, cannot engage in price discrimination. When the politician reveals her true benefits but requires the bureaucrat to supply at a uniform price, budget maximization by the bureaucrat will lead to output t_1 and budget a_1*(t_1), as indicated in figure 4.1. In this case, the bureaucrat will set the price of the service in such a way that the politician opts for the maximal output that can be produced at that price without a loss. This implies that, in the absence of income effects, at output t_1 the price of the service, as measured by the slope of the ABCF, will equal marginal benefits, as measured by the slope of the BOF. Later, on p. 87, we shall also look at the consequences of income effects under the fixed price rule. Before the analysis is continued in that direction, it is useful to consider other characteristics of market structure than price discrimination, and other bureaucratic objectives than budget maximization.

In the model to be developed in this chapter, we shall assume a complete ABCF and consider the effects on outcomes separately with and without bureaucratic price discrimination.

Independence

The idea of bureaucratic independence was first criticized by Thompson (1973). In a review of Niskanen's original book, Thompson argues that in government there can be no question of a bureaucratic monopoly of supply in the proper sense. Given the competence rules that govern the relations between politicians and bureaucrats in democratic governments, the former could simply order the latter to produce certain outputs for certain budgets. Indeed, as Thompson pointed out, the idea of bureaucratic monopoly in Niskanen's original theory requires a state of total ignorance on the part of the 'sponsor' with respect to production costs. According to Thompson, there is in reality no question of monopoly, but merely of a certain bureaucratic capacity to misrepresent costs. In this interpretation, bureaucrats are only able to act as if they were price-discriminating monopolists as long as they can effectively shield information on real (minimal) production costs from the politicians who decide on their budgets. The moment this information reaches these actors, in spite of bureaucratic efforts to the contrary, monopolistic opportunities evaporate. Thompson did not find it plausible that bureaucrats would possess this type of unlimited capacity for concealment.

Thompson's criticism has been elaborated by Breton and Wintrobe (1975). These authors pointed at the institutions that in reality have been set up to provide politicians with independent cost information: one can think of executive and legislative budget bureaux and of courts of audit. Breton and Wintrobe accordingly amended the Niskanean approach so as to allow for monitoring devices. Furthermore they assumed that politicians alone ultimately decide on budgets, and that these actors will only invest in information and control up to the point of equality between the marginal costs and marginal benefits of such investments.

The question arises whether this approach can still be seen as an elaboration of the Niskanean model. In this respect, it is important to distinguish between two different roles of information in a situation of bilateral bargaining. In a proper bilateral monopoly, information is important because it influences the strategies of the players. Often it will also determine dominance. A party who has better information about her opponent's 'borderline' than the opponent has about hers will tend stick to her offer and pretend that it is final. Even if the opponent does not accept this and makes a further bid of her own, information remains important for the outcome. In the latter case, dominance will also be determined by factors such as bargaining skills and motivations, but the loss of the ultimately yielding party will still be constrained by her opponent's information. We shall come to this role of information shortly. In the Breton and Wintrobe approach, the role of information is different. Here, the relation between the parties is primarily determined by hierarchy: the politician can simply compel the bureaucrat to supply what she demands. In this approach, information determines the bureaucratic room for manoeuvre. In particular, the bureaucrat can manipulate her ABCF only in so for as the politician lacks information about real (minimal) total costs. Information is not a factor that affects outcomes in an otherwise undetermined bargaining game, but a condition that defines a rule of the game.

In later work, the latter approach has led to the 'principal–agent model'. In this model, the demander is called the principal and the supplier the agent; decision-making by the principal on the basis of apparent, higher than real, costs reported by the agent, is called 'adverse selection'. The essential difference between the bilateral monopoly model and the principal–agent model of bureaucratic behaviour is that in the former the bureaucrats are conceived as independent actors who cannot be obliged to comply with the directives of politicians by virtue of hierarchy, whatever the latter's investments in information. This implies that the politicians must secure their interests by strategy rather than by hierarchy.

Looking at the relation between political authorities and administrators of public agencies in actual governments, the model of bilateral monopoly seems particularly appropriate in cases where political authorities do not effectively control the production process. In Niskanen's view, this applies to the departments, bureaux and offices of the US federal government. It also applies to 'quangos', public enterprises and foundations, as well as to the new-style agencies that have been formed since the mid-1980s in British and Dutch central governments. On the other hand, the model seems less applicable to agencies that are organized as regular departmental divisions in parliamentary systems. In the latter systems, ministers must primarily be considered as political authorities. Moreover, they can and do intervene in the production process of these agencies, for instance through organizational measures and through decrees about the use of production factors (numbers of staff, office equipment, etc.). Under these circumstances the principal–agent model offers a more plausible basis for analysis.

In the present volume the principal–agent model will not be developed and explored further. This implies that our analysis and conclusions will primarily be concerned with public agencies that are controlled by inspection of outputs rather than by direct intervention in the process of production.

Dominance with complete information

Finally, the assumption of bureaucratic dominance has to be addressed. Even when it is assumed that the bureaucrat can act independently in budgetary matters so that her relation to the politician is one of genuine bilateral monopoly, it can still be argued that the politician is the dominant party.

Consider, for instance, the extreme case where the politician manages to hide all information about her benefits from the bureaucrat. Miller and Moe (1983) have denoted this political strategy as the 'demand-concealing' strategy, as opposed to the 'demand revealing' strategies in which the politician puts constraints upon the ABCF that she is willing to accept, but is not secretive about her own benefits. A politician who succeeds in the former strategy and who has complete information about the TCF can make a final all-or-nothing offer to the bureaucrat. This leads to the acceptance of the optimal output of the politician, which is q_1 in figure 4.1, and the corresponding budget $c_1(q_1)$. Note that if there are no income effects, q_1 is the output that maximizes the excess of total benefits over total costs or 'political surplus' (the term 'consumer's surplus' remains reserved for the excess of individual value over individual (tax) price; political surplus thus equals consumer's surplus divided by individual tax share). Note that if there are income effects and the service is a normal (not inferior) good, the optimal output q_1 will generally be somewhat larger than the output at which the slope of the TCF equals the slope of the BOF.

The assumption of bureaucratic dominance is motivated by Niskanen as follows:

Although the nominal relation of a bureau and its sponsor is that of a bilateral monopoly, the relative incentives and available information, under most conditions, give the bureau the overwhelmingly dominant monopoly power. (Niskanen, 1971, p. 30)

The supposition implied in this argument is debatable. Particularly as far as information is concerned, it is not clear why politicians would be entirely ignorant about bureaucratic costs, whereas bureaucrats would be fully informed about political benefits. It has been mentioned already that politicians avail themselves of monitoring devices such as budget bureaux. They can also order evaluation studies and make use of external expertise. On the other hand, it cannot be denied that the bureaucrat has a strong position in the bargaining process. Since it is the bureaucrat who has to produce the services, and not the budget bureau or an external evaluator, ultimately she tends to be considered as the decisive expert on costs. It must also be kept in mind that in order to be effective, monitoring activities have to directed at the entire TCF and not just at the costs of the current output level. The productive (in)efficiency of current production – its 'X-(in)efficiency' in the terminology of Leibenstein (1966, 1978) – says nothing about its allocational (in)efficiency. It is not even possible to infer from a given degree of productive inefficiency whether output is too small or too large. Monitoring has therefore to be directed at the real (minimal) costs of the actual output as well as at the real (minimal) costs of alternative outputs.[4]

A less extreme assumption than dominance with complete information is dominance with limited information. A dominant bureaucrat with limited information is able to make the final offer, but her information about political benefits is not entirely accurate. In particular, the politician has been able to conceal a part of her benefits so that the bureaucrat estimates her benefits as smaller than they really are. This leads to a kinked ABCF, as indicated in figure 4.2 by a_1, and subsequently to a budget maximizing output of s_1 and a budget of $a_1(s_1)$. Recall that in order to induce the desired effect upon the politician's optimal output, the slope of the ABCF curve must be smaller than the BOF curve before the kink point, and larger than that of the BOF curve after the kink point. Since the bureaucrat does not know the BOF, she has to make the change of slope at the kink point somewhat larger than strictly required if her estimate of the BOF – which is the lower bound of the uncertainty margin – were true. In figure 4.2 it is assumed that the bureaucrat's uncertainty margin is a proportional part of the total benefits of the service to the politician.[5]

In the model to be developed in this chapter we shall assume that the bureaucrat is either completely dominant or dominant with limited information.

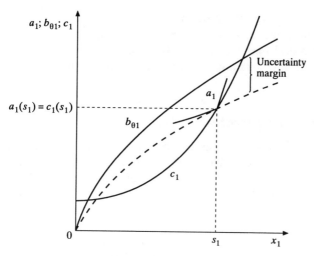

Figure 4.2 The Apparent Budgetary Cost Function of a dominant budget maximizing bureaucrat with limited information

Objectives of bureaucrats

Paraphrasing Adam Smith, Buchanan once remarked that 'it is not due to the benevolence of the bureaucrat that we expect our research grant, our defense contract or our welfare check' (Buchanan's foreword in Tullock, 1965).[6] The question arises, however, what else it is that motivates the bureaucrat to deliver these services.

It has been mentioned already that Niskanen in his seminal 1971 study proposed 'budget maximization'. This proposal was motivated as follows:

Among the several variables that may enter the bureaucrat's utility function are the following: salary, perquisites of the office, public reputation, power, patronage, output of the bureau, ease of making changes, and ease of managing the bureau. All of these variables except the last two, I contend, are a positive monotonic function of the total budget of the bureau during the bureaucrat's tenure in office. The problems of making changes and the personal burdens of managing a bureau are often higher at higher budget levels, but both are reduced by increases in the total budget. (Niskanen, 1971, p. 38)

The assumption of budget maximization has appeared to be the most controversial part of the entire Niskanean model. Since the publication of Niskanen's original book, a lively debate has gone on in the economic and political literature about the empirical relevance of this assumption.

It is important to distinguish between three different themes of this debate, namely:

1. The essence of the assumption
2. The appropriate procedure to test the assumption
3. The empirical relevance of the assumption.

Some important contributions to each of these themes will now be reviewed.

The essence of the assumption

Commentators have emphasized one of two propositions that were originally put forward by Niskanen. The first is the proposition that Blais and Dion in their (1991) survey of the literature, have called the 'formal model'. This states that bureaucrats want to maximize their budgets. The second is the proposition that Blais and Dion have called the 'informal model'. This states that bureaucrats want large budgets, not necessarily maximal ones.

The main difference between these propositions is that the second (the 'informal model') allows other bureaucratic objectives alongside the size of the budget. If the nature of these other objectives and their weight in comparison to the size of the budget are not specified, this proposition does not allow precise predictions about outcomes. This explains the term 'informal model'. However, such a lack of specification is not inherent in this view of the essence of the assumption. Indeed, in one of the first and most important comments on the Niskanean model, Migué and Bélanger (1974) proposed just such a specification.

Migué and Bélanger argued that the factors that figure in the utility functions of bureaucrats are related not only to the size but also to the use of the budget. They pointed out that even if every factor in the utility function of the bureaucrat costs money, the budget would not necessarily have to rise in order to increase the bureaucratic utility. They emphasize that the bureaucrat is primarily interested in discretionary resources, which she can use as she sees fit in order to maximize her utility. She can obtain these resources by realization of what Migué and Bélanger call a 'managerial discretionary profit'. The latter concept was adopted from the corporate capitalism discussion of the 1950s and 1960s.[7] This refers to the expenditure margin, at a given output level, implied by the presence of producer's surplus. In a bureau, as in a private corporation where management is separated from ownership, producer's surplus cannot be taken home in pecuniary form by the bureaucrat or manager. However, it can still be appropriated in the form of expenditures that are not strictly needed to produce a given output. One can think of additional staff, travel abroad, or reduction of the level of effort. It is also possible to add part of the surplus to private income, namely by raising the pay level of staff above the market level, for instance by generous scaling of job requirements. This approach leads to a bureaucratic maximand that contains both managerial discretionary profit and output as independent variables.

The appropriate procedure to test the assumption

On this theme, the literature shows two views. The direct approach rejects Friedman's principle that an economic theory ought to be assessed by testing of its inferences rather than of its assumptions (Friedman, 1953). In this approach, interview responses and behaviour in budgetary negotiations (for instance, annual budgetary requests) are considered as useful data to test the assumption. A problem with interview data is, of course, that bureaucrats may conceal their true motives when they are interrogated about them. A problem with request data is that they are hard to interpret in terms of the Niskanean model. On the basis of various studies, Blais and Dion claim that 'there is ample evidence that bureaucrats systematically request larger budgets', and they adduce the alleged evidence in support of their second proposition (the 'informal model'). However, even apart from the question whether this claim is justified, evidence to the effect that bureaucrats would always seek larger budgets than they currently have supports the second proposition only under specific cost, benefit, and market conditions. Under other conditions, it does not. If, for instance, political demand for a service is rising rapidly, a small budgetary increase may yield a budget that is smaller than the 'large budget' as predicted by some specific form of the second proposition (and *a fortiori* smaller than the 'maximal budget' as predicted by the first proposition). The crucial point is that the Niskanean model does not say anything about the characteristics of maximizing behaviour but only about its results (maximal budgets given the constraints from market structure).

In order to avoid these problems, the direct approach often focuses on the connection between between the size of the budget and factors such as salary, perquisites of office, etc. This connection was mentioned by Niskanen as the rationale of the proposed assumption (recall the quotation on p. 75 above). A difficulty with this approach is that if the connection is falsified in the light of empirical evidence, the assumption of bureaucratic budget maximization can still be true, although it would then need a better explanation.

The indirect approach attempts to assess the assumption by testing hypotheses that can be inferred from it. In the literature, this approach is sometimes described as the testing of bureaucratic 'success' as opposed to bureaucratic motivation. Hypotheses that have been tested in empirical work are particularly concerned with allocational inefficiency (oversupply) and with productive inefficiency (discrepancy between apparent and real costs).

The empirical relevance of the assumption

In the course of the 1970s and 1980s a number of empirical studies were published that shed more light upon the motivation of bureaucrats and the relation of motivation to the size of the budget. Some important results of these studies will now be summarized.

The direct approach

First, in general no positive correlation has been found between the size of the budget of an agency and the private income (salary) or working conditions (particularly number of subordinates) of its personnel. The crucial variable for the attainment of these advantages seems to be promotion within the bureaucratic hierarchy ('getting ahead') rather than budgetary prosperity of the agency. Furthermore, promotion is typically accompanied by greater responsibility, which may be even more important for bureaucratic utility than income and working conditions.[8] These results do not contradict the fact that bureaucratic utility is partially dependent on income and working conditions, but they do refute that these job characteristics are a positive monotonic function of the size of the budget.

Secondly, bureaucratic motivation is not uniform. The distinction between top executives and subordinates is particularly important in this respect. Agency administrators, who are the relevant bureaucrats in the Niskanean model, typically belong to the former category. For them, promotion means shifting to the top job in a more important agency or transferral to a similarly attractive position in the private sector, rather than climbing to the next rung of the hierarchical ladder. This implies that they have to build support outside their own agency. The succesful agency administrator simultaneously seeks to build a reputation of efficient manager and to develop mutually beneficient relations with external clients. For the former purpose, she must assure the loyalty of the agency's workforce, which is essential for the smooth conduct of operations. For the latter purpose, she must see to it that external clients are properly served. In this connection, external clients must not only be seen as the consumers of the services supplied by the agency but also as the producers in the private sector who are dependent on subsidies and contracts from the agency.[9]

The bureaucrat who pursues a career as an agency administrator takes on different appearances in different political systems.[10] In the US federal government, she is the presidential appointee who switches to and from public agencies and private business, think tanks, law firms and universities. She is at the same time an expert in her own policy field and a participant in the political debate. She remains a bureaucrat, however, in that she does not seek elected office and remains dependent on nominations for promotion. In contrast to the (pure) 'politico', who usually serves in an advisory rather than in an executive role, she typically associates herself with the special interests served by her agency; hence she has been called an 'amphibian' (Campbell, 1986). Together with the external clients of the agency and their Congressional representatives she makes up the 'iron triangle' (Aberman, Putman and Rockman, 1981) that has been identified as the most formidable obstacle to policy change in the US federal government.[11]

In European parliamentary systems, such as the UK and the Netherlands we must think of the administrators of 'quangos', public enterprises and foundations and new-style agencies. These officials are usually appointed by ministers or by supervisory boards. They resemble the 'amphibians' in American government in that they are experts in their own policy field and maintain close ties with interest groups of clients in the private sector and with friendly members of parliament but they do not switch as often to jobs outside the public sector. Their careers rather tend to proceed within ministerial departments and various types of public agencies.

In view of these career patterns, the administrator of a public agency will be interested in the acquisition of discretionary resources as well as in a large output. Discretionary resources can be used to provide job protection and opportunities for promotion to agency personnel and thus to secure a smooth conduct of operations. A large output is needed to serve consumers. Both discretionary resources and output can be used to serve clients in the private production sector through subsidies and contracts. This implies that the empirical results in this area are roughly consistent with the assumption of Migué and Bélanger noted on p. 76 above. By shedding a new light upon the roles of output and managerial discretionary profit as bureaucratic objectives, these results suggest a credible explanation of the Migué–Bélanger assumption, and thus contribute to its plausibility.

It is remarkable that when the empirical research effort about the relation between the budget and bureaucratic utility had hardly begun, Niskanen had already accepted the Migué and Bélanger amendment on the basis of common sense arguments (Niskanen, 1975).[12] In particular, Niskanen recognized that both personal income and perquisites were dependent on output and discretionary resources, so that the size of the budget could be omitted altogether as a separate argument in the bureaucratic maximand. More recently, Niskanen has gone a step further, by proposing that overexpansion of output simply be conceived of as a special way of spending discretionary resources, which is particularly sought by bureaucrats who can be characterized as 'zealots' in the Downsian sense (Niskanen, 1991). Of course, the latter consideration does not change the form of the Migué–Bélanger bureaucratic maximand, but it underscores the plausibility of its rationale in the light of recent empirical findings.

The indirect approach

This approach has focused on allocational inefficiency (over-supply) as a consequence of bureaucratic budget or output maximization, and on productive inefficiency as a consequence of bureaucratic maximization of managerial discretionary profit. Four main research procedures have been used to identify oversupply and productive inefficiency; the first of these focuses on oversupply and the other three on oversupply and productive inefficiency simultaneously.

The first procedure attempts to estimate the cost elasticity of political demand. This approach is based upon an insight of McGuire (1981), who showed that the cost elasticity of demand is an important indicator of oversupply. The reasoning is that if the bureaucrat maximizes the budget, demand is necessarily cost elastic (implying a cost elasticity of less than −1), so that a decrease in real average costs unambiguously leads to an increase in total budget.[13] The cost elasticity of demand can be tested empirically.[14]

The second procedure compares outputs and costs of identical services supplied by public agencies and private firms. Studies in this area often focus on services which under the condition of public provision are supplied by municipal agencies because in this sphere comparability can be secured relatively well. Examples are fire protection services, refuse collection, and electricity production.[15]

The third procedure compares expenditures in large and small local governments in metropolitan areas. This approach is based upon the Tiebout (1956) model about the expenditures of local governments. The central idea of this model is that citizens 'vote with their feet' in order to acquire an optimal package of public services for the lowest price. It follows from this model that *per capita* outputs, expenditures and costs should be lower if a metropolitan area is split up in independent municipalities, because this enables inhabitants to move easily to another government and thus destroys the monopoly power of municipal agencies.[16]

The fourth procedure investigates the relation between the rate of growth of public expenditures or tax revenues on the one hand and election outcomes for executive officers on the other.[17] The idea is that if the model and its bureaucratic maximand are true, election results will be worse for the incumbent officer to the extent that the growth rate of expenditures or revenues is larger. Although this idea seems to be plausible at first sight, on closer inspection it appears that various additional assumptions are necessary to infer the hypothesized result from the model. For one thing, it has to be assumed that opposition candidates either have better information about the real (minimal) costs of services than incumbents, or that they can make more credible claims to tame the bureaucracy.

The problem of alternative explanations arises in different forms in each of the research procedures mentioned. In the first and second procedure – bureaucratic behaviour as a cause of cost elastic demand, and of price or output differences between private and public supply – the most straightforward alternative explanation is that oversupply or inefficiency is due to political rather than to bureaucratic behaviour. Apart from the fact that politicians may have quite different preferences depending on whether they belong to the beneficiaries of a service, they may also deliberately give up some political surplus in order to provide benefits to interest groups (recall p. 42). In this respect, an even more sceptical hypothesis has been proposed by Fiorina and Noll (Fiorina, 1977; Fiorina and Noll, 1978). According to these authors, politicians may be little interested in bureaucratic oversupply and inefficiency under normal circumstances because they want to be seen to take resolute action in response to incidental outbursts of dissatisfaction among citizens. Such outbursts will only occur, and far-reaching measures will then only be possible, when 'sufficient' oversupply and inefficiency have been built up in advance.

In the third procedure – bureaucratic behaviour as determinant of expenditure differences between small and large municipalities in metropolitan areas – the most straightforward alternative hypothesis is that the relatively low expenditures in small municipalities are due to a special form of political behaviour, namely tax base maximization (Buchanan, 1971; Sjoquist, 1982). According to this hypothesis, the relatively low level of expenditures in small municipalities is due to political strategies aimed at the prevention of free-riding by citizens of neighbouring municipalities. These strategies would amount to the non-cooperative solution to a Prisoner's Dilemma game. In this game politicians – in accordance with citizens – would rather keep the output of services at a suboptimal level than allow the citizens of neigbouring municipalities to use the services at the cost of their own municipality.

In the fourth procedure – bureaucratic behaviour as a determinant of election results of executive officers – the most straightforward alternative hypothesis is that the growth rate of expenditure and revenues is dependent, among other things, on inflation and unemployment. Since inflation and unemployment are highly unpopular among citizens, the probability is high that they will vote against them.

Some of the studies mentioned partially or wholly succeed in excluding the alternative explanations by a research design that controls for the alternative explanatory variables. Others, however, do not. Looking at the results of empirical research concerning bureaucratic motivation and behaviour, the impression grows that studies in the sphere of comparison between private and public supply (the second procedure) and in that of comparison between large and small municipalities in metropolitan areas (the third procedure) offer the most convincing evidence of the assumptions about bureaucratic objectives as proposed by Niskanen, Migué and Bélanger. Since the Niskanean maximand can be considered as a special case of the maximand proposed by Migué and Bélanger, we shall make use of the latter in the model to be developed in the remainder of this chapter.

A partial approach to the public supply of public goods

The analysis will now be continued on the basis of some formal models. In the following sections of this chapter the focus will particularly be upon the effect of bureaucratic strategies on the shift of political ideal points in the output space of publicly provided services. The present section treats a model that aims to describe the behaviour of a single bureaucrat who provides a pure public good.

In chapter 3 it was assumed that politicians could purchase services in internal markets at a constant cost price per unit. This assumption will now be replaced by the assumption that services can be purchased from public agencies for budgets indicated by the ABCFs of the responsible bureaucrats. The ABCF incorporates the bargaining strategy of the bureaucrat; it may be linear and pass through the origin, resulting in a constant unit price, but it may also take other forms.

A partial model for this case can be formulated as follows:

Model IV

$$\max u_\theta(x_1, m_\theta) \tag{1}$$

$$\max u_1(d_1, x_1) \tag{2}$$

$$p_{\theta 1} x_1 + m_\theta = g_\theta \tag{3}$$

$$c_1 = c_1(x_1) \tag{4}$$

$$p_{\theta 1} \equiv \tau_\theta a_1(x_1)/x_1 \tag{5}$$

$$d_1 \equiv a_1(x_1) - c_1(x_1). \tag{6}$$

Expression (1) is the maximand of the politician. It is identical to expression (1) of model I of chapter 3 and is subject to the same restrictions.

Expression (2) is the maximand of the bureaucrat. It is of the Migué–Bélanger type in that it distinguishes output (x_1) and managerial discretionary profit (d_1) as bureaucratic objectives. The relative weight of both objectives depends on the shape and parameters of the maximand. Similarly to the political maximand, it is assumed to be monotonically increasing, continuous and quasi-concave.

Expression (3) is the budget constraint of the politician, which is identical to equation (2) of model I.

Expression (4) is the Total Cost Function (TCF) of the public good. Output should again be interpreted in the sense of 'scale'. The TCF is assumed to be continuous, monotonically increasing and convex at higher ouput levels. A TCF of this shape can be derived from a usual production function that is continuous, monotonically increasing and concave at higher output levels.

Expression (5) provides the definition of the individual tax price of the good. It says that the tax price equals the average apparent budgetary costs of the good per unit times the tax share of the politician.[18]

Equation (6) defines managerial discretionary profit as the difference between apparent budgetary costs and (real) total costs.

The model assumes that not only outputs (x_1,m_θ) and managerial dicretionary profit (MDP) (d_1) are endogenous, but also apparent costs ($a_1(x_1)$), and hence the entire shape of the ABCF. Gross private income (g_θ) and the tax share of the politician (τ_θ) are exogenous.

The consequences of the model will be considered under two different conditions of market structure as discussed before, namely with and without price discrimination. The former condition is illustrated in figure 4.3.

Figure 4.3a shows the TCF and the BOF of the politician in a cost–benefit diagram. The area between the curves of these functions indicates the room for strategic cost revelation. Figure 4.3b illustrates the magnitude of this room for manoeuvre in a separate diagram, and confronts it with a conventional indifference field that represents the preferences of the bureaucrat for combinations of output and MDP. The concave function $f_{\theta 1}$ relates the differences between the values of the BOF and the TCF of figure 4.3a to output. It will be called the Political Surplus Function (PSF). The PSF is concave because it results from the subtraction of the convex TCF from the concave BOF.[19] The point indicating the bureaucrat's optimal combination is located at the highest feasible indifference curve given the stategy constraint. This point is reached at output t_1 in figure 4.3b and can be attained by choosing the kinked ABCF

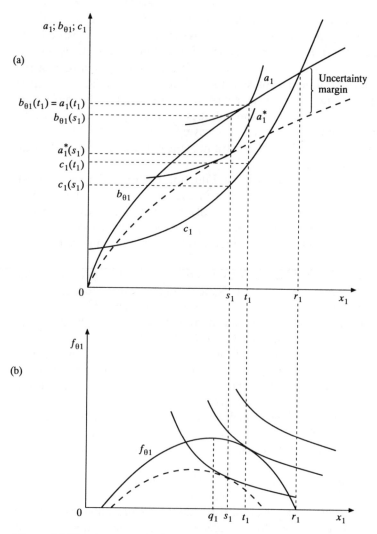

Figure 4.3 The Apparent Budgetary Cost Function of a dominant, output and MDP maximizing bureaucrat with complete or limited information

indicated in figure 4.3a by a_1. Just as the ABCF that the budget maximizing bureaucrat will choose, this ABCF has a smaller slope than the politician's BOF before the kink and a larger slope than that BOF after the kink; furthermore, the value of the ABCF exceeds that of the TCF at every output so that apparent costs will always cover real costs (recall p. 70). When confronted with this ABCF, the politician will be induced to choose the output preferred by the bureaucrat. This will in turn lead to an MDP of $a_1(t_1) - c_1(t_1)$.

Note that the bureaucratic maximand originally proposed by Niskanen can be seen as a special case of the Migué–Bélanger maximand. Since in Niskanen's view only the size of the budget is relevant to the bureaucrat and since the TCF increases monotonically with output, the Niskanean maximand would imply a field of vertical indifference curves of the bureaucrat in figure 4.3b. Under the cost–benefit conditions shown in figure 4.3b, this would lead to an optimal combination of output and MDP of $(r_1, 0)$.

It appears then, that under the condition of complete bureaucratic dominance the politician's ideal point will be shifted upwards from the position it would take if the good were supplied at its (real) cost price. The latter position would be at output q_1 in figure 4.3, which is the output where in the absence of income effects the surplus function $f_{\theta 1}$ attains its top (if there are income effects the allocational optimal position q_1 is at a somewhat higher output than where the surplus function $f_{\theta 1}$ attains its top due to positive political surplus).

Assume next that the politician succeeds in concealing some information about her preferences so that the bureaucrat has limited information. In that case the bureaucrat might think that the BOF of the politician looks, for instance, like the dotted curve indicated in figure 4.3a.

Accordingly, she will estimate the room for strategic cost revelation as indicated by the dotted surplus curve in figure 4.3b. This will then result in an ABCF as indicated by a_1^* in figure 4.3a. Confronted with this ABCF, the politician will opt for output s_1. In this case, the difference between political benefits and bureaucratic costs will not be captured entirely by the bureaucrat in the form of MDP, but rather be divided between the politician and the bureaucrat in the form of political surplus, namely $b_{\theta 1}(s_1) - a_1{}^*(s_1)$, and MDP, namely $a_1{}^*(s_1) - c_1(s_1)$, respectively.

Consider next the case where the bureaucrat is required to call a fixed price per unit as proposed by Miller and Moe. The resulting situation can be illustrated by a price–output diagram, as shown in figure 4.4.

Figure 4.4 shows the Individual Demand Function (IDF), the Marginal Revenue Function (MRF) and the Average Evaluation Function (AEF, also known as the 'All-or-nothing' IDF) of the politician. The vertical axis measures price in terms of tax price ($p_{\theta 1}$) (see expression (5) of model IV). The AEF expresses average tax price as a function of output under the assumption that the supplier applies perfect price discrimination of the second degree (so that political surplus is entirely elimated). Consequently, average tax price according to the AEF equals average benefit (total benefit according to the BOF divided by output) times individual tax share. Figure

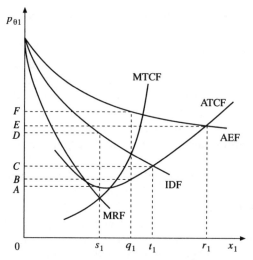

Figure 4.4 Demand for and supply of a publicly provided good

4.4 shows also the marginal and average 'tax costs' of the good, indicated by the marginal and average tax cost function (MTCF and ATCF), respectively. Tax costs, similarly to tax prices, take the politician's tax share into account, so tax costs are real costs times the politician's tax share.

Assuming that the bureaucrat can set the price, and hence the tax price, as she wishes, it appears from figure 4.4 which outputs and MDPs will follow from various bureaucratic objectives. On the basis of the Migué–Bélanger maximand, two extreme cases can be distinguished, namely that the bureaucrat maximizes output or that she maximizes MDP. In the former case, she will set the tax price at OC, in the latter case at OD. Given the individual demand function of the politician, this will lead to outputs of t_1 and s_1 respectively. At output t_1 average revenue (as indicated by the IDF) equals average tax costs (as indicated by the ATCF) and output is maximized. In this case production is efficient. At output s_1 marginal revenue (as indicated by the MRF) equals marginal tax costs (as indicated by the MTCF) and MDP is maximized. In this case, the bureaucrat behaves like a private monopolist on the understanding that profit is not visible but concealed as MDP. Figure 4.4, which indicates costs and prices at the individual level, does not indicate MDP directly, but it does indicate MDP times tax share, which is a proportional indicator of MDP. Since MDP is the difference between budget (output times average tax price) and total costs, MDP times tax share appear in figure 4.4 as output times the difference between average tax price (as indicated by the IDF) and average tax costs (as indicated by the ATCF). If the bureaucrat sets the price at OD, this indicator amounts to: $s_1 \times (OD - OA) = s_1 \times DA$, as shown in figure 4.4. From the point of view of the politician, optimal output is neither t_1, nor s_1, but q_1, at which marginal benefits (as indicated by the IDF) equal marginal tax costs (as indicated by the MTCF). It is interesting that q_1 lies necessarily between s_1 and t_1. This implies that some intermediate variant of the Migué–Bélanger bureaucratic maximand may result in an output that may come close to the allocationally optimal output.

It appears also from figure 4.4 that the outcomes with and without price discrimination, are different. With price discrimination output maximization will lead to output r_1 and maximization of MDP will lead, in the absence of income effects, to output q_1, the allocationally optimal output. At r_1 average revenue (as indicated under the condition of price discrimination by the AEF) equals average tax costs (as indicated by the ATCF) and at q_1 marginal revenue (as indicated under this condition and in the absence of income effects by the IDF) equals marginal tax costs (as indicated by the MTCF). The IDF can under this condition, and in the absence of income effects, be considered as a marginal revenue function because it indicates the tax price that the politician is willing to pay for the marginal unit. In the presence of income effects, equalization of marginal revenue and marginal tax costs will of course lead to an output that is somewhat lower than the allocationally optimal output q_1 (namely the output at which marginal benefits as measured by the CMEF for initial situation zero – the derivative of the TEF – equal marginal tax costs; recall p. 50). Output r_1 is attained at an average tax price of OE and output q_1 at an average tax price of OF. At output r_1 production is efficient. At output q_1, MDP times tax share is indicated by output times the difference between average apparent tax costs (OF) and average real tax costs (OB), which amounts to $q_1 \times FB$.

The bilateral monopoly model without price discrimination may lead to different outcomes for the cases where the bureaucrat maximizes budget and output. If price discrimination is possible, this is not the case. Under the latter condition output is maximized, as mentioned before, at the intersection of AEF and ATCF (at output r_1 in figure 4.4). Since under this condition – and in the absence of income effects – the IDF indicates marginal revenue and since in view of the shape of the utility function of the politician – particularly the fact that it is monotonically increasing so that that the politician is 'insatiable' – the IDF is always positive at r_1, output maximization and budget maximization coincide.[20] However, if price discrimination is not possible, output is maximized at the intersection of IDF and ATCF (at output t_1 in figure 4.4). Since under this condition the MRF indicates marginal revenue and since it is possible that the MRF is negative at output t_1, budget maximization may lead to a lower than output maximization. In that case, the budget will be

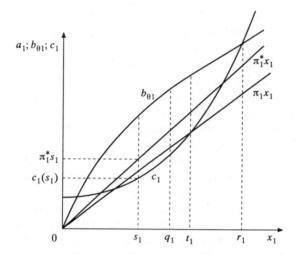

Figure 4.5 The linear Apparent Budgetary Cost Function of a dominant bureaucrat with complete information

maximized at the output where marginal revenue, as indicated by the MRF, is zero.

It may be illuminating to illustrate the consequences of the monopoly model without price discrimination also by the use of a cost–benefit diagram. This has been done in figure 4.5.

Figure 4.5 shows the two linear ABCFs that the bureaucrat can choose when she wants to maximize output *casu quo* MDP. The ABCF of the form $a_1(x_1) = \pi_1 x_1$ leads to maximal output. The slope parameter π_1 denotes the required price (average apparent costs). This parameter corresponds to the ordinate OC in figure 4.4. The ABCF of the form $a_1(x_1) = \pi_1^* x_1$ leads to maximal MDP. Again the slope parameter π_1^* denotes the required price. This parameter corresponds to the ordinate OD in figure 4.4. The outputs indicated on the horizontal axis correspond to the outputs indicated upon the horizontal axis of figure 4.4. In the absence of income effects, the BOF and the output maximizing ABCF have the same slope at t_1, and the BOF and the MDP maximizing ABCF have the same slope at s_1. MDP at t_1 is zero and MDP at s_1 is $\pi_1^* s_1 - c(s_1)$.

The argument in this section is summarized in the mathematical appendix by way of a numerical example (pp. 228–35).

A general approach to the public supply of public goods

The analysis of bureaucratic supply will now be extended to the case of n pure public goods. It will be assumed that each of the public goods is being provided by a separate agency and a separate bureaucrat. In this respect there is no complete analogy with the general approach to demand as pursued in chapter 3. There, it was assumed that each politician received benefits from a number of goods. Here, it will not be assumed that each bureaucrat incurs costs from a number of goods. The analysis will rather focus upon the shift of political ideal points as a consequence of bureaucratic strategies chosen by different bureaucrats for different goods. This implies that we shall not use multivariate real and apparent cost functions. Since in reality agencies sometimes provide more services and since the production processes of these services are often interdependent, it has to be conceded that this is a simplification of reality. It is felt, though, that the elimination of this simplification would not lead to fundamentally different results and would merely complicate the argument.

Although it will be assumed that each of the goods is provided by a separate bureaucrat, the present section will not consider interaction among the bureaucrats. At the present stage it will rather be assumed that each bureaucrat pursues her individual strategy towards the politician without taking into account of how these strategies might affect the strategies of other bureaucrats. The latter assumption will be dropped in chapter 6.

A model of supply for n public goods can be formulated as follows:

Model V

$$\max u_\theta(\bar{x}, m_\theta) \tag{1}$$

$$\max u_i(d_i, x_i) \qquad i = 1, 2, \ldots, n \tag{2}$$

$$\bar{p}_\theta \cdot \bar{x} + m_\theta = g_\theta \tag{3}$$

$$c_i = c_i(x_i) \qquad i = 1, 2, \ldots, n \tag{4}$$

$$p_{\theta i} \equiv \tau_\theta a_i(x_i)/x_i \qquad i = 1, 2, \ldots, n \tag{5}$$

$$d_i \equiv a_i(x_i) - c_i(x_i) \qquad i = 1, 2, \ldots, n. \tag{6}$$

Expressions (1) and (3) are analogous to the corresponding expressions of model IV, but contain a vector of outputs $(\bar{x})$ instead of a single output (x_1). Expressions (2), (4), (5) and (6) are identical to the corresponding expressions of model IV, on the understanding that the model contains as many of each of these expressions as there are public goods and bureaucrats

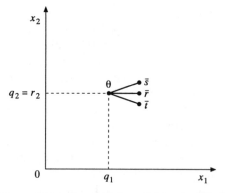

Figure 4.6 Ideal points of a politician in an output space for two public goods if the costs of one of the goods are revealed strategically

in the system. In this way, the model expresses the fact that each bureaucrat supplies a single good. Accordingly, the real and apparent cost functions – $c_i(x_i)$ and $a_i(x_i)$ – remain monovariate functions of output. The restrictions on the shape of the utility and cost functions mentioned in regard to model IV are applicable here.

In principle, the consequences of the present model could also be examined for the separate cases (a) with and without price discrimination, and (b) with and without complete information about political benefits on the part of the bureaucrat. However, there is no necessity to do this, now we have seen that all cases result in similar outcomes, namely an upward shift of the politician's ideal point along the output coordinate in comparison to the allocationally optimal outcome. The size of this shift may vary between the four possible cases, but for the purpose of the present analysis this variation is not important. At this point, the focus will rather be upon the nature of the shift in a multidimensional output space. Therefore we have to consider alternative combinations of bureaucratic strategies.

Suppose first that the politician has to choose a combination of two public goods, one of which is supplied strategically according to apparent costs that deviate from real costs and the other according to real costs. It may be supposed, for instance, that the production process of the latter good is subject to efficient monitoring devices, so that the bureaucrat providing this good has little opportunity to misrepresent costs. In this case, the politician's ideal point will be located as indicated in figure 4.6.

In figure 4.6 output combination $\bar{q}\,(= (q_i, q_2))$ indicates the allocationally optimal output. Figure 4.6 shows three possibilities with respect to the output combination induced by strategic supply. The first is that the utility function of the politician satisfies the condition of separability. In this case, the politician is said to have 'separable preferences'. The condition can be denoted as follows:

$$\delta^2 u_\theta/(\delta x_i \delta x_j) = 0 \text{ for } i,j = 1,2, i = \neq j.$$

Under this condition, the utility of each good is not dependent upon the available output of the other good. If this condition applies and if the costs of the second good are revealed sincerely, whereas those of the first good are revealed strategically, the ideal point of the politician is located at $\bar{r}$ in figure 4.6. Since $r_2 = q_2$, it appears from figure 4.6 that the politician opts for the same output of the second good regardless of her preferred output of the first.

However, if the preferences of the politician are not separable, two other possibilities arise. One is that the goods are to a certain extent substitutes for each other; the other is that they are to a certain extent complements of each other. In the former case an increase (decrease) in one of the outputs leads to an decrease (increase) in the preferred output of the other, in the latter case an increase (decrease) in one of the outputs leads to an increase (decrease) in the preferred output of the other.

Under these conditions, the utility of each good is dependent upon the available output of the other. The conditions can be denoted as follows:

Substitutes: $\delta^2 u_\theta/(\delta x_i \delta x_j) < 0$ for $i,j = 1,2, i \neq j$
Complements: $\delta^2 u_\theta/(\delta x_i \delta x_j) > 0$ for $i,j = 1,2, i \neq j$.

If either of these conditions applies and if, again, the costs of the second good are revealed sincerely, whereas those of the first good are revealed strategically, the politician's ideal point is located at either $\bar{s}$ or $\bar{t}$. At $\bar{s}$ the goods are complements, at $\bar{t}$ they are substitutes. Since $s_2 > q_2$ and $t_2 < q_2$, it appears from figure 4.6 that the politician opts for either more or less of the second good when her preferred output of the first good increases.

Suppose next that the politician has to choose a combination of outputs of two public goods, both of which are supplied strategically. In this case, the politician's ideal point will be located with respect to the allocationally optimal output combination, as indicated in figure 4.7.

In figure 4.7, output combination $\bar{q}$ indicates again the allocationally optimal output. Figure 4.7 also shows three possibilities with respect to the output combination induced by strategic cost revelation, corresponding to the conditions of separable preferences ($\bar{r}$), complementary goods ($\bar{s}$) and substitute goods ($\bar{t}$). Since in the case of complementary goods the shift from the allocationaly optimal outputs will be larger in both dimensions than in the case of separability, the resulting total shift will be larger as well. Analogously, in the case of substitute goods the resulting total shift will be smaller than the total shift in the case of separability.

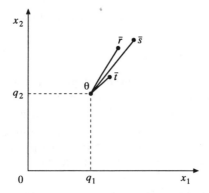

Figure 4.7 Ideal points of a politician in an output space for two public goods if the costs of both goods are revealed strategically

Just as in the one-dimensional case, it appears that the ideal point of the politican shifts upwards under strategic bureaucratic cost revelation. The size of the shift depends not only on the possibility of price discrimination and the degree of informational advantage, but also upon the substitutability or complementarity of the goods.

The public supply of private and group goods

Consider now the consequences of model V for the location of the politician's ideal point for private goods, with or without externalities, and group goods. After what has been said in chapter 3 about the demand for these types of goods, it should not be surprising that these consequences are dependent on who the consumers are. If the politician under consideration belongs to the consumers of some or all of these goods her ideal point will move in a different way under the influence of bureaucratic strategies than if she benefits at best from an external effect.

As we have seen, the partial cost–benefit diagram of a politician who belongs to the consumers of a service looks the same regardless of whether the service is a private good, a group good or a pure public good. However, due to low tax prices and corresponding high partial BOF values, the difference between total benefits and total costs will typically be quite large if the good has a limited number of (eligible) consumers.[21] As mentioned on p. 56, tax prices depend on the number of consumers, so that in principle the room for bureaucratic cost manipulation will be larger to the extent that the number of consumers is smaller.

We have seen also that if the politician does not belong to the consumers of the service, the partial BOF-values are zero throughout or, in the case of externalities, almost zero throughout, and the optimal output of the

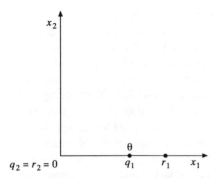

Figure 4.8 Ideal points of a politician in an output space for two private or group goods if the costs of one or both goods are revealed strategically

politician will be zero, or almost zero, regardless of bureaucratic strategies.

As soon as more private or group goods enter the picture, it is rarely the case that the politician belongs to the consumers of each one of them. It is, on the contrary, characteristic for decision-making about such goods that different politicians belong to the consumers of different goods. In order to examine this possibility, goods not consumed by the politician under consideration were, of course, introduced in the demand models II and III of chapter 3. The analysis of the present section builds on these results.

Suppose, to begin with, that in a supply model for two goods the bureaucrat supplying the first good engages in strategic cost revelation, whereas the bureaucrat supplying the second good does not. On p. 59 it was shown that if a politician has to choose between output combinations of two goods that are available at cost price and if she is a consumer of the first good but not of the second, her ideal point in the output space will be located upon or, in the case of externalities of type II, close to, the output axis of the first good. If, in such a situation, the bureaucrat supplying the first good turns to strategic cost revelation, the politician's ideal point will shift upwards along the output axis of that good. As in the case of a pure public good, the size of the shift will be dependent on the possibility of price discrimination and the degree of informational advantage, but for the purpose of the present analysis this distinction is not important. This is illustrated in figure 4.8, where the ideal point shifts from $\bar{q}(=(q,0))$ to $\bar{r}(=(r,0))$.

If the politician were to decide alone, that is to say if her preferences were decisive for the political authority as a whole, the upward shift of her ideal point would of course be in the bureaucrat's interest. However, in reality this is usually not the case. If not, it is doubtful whether the bureaucrat would engage in strategic cost revelation. To see this, it should be noted that the politician does (almost) not benefit from the second good which is supplied by a different bureaucrat. If in the initial situation outputs of both goods are being supplied, a bureaucratic strategy that would diminish the politician's political surplus from the first good will be very risky. Since the politician has to pay a tax price for the second good although she does not benefit, her preferred output of it is (almost) zero and a positive output leads to a 'negative political surplus' or political deficit for her. By choosing such a strategy, the bureaucrat could easily turn the total political surplus of the politician from both goods negative, and thus motivate her to opt for the termination of public provision of both goods altogether. Of course, the politician will under this condition still prefer to purchase only the first good and her optimal output of it will still be larger than under sincere cost revelation, but this outcome will emerge only if the politician decides on her own. As soon as other politicians, who are only interested in the second good, enter the picture, the termination of all public provision might be an acceptable compromise. The question of what will happen under these circumstances can only be answered when decision-making by a political committee is taken into account, and will be pursued in chapter 6.

Suppose next, that in the same model, the bureaucrat supplying the second good engages in strategic cost revelation, whereas the bureaucrat supplying the first good does not. If the politician's ideal point is on the output axis of the first good, for instance at $\bar{q}$ in figure 4.8, it will remain in its place and if, in the case of an externality of type II, it is not exactly on that output axis, but close to it, such a stategy will press it even closer to the axis. The ideal point will thus hardly shift. However, if in the initial situation substantial outputs of both goods are being supplied, the politician's total political surplus from both goods may easily turn negative. Again, it is doubtful whether the bureaucrat will engage in such a risky strategy.

Suppose next, that in the same model, one of the bureaucrats considers engaging in strategic cost revelation, whereas the other bureaucrat for some reason has already chosen such a strategy. This would change nothing for the former bureaucrat. If in the initial situation both goods are being supplied in substantial amounts, the politician's total political surplus from both goods might already be very small or negative, and strategic cost revelation by one more bureaucrat will worsen the situation. Of course, it also remains true that, apart from changes in political surplus, the politician's ideal point will shift upwards or remain roughly in its place depending on whether or not she is a consumer of the good.

Suppose, finally, that the politician does not consume either good. On p. 60 it was shown that if a politician has to choose between output combinations of two goods that are available at real cost price, and if she is not a consumer of either of the goods, her ideal point will be located in or, in the case of externalities of type II, close to, the origin. If, in such a situation, a bureaucrat supplying one of the goods turns to stategic cost revelation, the politician's ideal point will remain in the origin or be pushed towards an output axis close to the origin. The same will happen if a bureaucrat supplying one of the goods turns to strategic costs revelation, whereas the costs of the other good are, for some reason, already being revealed strategically. Although in none of these cases will there be a sizeable shift of the politician's ideal point, such strategies will increase the politician's total political deficit. Note, however, that with respect to a politician who does not consume either good, there is no special risk involved in strategic cost revelation because such a politician will opt for zero outputs of both goods regardless of tax costs.

In a supply model for more than two private or group goods, similar reasonings apply. A bureaucrat switching to strategic cost revelation will push the ideal point of a politician who consumes the good concerned upwards along the dimension of that good, but will hardly affect the ideal point of a politician who does (almost) not benefit. In such models, every switch from sincere to strategic cost revelation is very risky if the committee consists of more than one politician because it increases the probability that the termination of the public provision of a certain group of goods will improve the political surplus of a decisive group of politicians.

The analysis of the consequences of bureaucratic strategies for the location of the politician's ideal point in the output space of publicly provided services is now complete. Whether or not a bureaucrat will actually engage in strategic cost revelation under the various conditions considered in this chapter does not only depend upon the reactions of individual politicians but also upon the reactions of committees of politicians, such as cabinets and chambers of parliament. The analysis of decision-making in political committees has therefore to be explored.

Guide to the literature
The modern theory of bureaucracy starts with Weber and von Mises. Weber's most important contributions in this area are part I of his *Wirtschaft und Gesellschaft* (1921), published in English under the title *The Theory of Social and Economic Organization*, and part III, chapter 6 of *Wirtschaft and Gesellschaft*, published in English in *From Max Weber: Essays in Sociology* (1948). Von Mises' seminal contribution is *Bureaucracy* (1944). The economic theory of bureaucracy in the proper sense started with Tullock, *The Politics of Bureaucracy* (1965) and Downs, *Inside Bureaucracy* (1967). Niskanen developed his theory of bureaucracy in *Bureaucracy and Representative Government* (1971); the basic ideas had already been published in 'The peculiar economics of bureaucracy' (1968). Niskanen's book was reviewed by Thompson (1973) and by Tullock (1970b). For a critical review, see Margolis (1975). A not entirely scientific, but still influential, contribution to the early literature on bureaucracy is Parkinson, *Parkinson's Law* (1957).

The basic papers about the structure of the internal market are Miller and Moe, 'Bureaucrats, legislators and the size of government' (1983) which treats price discrimination and dominance, and Breton and Wintrobe, 'The equilibrium size of a budget maximizing bureau' (1975) which treats bureaucratic independence. Surveys of the literature about the principal–agent model with particular attention to applications in public organizations are Moe, 'The new economics of organization' (1984) and Miller and Moe, 'The positive theory of hierarchies' (1986). A view about the budgetary bargaining proces in which neither the politician nor the bureaucrat is dominant is provided in Miller, 'Bureaucratic compliance as a game on the unit square' (1977). In this view, the politician decides about the budget and the bureaucrat about the output (and thereby about MDP). This leads to a non-zero-sum two-person game that may not have a unique equilibrium. This approach implies that the politician is capable of strategic (non-sincere) benefit revelation, which seems somewhat problematical from an empirical point of view. Surveys of alternative models of internal market structure are Bendor, 'Review article: formal models of bureaucracy' (1988); Conybeare, 'Bureaucracy, monopoly and competition: a critical analysis of the budgetary maximizing model of bureaucracy' (1984); Blankart, 'Zur ökonomische Theorie der Bureaucratie' (1975); Moene, 'Types of bureaucratic interaction' (1986); and the contribution by Miller and Moe (1983) mentioned above. Weingast has argued in 'A principal–agent perspective on Congressional–bureaucratic relations' (1984) that the principal–agent model is applicable to the relation between Congress and agency administrators in the US federal government. The same approach is followed in Bendor, Taylor and van Gaalen, 'Bureaucratic expertise versus legislative authority: a model of deception and monitoring in budgeting' (1985) and 'Politicians, bureaucrats and asymmetric information' (1987). In 'Congressional oversight overlooked: policy patrols versus fire alarms' (1984), McCubbins and Schwarz have emphasized that political oversight of bureaucratic performance is for a large part taken care of by affected third parties. In their view, legislators spend little effort in reviewing activities themselves, but mainly react to complaints of third parties ('fire alarm oversight' as opposed to 'police patrol oversight'). In *The Logic of Bureaucratic Conduct* (1982), Breton and Wintrobe have amended the model of their seminal 1975 paper by allowing for 'trade' in 'efficient informal services' by bureaucrats in exchange for 'policy characteristics', such as output, and income in kind or in money (salary). This idea seems compatible with the model presented in this chapter, and could be used to elaborate the concept of the 'uncertainty margin'.

Essential theoretical papers about bureaucratic motivation and objectives are Migué and Bélanger, 'Toward a general theory of managerial discretion' (1974) and Niskanen, 'Bureaucrats and politicians' (1975). The observation that profit or MDP maximization by a monopolist in a market with second degree price discrimination leads to optimal allocation was first made in Holcombe and Price, 'Optimality and the institutional structure of bureaucracy' (1978). Surveys of the empirical literature on the basis of the indirect approach are Orzechowski, 'Economic models of bureaucracy: survey, extensions and evidence' (1977) and Kiewiet, 'Bureaucrats and budgetary outcomes: quantative analyses' (1991). An interesting collection of papers about the Niskanean bureaucratic maximand, including some surveys of empirical studies as well as a retrospection by Niskanen, is Blais and Dion, *The Budget-maximizing Bureaucrat. Appraisals and Evidence* (1991).

An extensive, though somewhat eclectic, survey of the economic theory of bureaucracy is Jackson, *The Political Economy of Bureaucracy* (1982). Useful surveys of the theoretical as well as the empirical literature about the bilateral monopoly model is provided in chapter 14 of Mueller, *Public Choice II* (1989). A useful theoretical survey is Chan and Mestelman, 'Institutions, efficiency and the strategic behaviour of sponsors and bureaux' (1988).

5 Political decision-making

Elements of game theory

Political authorities are often collective bodies: cabinets, councils, houses of parliament, etc. The analytical tools for the study of interaction among members of collective bodies will be taken from the theory of games, especially from the theory of a specific type of n-person game that will be introduced and described in the present section and that will be called a 'budgetary game'. In the next section some additional concepts with respect to budgetary games will be defined, namely those of the preference set, the dominant set and the Pareto superior set. With the help of these concepts it will be possible to review in the following sections some elementary game-theoretic results and to consider the consequences of these results for the problem of stability in budgetary games.

Up to this point the theory of public demand has been considered only at the level of the individual politician. In reality, we observe collective bodies. These bodies do not only decide for themselves but for all citizens of government. This state of affairs raises the question of how individual politicians interact with one another as members of a committee in the process of reaching decisions, and this question leads to the analysis of collective decision-making in the proper sense. As it turns out, game theory is an almost indispensable analytical tool when entering this domain.

The required elements of game theory will be introduced in a way that is understandable to the reader who has no prior knowledge. On the other hand, only those elements will be described that are strictly necessary to follow the argument. This implies, among other things, that matters will not be introduced in a more or less systematic way, starting with games in extensive and normal form and then successively proceeding to the various basic types of games. Instead, the present section immediately introduces a very specific and, from the mainstream game-theoretical perspective, very eccentric type of game, that cannot be found in most introductory textbooks in the field. The intended type of game can be specified as follows: the game is (a) n-person, (b) cooperative, (c) economic and (d) simple and majoritan. For reasons that will become clear, this type of game will be called a 'budgetary game'. The game will be introduced by reviewing its various properties.

N-person games

'N-person-games' is the conventional name for games of more than two players. Although the special analytical tools that have been developed to study games of more than two players are perfectly applicable to games of only two players or even one player, the latter types of games can for many purposes more fruitfully be studied on the basis of a different analytical apparatus.

Cooperative games

Secondly, the budgetary game is called 'cooperative'. In cooperative games the players are allowed to communicate freely among each other, and to make binding agreements before choosing their strategies.

Foremost among the analytical devices of n-person, cooperative game theory is a notion called the 'characteristic function'. This function provides information about the 'value' of the game to the various coalitions of players that may be formed. The basic idea of the characteristic function is that coalitions of players may combine their strategies in such a way that they are able to guarantee certain results regardless of how well players outside the coalition are doing. The most favourable result that the coalition is able to secure for itself in this way is the 'value' of the game to the coalition in the sense of the characteristic function. Some short remarks about the characteristic function are now in order.

There are several ways in which the value of a game can be measured. The easiest way is through a single real number that in some way indicates the 'joint pay-off' the coalition is able to secure for its members. In this case the characteristic function is a real-valued function that maps the set of 2^n possible coalitions into the straight line that represents the scale of 'joint pay-off' to the coalition members. As a formal convention it is usually assumed that the value of the empty coalition is zero. Of course, this form of the characteristic function is meaningful only under quite restrictive conditions. In particular, it requires that the pay-off can be treated as a so-called 'transferable utility'. This implies two things: (a) that it is possible to characterize the preferences of the players in terms of cardinal individual utility,[1] and (b) that there exists a perfectly divisible and unrestrictedly transferable commodity, for which all players hold linear utility.[2] Only under these conditions does it make sense to characterize the value of a coalition in terms of a single quantity, which is invariant under alternative distributions among its members. Although scholars in the field of game theory seem to be divided about the gravity of the limitation of empirical relevance resulting from these conditions in particular applications, there is no reason to worry, since value can be measured in less restrictive ways. In the case of budgetary games this will indeed be appropriate, but for the purpose of discussion it is useful to stick for a while with the characteristic function in its simplest shape.

It is a logical consequence of the idea of 'cooperation' among players that the characteristic function satisfies the condition of 'superadditivity'. To appreciate the meaning of this condition, it is useful to introduce some symbolism.

The real-valued characteristic function will be denoted by $v(S)$. The argument S in this expression denotes a particular coalition of players, that is a subset of the set of all players (including the empty coalition). The set of all players, called the 'grand coalition' is usually denoted by N. Sticking with the convention to denote individual actors by lower case Greek letters, it follows:

$$N = \{1, 2, \ldots, v\}$$

where v denotes the last player, and

$$S \subseteq N.$$

A characteristic function is said to be superadditive when it satisfies:

$$v(S \cup T) \geq v(S) + v(T) \text{ for every } S, T, S \cap T = \varnothing.$$

Superadditivity follows from the fact that the set of outcomes a coalition can guarantee can never shrink when the coalition picks up additional members. This is the case because by picking up additional members, the coalition adds to the set of available combined strategies without losing any.

A special kind of game emerges if the condition of superadditivity is not for at least some coalition satisfied by strict inequalities, so that:

$$v(S \cup T) = v(S) + v(T) \text{ for every } S, T, S \cap T = \varnothing.$$

In such a game, called 'inessential', it makes no sense to any player to join any coalition. So all players stay apart and receive their own value:

$$v(\{\xi\}) \text{ for every } \xi, \xi \in N.$$

All other games, for which it thus holds that at least some coalition does make sense to some players, are called 'essential'.

In some games the characteristic function is not a good indicator of the strength of coalitions in spite of its relevance as an indicator of their capabilities. This may particularly (but not exclusively) be the case if the game is not 'constant-sum', so that the value of the game to a coalition and that to its countercoalition do not sum up to the same number for all pairs of coalitions and countercoalitions (the constant-sum condition can be written as $v(S) + v(N - S) = v(N)$ for every $S,S \subseteq N$). In such a game, the players excluded from a certain coalition might not be motivated, as they are in constant-sum games, to form a countercoalition and to do whatever they can to keep the coalition from which they are excluded, at its minimum, because this might not be in their own interest. It might be tempting to define the value of the game to a coalition in this case as the pay-off the coalition will receive if the players outside the coalition maximize their own results. However, such a definition would be unwarranted, since it would not take into account the threat capacity of the excluded players following from the possibility of acting in concert – by formation of the countercoalition – and of inflicting maximal harm upon the coalition (the 'brag strategy'). In practice, this is of course the type of game where not only the skills but also the moral properties of the players become of paramount importance.

Let us now see what kind of measure is possible when the assumption of 'transferable utility' is dropped and no more than ordinal utility is assumed at the level of the individual player.

One alternative is to measure value in terms of a set of pay-off vectors, namely the set of pay-off vectors resulting from the outcomes the coalition can guarantee.[3] The value of the game to the empty coalition is then assumed to be the empty set $v(\varnothing) = \varnothing$. This measure renders the characteristic function into a set-valued function. The sets in its codomain are called characteristic sets. Each characteristic set consists of a number of pay-off vectors and each pay-off vector consists of a row of pay-offs to the players which are individual utilities. Usually it is assumed that if a characteristic set includes a pay-off vector that assigns a certain pay-off to a coalition member it also includes all pay-off vectors that, *ceteris paribus*, assign lower pay-offs to that coalition member. This so-called 'assumption of free disposal' is based on the reasonable idea that it is always possible for a player to 'throw utility away'.

It deserves attention that according to this measure the pay-off vectors in the characteristic set not only describe the individual pay-offs to the members of a coalition but also those to the players excluded from that coalition. Note that this is just a consequence of the chosen way of operationalization. Another possibility would be to restrict the pay-off vectors in the characteristic set to the individual pay-offs of the coalition members. The latter convention seems more in accordance with the basic idea of a characteristic function, but it has the inconvenient consequence that the characteristic sets do not belong to the same utility space. Since the pay-offs to the players outside the coalition are not relevant to the purposes the characteristic function has to serve – recall that the function purports to indicate the pay-offs that the coalition can secure for itself – it is usually assumed that the pay-offs of the excluded players can be of any magnitude. Another convention could be to assign, arbitrarily, zero pay-off to the excluded players. In view of the ordinal character of the individual utility indices, 'zero' has of course no intrinsic meaning in this formulation. It must be emphasized that this extension of the pay-off vectors in the characteristic set to the excluded players is a purely formal convention, that facilitates reasoning about characteristic sets because it places them in the same utility space, but that it has nothing to do with the underlying game. In particular, it does not mean that the individual pay-offs assigned to the excluded players in a characteristic set could ever be realized according to the rules of the game.[4]

Of course, the characteristic function in the present set-valued form must also be superadditive. The condition of superadditivity can be written as follows:

$$v(S \cup T) \supseteq v(S) \cap v(T) \text{ for every } S, T, \ S \cap T = \varnothing.$$

A geometrical illustration is given in figure 5.1.

Figure 5.1 shows the utility space for a two-person game. The players are θ and ψ. The coordinates have only ordinal meaning. The characteristic sets (of the non-empty coalitions) take the form of half-spaces indicated by the shading at one side of the dividing lines. Since the intersection of $v(\{\theta\})$ and $v(\{\psi\})$ is included in $v(\{\theta, \psi\})$, superadditivity holds.

Economic games

The third specification concerns the type of outcomes (endstates) games can have. When these outcomes are 'commodity bundles' accruing to the players, the games are called 'economic games'.

When analysing economic games it is important not to confuse the utility space in which the pay-off vectors are defined with the commodity space in which the outcomes are defined. Some additional symbolism will be useful in this respect. Outcomes of economic games will be denoted by lower case letters, indicating commodity vectors. Each component of such a vector represents a quantity of a private or public good benefiting one or more of

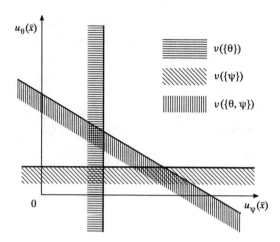

Figure 5.1 Superadditivity of a set-valued characteristic function

the players. So if there are n goods, the dimensionality of the commodity vector is n: $\bar{x} = (x_1, x_2, \ldots, x_n)$.

The utility functions that relate individual pay-offs to commodity bundles are called 'pay-off functions'. Sticking to the convention that utility functions are denoted by the letter u, the pay-off to player ζ resulting from commodity bundle $\bar{x}$ can be symbolized by $u_\zeta(\bar{x})$.

Simple majority games

The fourth and last property of the budgetary game to be introduced concerns the specification of the characteristic function: the budgetary game is a so-called 'simple game'.

In order to clarify the essence of a simple game, it is useful to present first the traditional definition which applies to games in real-valued characteristic function form. Such a game is called 'simple' when its characteristic function takes on only two different values. Since in this case one value must be larger than the other, the coalitions in simple games can be categorized according to whether they are 'winning' or 'losing'.

Because of superadditivity each coalition composed of a subset of players of a losing coalition is losing as well. Also, since at least one coalition must be losing, the empty coalition is losing. Furthermore, superadditivity implies that if a coalition composed of a subset of players of a larger coalition is winning, the larger coalition is also winning. Since at least one coalition must be winning, the grand coalition is winning.

Summarizing, when the value of the game to a winning coalition is denoted by 1, the set of all coalitions by $\mathcal{N}$, the set of all winning coalitions by $\mathcal{W}$ and the set of all losing coalitions by $\mathcal{L}$, a simple game is characterized by:

$$\mathcal{W} \cup \mathcal{L} = \mathcal{N} \text{ and } \mathcal{W} \cap \mathcal{L} = \varnothing \tag{1}$$

$$v(S) = 0 \text{ for every } S, S \in \mathcal{L} \tag{2}$$

$$v(S) = 1 \text{ for every } S, S \in \mathcal{W} \tag{3}$$

$$\{T \mid T \subseteq S\} \in \mathcal{L} \text{ for every } S, S \in \mathcal{L} \tag{4}$$

$$\{T \mid T \supseteq S\} \in \mathcal{W} \text{ for every } S, S \in \mathcal{W} \tag{5}$$

$$\varnothing \in \mathcal{L} \tag{6}$$

$$N \in \mathcal{W}. \tag{7}$$

In view of the convention regarding the structure of the characteristic function adopted in this study, it is not possible to transpose the given definition of a simple majority game more or less directly to the case of a game in set-valued characteristic function form. This is a consequence of the convention to include the individual pay-offs to non-members of a coalition in the pay-off vectors composing the characteristic set. Since according to this convention the pay-offs to non-members of a coalition can be of any magnitude, the characteristic function of any game will by definition have as many characteristic sets, and thus values, as there are coalitions.

However, it is still possible to capture the essence of a simple game – namely that the value of the game to a coalition is either large or small depending on whether the coalition is winning or losing – in terms of the set-valued characteristic function. In view of the typical, 'cylindrical' shape of characteristic sets, a simple game can particularly be defined as a game for which it holds that: (1) the characteristic set of any losing coalition is empty and (2) the characteristic set of the union of any winning coalition and any other coalition is a subset of the union of the characteristic sets of both coalitions. Note that the first part of this definition is compatible with the definition of a characteristic function in set-valued form.

This definition of a simple game in set-valued characteristic function form implies that we have to substitute the following lines for lines (2) and (3) in the characterization of the simple game presented above:

$$v(S) = \varnothing \text{ for every } S, S \in \mathcal{L} \tag{2}$$

$$v(S \cup T) \subseteq v(S) \cup v(T) \text{ for every } S, S \in \mathcal{W}. \tag{3}$$

The set-valued characteristic function of a three-person simple game is illustrated geometrically in figure 5.2.

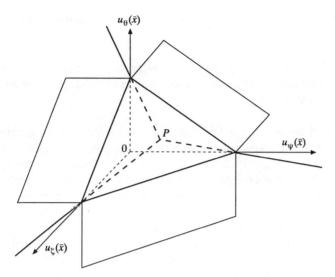

Figure 5.2 Characteristic sets of a three-person simple majority game

In figure 5.2 each of the two-person coalitions, as well as the grand coalition, is winning. The one-person 'coalitions' are losing. The characteristic sets of the two-person coalitions are half-spaces bound from above by a plane that intersects the utility coordinates of the players in the coalition and that is parallel to the utility coordinate of the excluded player. The characteristic set of the grand coalition is a triangular knotted cone with its three sides in the planes bounding the characteristic sets of the two-person coalitions and the vertex of its knotted point at P. Clearly, the three-person coalition does not offer better opportunities to the entire membership of a less inclusive winning coalition, which is the property of a simple game as specified in (3) above.

If the winning or losing of a coalition in a simple game solely depends upon the number of its members, the game is called 'symmetrical'.[5] If in a symmetrical simple game, the value of the game to a coalition depends on whether the coalition includes an absolute majority of the players, the game is called a simple majority game. Note that in a simple majority game with an even number of players it is not true that the countercoalitions of all losing coalitions are winning. Simple games for which the latter does hold, for instance simple majority games with an odd number of players, are called 'strong'. A somewhat weaker property that a symmetrical simple game may exhibit is that it is 'proper'. For proper games it is true that when a coalition is winning, its countercoalition is losing. Note that simple majority games are proper, but not necessarily strong.

We have now arrived at the point where the 'budgetary game' can be defined:

> The budgetary game is the n-person, cooperative, economic, simple majority game that has bundles of public and private goods as outcomes.

It should be noted that this definition clears the way for making the connection with the analysis of the preceding chapters. When the commodity space of the budgetary game in the sense of this definition is interpreted in terms of the various private and public good spaces of those chapters, the analysis can be pushed ahead into the domain of collective decision-making in the proper sense. In accordance with this interpretation the players will henceforth be referred to as 'politicians' and the set of all players the 'committee'. Furthermore the strategies of the players will be called 'voting strategies', the commodity combinations 'budgetary proposals', the pay-off functions 'preference functions' and the space itself the 'attribute space' of the budgetary game.

Furthermore, since the game is simple, the characteristic set of every losing coalition is empty. This feature of the budgetary game reflects the fact that minority coalitions cannot guarantee any outcome.

Domination and Pareto superiority in budgetary games

One of the main purposes of (applied) game theory is the explanation of the existence or absence of equilibrium in social situations that broadly satisfy its assumptions. Game theory serves that purpose by clarifying why rational actors in game-like situations prefer one course of action or strategy to another. The main approach to such a clarification is the comparative analysis of the pay-off vectors resulting from alternative strategies.

In the area of cooperative n-person games, the analysis focuses on the joint (coordinated) strategies of coalitions. What particularly matters is the capacity of coalitions, in the sense of the pay-off vectors they can secure. Of course, this is precisely the type of information the characteristic function provides. Knowledge of this function should therefore make it possible to identify equilibrium vectors and the corresponding coalitions. However, when game models are applied in empirical research, complete information about the characteristic function is usually not available. Fortunately, incomplete information often suffices to derive non-trivial hypotheses. In a budgetary game, for instance, information about the (estimated) distribution of politician's ideal points in the attribute space suffices to derive hypotheses about voting strategies, coalitions, and outcomes (decisions) that can potentially be tested empirically. Sometimes, it is not even necessary to acquire data about actual ideal points in order to perform empirical research on the basis of the game model. If it can be established on theoretical grounds that certain types of publicly provided services necessarily induce certain distributions of ideal points, it is possible to test the game model by subsequent derivation of the types of strategies, coalitions and outcomes these distributions must yield.

The study of equilibrium is conducted by the formulation of conditions that pay-off vectors have to satisfy in order to qualify as equilibrium vectors. Such conditions are known as 'solution' concepts. In the remainder of this chapter some of these concepts will be treated, but as a first step it is useful to consider some analytical tools that will be needed. First, we shall define the 'preference set' of a politician with respect to a given proposal in the attribute space of a budgetary game. This definition will be based on the relation of individual preference. Secondly, we shall introduce some concepts that have the character of 'relations between pay-off vectors'. Two of such relations will be considered, namely those of 'domination' and 'Pareto superiority'. These relations will be used to define the 'dominant set' and the 'Pareto superior set' of a committee of politicians with respect to a given proposal in the attribute space of a budgetary game. Finally, some applications of these ideas to specific budgetary games will be discussed.

The 'preference set' of a politician with respect to a given proposal in the attribute space of a budgetary game can be defined as the set of proposals that the politician prefers to the given proposal. The preference set of politician ξ with respect to given proposal $\bar{x}$ will be denoted by $P_\xi(\bar{x})$. Accordingly, the definition of the the preference set can be denoted as follows:

$$P_\xi(\bar{x}) \equiv \{\bar{y} \,|\, u_\xi(\bar{y}) > u_\xi(\bar{x})\}.$$

The preference set is defined in terms of strict preference: only proposals are included that are strictly preferred to the given proposal, that is to say not the ones the politician is indifferent about. This implies that the preference set is an 'open set': its boundary (in the one-dimensional case, its boundary points) do not belong to it.

It follows from the definition of the preference set that if $\bar{x}$ is the ideal point of the politician, the preference set with respect to $\bar{x}$ is empty; so: $P_\xi(\bar{x}) = \varnothing$.

A particular preference set is the one with respect to the proposal of zero outputs of all services: $P_\xi(\bar{o})$ with $o_i = 0$ for every i. This preference set is called the 'individually beneficial set', and it consists of all (combinations of) outputs the politician prefers to forgoing the service(s) entirely. The intersection of the individually beneficial sets of a coalition of politicians in a committee is called the 'collectively beneficial set' of the coalition.

A pay-off vector dominates another pay-off vector if and only if the former assigns higher pay-offs to a coalition of politicians than the latter and if, moreover, the former is included in the characteristic set of that coalition. This definition can be extended to the sphere of outcomes: a proposal dominates another proposal if and only if the pay-off vector associated with the former dominates the pay-off vector associated with the latter. Since the budgetary game is a simple majority game and hence every pay-off vector associated with a proposal in the attribute space is in the characteristic set of every majority coalition, the latter definition can also be stated as follows: a proposal dominates another proposal if and only if the pay-off vector associated with the former assigns higher pay-offs to a majority of the politicians in the committee than the latter.

On the basis of the relation of domination, the 'domination set' of a committee with respect to a given proposal in the attribute space of budgetary game can be defined as the set of proposals that dominate the given proposal.

The dominant set of a committee with respect to given proposal $\bar{x}$, will be denoted by $D(\bar{x})$. If the number of committee members in coalition S is denoted by $|S|$, the definition of the dominant set can be denoted as follows:

$$D(\bar{x}) \equiv \{\bar{y} \mid u_\xi(\bar{y}) > u_\xi(\bar{x}) \text{ for every } \xi, \xi \in S \text{ and some } S, |S| > |N|/2\}.$$

A special kind of domination is Pareto superiority. A pay-off vector is Pareto superior to another pay-off vector if and only if the former assigns higher pay-offs to all members of a committee and if, moreover, the former is included in the characteristic set of the grand coalition. Again, this definition can be extended to the sphere of outcomes. Since the budgetary game is a simple majority game and hence every pay-off vector associated with a proposal in the attribute space is in the characteristic set of the grand coalition, the corresponding definition can be stated as follows: a proposal is Pareto superior to another proposal if and only if the pay-off vector associated with the former assigns higher pay-offs to all politicians in the committee.

On the basis of the relation of Pareto superiority, the 'Pareto superior set' of a committee with respect to a given proposal in the attribute space of a budgetary game can be defined as the set of proposals that are Pareto superior to the given proposal.

The Pareto superior set of a politician with respect to a given proposal $\bar{x}$ will be denoted by $S(\bar{x})$. Accordingly, the definition of the Pareto superior

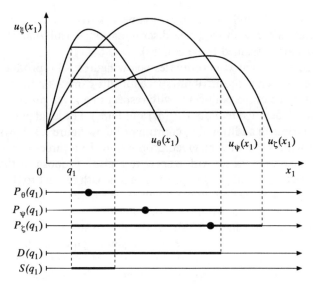

Figure 5.3 Dominant and Pareto superior sets of a committee deciding on a single public good

set can be denoted as follows:

$$S(\bar{x}) \equiv \{\bar{y} \mid u_{\xi}(\bar{y}) > u_{\xi}(\bar{x}) \text{ for every } \xi, \xi \in N\}.$$

Some applications of these ideas will now be presented. Just as in chapters 3 and 4, both a partial and a general approach will be pursued. In both instances examples of three-person games will be considered.

Figure 5.3 illustrates the pure public good case. Figure 5.3 shows the Preference Functions (PFs) of three politicians: θ, ψ and ζ in a given initial situation. Since the PF depends on the subjective evaluation of the public good, the three functions will in general not coincide.

On p. 61 it was mentioned that if the good is available at a constant tax price, the PF is unimodal ('single-peaked'). Although we have seen in chapter 4 that goods supplied by public agencies are often not available at a constant price, and hence not at a constant tax price, it turns out that the resulting PF can still be unimodal. In the mathematical appendix (pp. 224–8) it is shown that it is a sufficient condition for the unimodality of the PF that the political maximand is quasi-concave and that the Apparent Budgetary Cost Function (ABCF) is convex. This implies that unimodal PFs will result from sincere cost revelation if the Total Cost Function (TCF) is (weakly) convex (including linear), but also from a monopolistic bureaucratic strategy with or without price discrimination. In the former case, the ABCF will coincide with the TCF, in the latter it will not coincide with the TCF but will still be convex (namely kinked with price discrimination and linear without price discrimination; recall that the kinked ABCF was also assumed to be convex).

The upper three additional x_1 coordinates below figures 5.3 reproduce the x_1-coordinate – which is the attribute space for this game – and show the three preference sets of the politicians with respect to a given proposal q_1 of the public good (denoted by $P_\theta(q_1)$, $P_\psi(q_1)$ and $P_\zeta(q_1)$). The ideal points are also shown. The fourth additional x_1 coordinate below figure 5.3 shows the dominant set with respect to the given proposal q_1. In a three-person budgetary game the dominant set with respect to a given proposal is the union of the intersections of all pairs of preference sets with respect to that proposal. All proposals in the dominant set will receive at least a two: one majority when voted against a given proposal outside the dominant set. The fifth x_1 coordinate below figure 5.3 shows the Pareto superior set with respect to the given proposal. In a three-person budgetary game, the Pareto superior set with respect to a given proposal is the intersection of the three preference sets with respect to that proposal. The set must be a subset of the dominant set with respect to the same proposal. The proposals that it contains must receive unanimous support when voted against a given proposal outside the Pareto superior set.

The next example concerns a three-person committee deciding on the purchase of a private or group good that is not consumed by a majority of the committee. Such a good will be called a 'minority private good' or a 'minority group good', as opposed to a private or group good that is consumed by a majority of the committee, which will be called a 'majority private good' or a 'majority group good'.[6] The example is illustrated in figure 5.4.

Again below figure 5.4 the preference sets with respect to a given proposal, the ideal points and the dominant set are shown. As far as the Pareto superior set is concerned, it turns out that with respect to the given proposal it is empty.

Proceeding now to the general approach, a three-person game representing a committee deciding about the purchase of two pure public goods will be considered first. Just as in chapters 3 and 4 it may be assumed that these two goods are only a subset of the total number of public and private goods that are purchased by the committee in question, but that for the purpose of the present analysis, the outputs of all other public and private goods are held constant.

Figure 5.5 illustrates the case of two public goods. The figure shows the preference sets of three politicians. This results in three different preference sets with respect to the same proposal (q_1,q_2). The various shaded regions indicate the dominant and Pareto superior sets with respect to this proposal. Again, the dominant set is the union of the intersections of pairs of

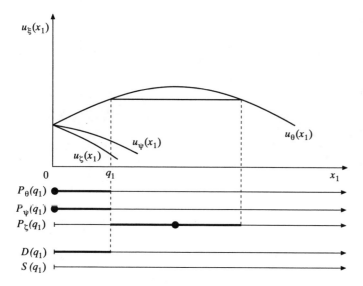

Figure 5.4 Dominant set in a committee deciding on a single private or group good

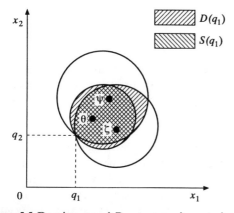

Figure 5.5 Dominant and Pareto superior sets in a committee deciding on two public goods

preference sets and the Pareto superior set is the intersection of all three preference sets.

The next example concerns the case of two private or group goods. It is assumed that the first politician consumes the first good but not the second, the second politician consumes the second good but not the first, and the third politician consumes neither good.

This case is illustrated in figure 5.6.

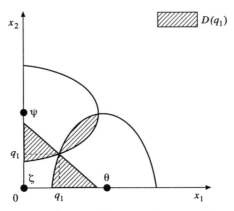

Figure 5.6 Dominant set in a committee deciding on two private or group goods

The dominant set with respect to the given proposal (q_1,q_2) is indicated again by the shaded region. The Pareto superior set with respect to the given proposal is empty.

Presolutions

As mentioned before, in game theory the search for equilibrium proceeds by exploring the consequences of conditions that pay-off vectors have to satisfy in order to qualify as 'solution' concepts. Some of these conditions seem so overly reasonable that almost all proposed solution concepts employ them. Shubik (1982) has proposed calling such conditions 'presolutions'. Three of those will now be reviewed, namely the conditions of (1) feasibility, (2) individual rationality and (3) Pareto optimality (not to be confused with Pareto superiority which, as we have seen, is not a property of separate pay-off vectors but rather of relations between pay-off vectors).

A pay-off vector satisfies the condition of feasibility if it is attainable by any coalition of players. In view of the fact that any pay-off vector that is attainable by a coalition is also attainable by the grand coalition – by virtue of superadditivity – the condition can also be expressed by saying that a pay-off vector is feasible if it is attainable by the grand coalition or, in terms of the set-valued characteristic function, if it belongs to the characteristic set of the grand coalition.

Since in the budgetary game every pay-off vector associated with a budgetary proposal belongs to the characteristic set of the grand coalition, the condition is automatically satisfied for every such pay-off vector. When the expression is transferred from the utility space to the attribute space, it follows that the entire attribute space is feasible.[7]

The next condition is that of 'individual rationality'. It requires that a pay-off vector must not attribute an individual pay-off to any player which is smaller than any pay-off that that player can secure by staying apart and forming her own one-person coalition. In terms of the set-valued characteristic function, the individual pay-off of a player must not be smaller than the individual pay-off attributed to that player by any pay-off vector in the characteristic set of that player. Since in the budgetary game with $|N| > 1$, a single politician cannot secure any pay-off, the condition is automatically satisfied for every pay-off vector. When the expression is transferred from the utility space to the attribute space, it follows that the entire attribute space is individually rational.

The condition of 'Pareto-optimality' is somewhat more discriminatory. A pay-off vector satisfies this condition if it is feasible and if, moreover, no other feasible pay-off vector exists which is Pareto superior to it.

Since in the budgetary game every pay-off vector associated with a budgetary proposal is feasible, a pay-off vector associated with a proposal $\bar{x}$ is Pareto-optimal, if and only if:

$$S(\bar{x}) = \varnothing.$$

The same condition can be used to define the Pareto optimal set in the attribute space. Denoting the Pareto optimal set by 0, this definition can be written as:

$$O \equiv \{\bar{x} \mid S(\bar{x}) = \varnothing\}.$$

A geometrical illustration may be helpful. Figure 5.7 illustrates a two-person budgetary game. Figure 5.7a shows the PFs of two politicians in a given initial situation for a public good. Figure 5.7b shows the set of pay-off vectors in the utility space corresponding to the budgetary proposals in the attribute space.

A move in the attribute space along the output axis in the positive direction corresponds to a move in the utility space along the indicated utility possibility curve in the clockwise direction. In the output interval below q_1, the pay-off to both politicians is increasing, in the interval between q_1 and r_1, the pay-off to ψ is decreasing and that to θ is increasing, in the interval above r_1 both individual pay-offs are decreasing. At s_1, ψ is back at the pay-off level corresponding to the zero output of the public good and at t_1, θ is back at that level. Since the assumption of 'free disposal' was made, the characteristic set of the grand coalition is illustrated in figure 5.7b by the shaded area. This is the feasible set. The individually rational set includes the entire space and the Pareto optimal set is indicated by the segmemt AB of the convex curve. This curve is the upper bound of the area indicating the characteristic set of the grand coalition. Below figure 5.7a the

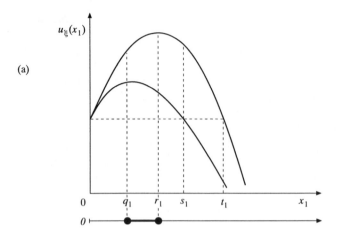

(a)

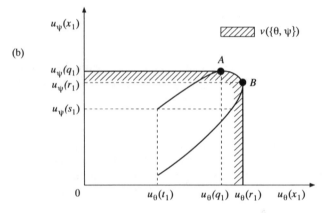

(b)

Figure 5.7 Presolutions of a two-person budgetary game for one public good

output axis is reproduced and the Pareto optimal set is indicated (O). The feasible and individually rational sets include the entire output axis. Apparently the Pareto optimal set in the uni-dimensional attribute space is the interval between the ideal points of the actors.

Figure 5.8 illustrates the Pareto optimal set in the attribute space in a three-person budgetary game.

Figure 5.8a shows the Pareto optimal set for a pure public good game, figure 5.8b for a private or group good game. In the latter case, the good is a minority private or group good that is consumed only by politician θ. The utility space is three-dimensional in such a game and cannot readily be illustrated geometrically. It is easy to understand, however, that the Pareto

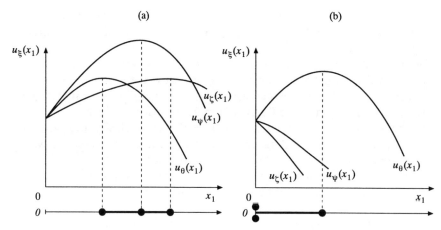

Figure 5.8 Pareto optimal set in a three-person budgetary game for one good

optimal set in the attribute space again equals the interval of the output axis
between the two most extreme ideal points. Indeed, it is true that for any
point outside this interval there is at least one point inside that is Pareto
superior to it: the lower extreme ideal point is Pareto superior to all points
below the lower extreme ideal point (in the private good case without
externalities there may be no such points) and the higher extreme ideal
point is Pareto superior to all points above the higher extreme ideal point.
Furthermore no point inside this interval is Pareto superior to any other
point inside it. The interval must thus indicate the Pareto optimal set.

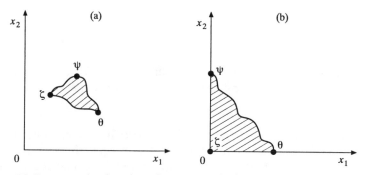

Figure 5.9 Pareto optimal set in a three-person budgetary game for two goods

Figure 5.9 finally illustrates a three-person budgetary game representing
a committee that decides about two public goods or two minority private or
group goods.

Again the feasible and individually rational sets cover the entire space. The typical shape of the Pareto optimal set is shown by the shaded area; figure 5.9a refers to the pure public good case, figure 5.9b to the private or group good case. Both figures show the contract curves between the ideal points, which consist of all points of tangency between the boundaries of the preference sets (indifference curves) of each pair of politicians between the respective ideal points. The Pareto optimal set consists of the area enclosed by the hull of the contract curves between all pairs of ideal points. Also in the present more-dimensional case the Pareto optimal set coincides with the region that induces empty Pareto superior sets.

In view of the elementary character of the three conditions mentioned thus far, von Neumann and Morgenstern, the founding fathers of game theory, introduced a separate term to denote the pay-off vectors satisfying all three of them: pay-off vectors which are feasible, as well as individually rational, as well as Pareto optimal are called 'imputations'. Most solution concepts that have been proposed as reasonable definitions of equilibrium are subsets of the set of imputations. As we have seen, in the case of the budgetary game the set of imputations coincides with the set of Pareto optimal pay-off vectors. The set of imputation proposals in the attribute space will therefore also coincide with the set of Pareto optimal proposals.

Some game-theoretic results

The single most convincing solution concept of n-person cooperative game theory is the 'core'. The core is defined as the set of feasible undominated pay-off vectors. Since in the budgetary game every pay-off vector associated with a budgetary proposal is feasible, a pay-off vector associated with a proposal $\bar{x}$ is in the core, if and only if:

$$D(\bar{x}) = \emptyset.$$

The same condition can be used to define the core in the attribute space. Denoting the core by C, this definition can be written as:

$$C \equiv \{\bar{x} \mid D(\bar{x}) = \emptyset\}.$$

In order to clarify the importance of the core in budgetary games, it is useful to make three observations about it. Subsequently, the existence of the core will be considered. The chapter will be concluded by some considerations concerning stability in the absence of a core.

The first observation is that the core is the set of pay-off vectors that is not only individually rational and Pareto optimal – or rational for the grand coalition – in the sense of the presolutions mentioned, but also rational for every other coalition. It may be said, therefore, that the core is 'collectively rational' for every coalition, or that it is included in the 'contract set' (the collectively rational set) of every coalition.

The second observation is that the core in the attribute space mainly coincides with a notion of equilibrium that is already much older than game theory, namely that of a so-called 'Condorcet winner'. This notion stems from a body of literature about voting that is not of game-theoretic nature and that goes back to the eighteenth-century French philosopher after whom it is called. A 'Condorcet winner' can be defined as a proposal that is strictly preferred by a majority of the voters to all other proposals in the attribute space. The close correspondence between the core and the set of Condorcet winners in a budgetary game follows from the fact that a proposal $\bar{x}$ which is preferred by a majority of the voters to another proposal $\bar{y}$, by definition dominates that proposal (since $\bar{x} \in P_\xi(\bar{y})$ for a majority of voters). However, the correspondence is not complete, since if the core includes more than one pay-off vector, these pay-off vectors do not dominate each other, so that they are not Condorcet winners. In fact the Condorcet criterion is a little stronger than the core criterion, since it not only requires that a proposal is not defeated by any other proposal but also that it does defeat every other proposal. A Condorcet winner is therefore by definition unique.

The third observation concerns the stability of the core. How stable is the core when applied to a budgetary game? Is it indeed an 'equilibrium' in the sense that there is a high probability that a decision-making process in a committee of politicians automatically converges to it if the process is starting elsewhere – that is to say with the consideration of an arbitrary other proposal – as well as in the sense that there is a high probability that the process does not leave it again as soon as it has arrived there? Indeed its game-theoretic rationale suggests that it is 'strategy-proof', in the sense that non-sincere voting does not destroy its equilibrium character. Nevertheless there are reasons for doubt, both of a theoretical and empirical nature.

The core may be vulnerable to certain kinds of conflicts between (subgroups of) politicians. Suppose, for instance, that a committee is considering a proposal $\bar{x}$, which is in the core and a proposal $\bar{y}$, which is not. Suppose, furthermore that a certain politician θ prefers $\bar{x}$ to $\bar{y}$ and that she could get $\bar{x}$ approved by the formation of a majority coalition S, all of whose members prefer $\bar{x}$ to $\bar{y}$ (so $u_\theta(\bar{x}) > u_\theta(\bar{y})$ and $u_\xi(\bar{x}) > u_\xi(\bar{y})$ for some θ, $\theta \in S$ and for every ξ, $\xi \neq \theta$, $\xi \in S$). Suppose, finally, that politican ψ is not in S and prefers $\bar{y}$ to $\bar{x}$ (so $u_\psi(\bar{y}) > u_\psi(\bar{x})$ for some ψ, $\psi \notin S$). Politician θ can now tell politician ψ: 'If you persist in $\bar{y}$, I shall put $\bar{x}$ to a vote and then it will receive a majority over $\bar{y}$.' Of course, this is the main argument underlying the core as a solution concept. But let us suppose that ψ does not yield to this argument and replies: 'If you put $\bar{x}$ to a vote, I will lure away ζ, who is a member of S, and if necessary other members of S, by proposing $\bar{z}$, so that you will end up worse than under $\bar{y}$.' Of course, this counter threat is a brag, becauszze if ψ can form a majority coalition, so that the other members of this coalition prefer $\bar{z}$ to $\bar{x}$, it is not possible that ψ herself prefers $\bar{z}$ to $\bar{x}$ as well. Indeed if this were possible, $\bar{x}$ would not be in the core. Nevertheless θ may believe ψ, for instance because ψ is known as a tough bargainer who never makes threats without sticking to them. Also ψ may put her threat into effect if she is not believed. In both cases the core proposal is not attained.

Experimental research suggests that particular environments that encourage strongly competitive behaviour might produce the phenomenon that actors get stuck in non-optimal positions because they cannot reach agreement about the division of spoils. Nevertheless, the general impression arising from the experimental literature is that the core, although it may incidentally fail, is in general a good predictor, especially in comparison to alternative solution concepts and, of course, under the condition that it exists.[8]

Since the problem of core existence is of utmost importance for the entire research effort concerning stability in budgetary games, it is necessary to pay attention to some of the results concerning this problem. Before turning to this, it is useful to summarize the exposition made so far, in the form of a formal model.

The model aims to capture in a few expressions the preceding game-theoretic argument about plausible outcomes of decision-making in a committee of politicians. The decision-making model can be written:

Model VI

$$\max u_\xi(\bar{x}, m_\xi) \qquad\qquad \xi = 1, 2, \ldots, v \qquad\qquad (1)$$

$$\bar{p}_\xi . \bar{x} + m_\xi = g_\xi \qquad\qquad \xi = 1, 2, \ldots, v \qquad\qquad (2)$$

$$c_i = c_i(x_i) \qquad\qquad i = 1, 2, \ldots, n \qquad\qquad (3)$$

$$a_i(x_i) = c_i(x_1) \qquad\qquad i = 1, 2, \ldots, n \qquad\qquad (4)$$

$$D(\bar{x}) = \varnothing \qquad\qquad\qquad\qquad (5)$$

$$p_{\xi i} \equiv \tau_\xi a_i(x_i)/x_i \qquad\qquad \xi = 1, 2, \ldots, v; \; i = 1, 2, \ldots, n \qquad (6)$$

$$D(\bar{x}) \equiv \{\bar{x} \mid u_\xi(\bar{y}) > u_\xi(\bar{y}) \text{ for every } \xi, \; \xi \in S$$
$$\text{and some } S, \; |S| > |N|/2\} \xi = 1, 2 \ldots, v. \qquad (7)$$

Expression (1) is the political maximand and (2) is the politician's income constraint. Both expressions are identical to the corresponding expressions in models I–V and are subject to the same restrictions. In this model, however, there are as many individual maximands and income constraints as there are politicians in the committee.

Expression (3) is the TCF for each service. It is subject to the same restrictions as the corresponding expression in models IV and V.

Expression (4) denotes the provisional assumption that costs are revealed sincerely, so that apparent costs equal real costs.

Expression (5) denotes the equilibrium condition, namely that a proposal will be reached which is undominated, that is a proposal in the core of the budgetary game.

Expression (6) defines the tax price of each service as a function of apparent costs and is identical to the corresponding expression in models IV and V.

Expression (7), finally, is the definition of the dominant set.

In the remainder of this chapter core existence will be discussed within the context of the budgetary game as specified by model VI.

The problem of core existence is one of the most thoroughly studied problems in n-person, cooperative game theory. For our purpose, the results concerning so-called 'spatial majority games' are especially relevant. A simple spatial majority game is a somewhat more general type of game than a budgetary game, but the resemblance is close. A solution of a spatial majority game is a set in an Euclidian 'policy space' that is not further defined in terms of publicly provided services. The policy space therefore has no natural origin, nor do the pay-off functions of the players have a natural shape. Any property of the policy space or the pay-off functions that may be required must be imposed by way of specific assumption.

The problem of core existence in spatial majority games can for the greater part only be dealt with by fairly advanced mathematical methods. For our exposition, however, it suffices to present a few important theorems without proofs or technical comment. Each theorem will be stated for the specific case of the budgetary game as described by model VI.

The first theorem to be presented is the well-known median voter theorem (Black, 1948, 1958), which can be stated as follows:

Median voter theorem

In a budgetary game for a single good the core exists if the preference functions of the politicians are unimodal. If the number of politicians is odd, the core consists of the ideal point of the politician who holds the median position (the 'median voter'). If the number of politicians is even, it consists of the median interval between adjacent ideal points.

It follows from the theorem that the core in the one-dimensional case either consists of a single point, or of a closed line segment. It consists of a single point if the number of politicians is odd, or if it is even and the median interval collapses to a single point. Otherwise it consists of a closed line segment.

The theorem requires that the politicians' PFs are unimodal ('single-peaked'). As mentioned on p. 109 the condition of unimodality of the PFs is satisfied if the political maximand is quasi-concave and the ABCF is convex (see the mathematical appendix, pp. 224–8). This implies that the condition will be satisfied if the service is supplied at real (minimal) costs in an internal market as assumed in model VI (ABCF = TCF), or if it is supplied in accordance with the monopolistic bureaucratic strategy with or without price discrimination.

The validity of the median voter theorem can be grasped by looking at what alternative coalitions in a three-person budgetary game, as illustrated in figure 5.10, could do to overturn the core proposal q_1.

The one-person 'coalitions' are powerless because they are losing. The two-person coalitions cannot do better than q_1 because in coalitions $\{\theta,\psi\}$ and $\{\psi,\zeta\}$ every deviation from q_1 is a loss for ψ and in coalition $\{\theta,\zeta\}$ every deviation from q_1 is either a loss for θ or for ζ. In the grand coalition $\{\theta,\psi,\zeta\}$, finally, every deviation from q_1 is a loss for ψ. Consequently no coalition can do better than q_1 so that q_1 is undominated.

The condition of unimodality of the PFs is sufficient but not necessary, as was already recognized by Black (1958) and later generalized by Niemi (1983). This is illustrated in figure 5.10 by the dotted alternative shape of the pay-off function of politician θ. The according pay-off function is bimodal but does not destroy the core at point q_1.

The importance of Black's theorem can hardly be exaggerated. It implies that whenever a decision-making process is restricted to a single service, and whenever there is reason to suppose that the PFs are unimodal, there is a fairly discriminating solution, with strong equilibrium characteristics both from an empirical and a theoretical point of view.

In the situation of a more-dimensional attribute space core existence is ruled by the pairwise symmetry theorem (Plott, 1967). This theorem can be stated as follows:

Pairwise symmetry theorem

In a budgetary game the core exists if the preference functions of the politicians are quasi-concave and if there is at least one point $\bar{q}$

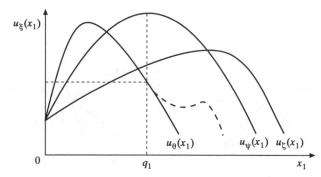

Figure 5.10 The core of a three-person budgetary game for one good

in the attribute space, such that the gradients at $\bar{q}$ of the preference functions of all politicians whose ideal points do not coincide with $\bar{q}$, can be divided in pairs of exactly opposite directions. The core consists of point $\bar{q}$ and, if there are more points that satisfy the stated condition, of all those points.

The pairwise symmetry theorem requires that the preference functions of the politicians are quasi-concave, so that the preference sets are convex. Quasi-concavity is a stricter condition than unimodality ('single-peakedness'). However, we have seen that preference functions are quasi-concave (and hence unimodal) if the services are supplied at real costs in an internal market as assumed in model VI (ABCF = TCF) or if they are supplied in accordance with the monopolistic bureaucratic strategy with or without price discrimination (see the mathematical appendix, pp. 224–8).

The pairwise symmetry theorem is illustrated for the case of a budgetary game for two goods in figure 5.11.

Figure 5.11a illustrates a five-person game. Figure 5.11a shows the ideal points of five politicians: $\theta, \psi, \zeta, \chi, \phi$ and the contract curves of the pairs of politicians $\{\psi, \zeta\}$ and $\{\chi, \phi\}$. The ideal point of θ is located at the point of intersection of both contract curves. The gradients of the preference functions at $\bar{q}$ are defined by:

$$\nabla u_\xi(\bar{q}) \equiv \left(\frac{\delta u_\xi}{\delta q_1}, \frac{\delta u_\xi}{\delta q_2} \right).$$

Since by definition the gradients of the preference functions of a pair of politicians point in opposite directions at every point of the contract curve,[9] and since the ideal point of θ coincides with the point of intersection of both contract curves, $\bar{q}$ is the core of this game. The directions of the non-zero gradients are indicated in figure 5.11a.

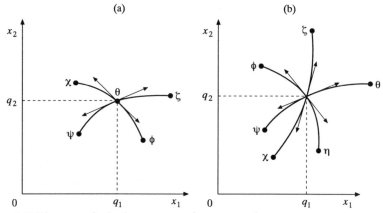

Figure 5.11 The core of a budgetary game for two goods

Figure 5.11b illustrates a six-person game. Figure 5.11b shows the ideal points of the six politicians $\theta, \psi, \zeta, \chi, \phi, \eta$ and the contract curves of the pairs of politicians $\{\theta, \psi\}$, $\{\zeta, \chi\}$ and $\{\phi, \eta\}$. Since the three contract curves intersect in the same point $\bar{q}$, the point of intersection is the point where pairs of gradients of preference functions point in exactly opposite directions and hence the core of this game. Again the directions of the gradients are indicated in figure 5.11b.

The intuitive rationale of the pairwise symmetry theorem is that every non-zero gradient or group of gradients at $\bar{q}$ indicates a potential advantageous move for a politician or group of politicians away from $\bar{q}$. Only when these 'forces' on $\bar{q}$ are neutralized by 'forces' in the opposite directions or by 'friction' holding $\bar{q}$ in its place, can $\bar{q}$ be an equilibrium proposal.

It follows from the pairwise symmetry theorem that in order to satisfy the conditions for core existence, the number of politicians in the committee must be even, or it must be odd with at least one ideal point coinciding with the core point.[10]

Just as in the median voter theorem, the pairwise symmetry theorem states a sufficient, but not a necessary condition for core existence. In particular, less symmetry is required to the extent that the number of ideal points that coincide with the core point exceeds the minimum number required by the pairwise symmetry theorem (which is one for an odd and zero for an even number of committee members). Furthermore, given the excess of ideal points coinciding with the core point, less symmetry is required to the extent that the number of committee members is smaller. This is illustrated in figure 5.12.

Figure 5.12 shows a five-person budgetary game that resembles the game

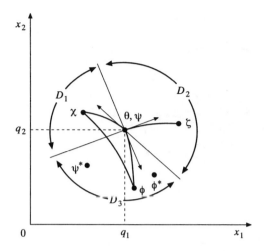

Figure 5.12 The core of a five-person budgetary game for two goods that does not satisfy the conditions of the pairwise symmetry theorem

of figure 5.11a. The differences between both games are that the ideal point of politician ψ coincides with that of θ and that the ideal point of politician ϕ has shifted slightly in the direction of a smaller output of both services. In order to facilitate the comparison between both configurations of ideal points the location of the ideal points of ψ and ϕ in figure 5.11a has been indicated in figure 5.12 by ψ^* and ϕ^*. Clearly, the (new) contract curve of the pair $\{\chi,\phi\}$ no longer passes through the coinciding ideal points of θ and ψ, so that the conditions of the pairwise symmetry theorem are not satisfied. Nevertheless, $\bar{q}$ is still the core of this game.

The fact that $\bar{q}$ is still the core of this game can be checked by constructing closed, convex, two-dimensional, pointed cones, that are bounded by pairs of lines tangent to adjacent contract curves at $\bar{q}$. Figure 5.12 shows the three cones that can so be constructed in the illustrated game, namely cones D_1, D_2 and D_3. It can be proved that if the absolute value of the number of gradients pointing into each cone minus two is less than the number of ideal points at $\bar{q}$, then $\bar{q}$ is the core[11] (Slutsky, 1979; Enelow and Hinich, 1983a). For the case of the illustrated game, this condition can be written as:

$$| N(D_j) - 2| \leq N(\bar{q}) \text{ for } j = 1,2,3.$$

In this expression $N(D_j)$ denotes the number of gradients of preference functions pointing into cone D_j and $N(\bar{q})$ the number of ideal points at $\bar{q}$.

Since in the illustrated game it holds that:

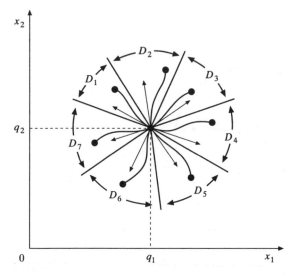

Figure 5.13 The core of a nine-person budgetary game for two goods that does not satisfy the conditions of the pairwise symmetry theorem

$$|N(D_j) - 2| = |1 - 2| = 1 \leq N(\bar{q}) = 2 \text{ for } j = 1,2,3,$$

it follows that $\bar{q}$ is the core of this game.

Figure 5.13 shows a nine-person game with the ideal points of two politicians coinciding with $\bar{q}$.

In this case the number of closed, convex, two-dimensional, pointed cones that are bounded by pairs of lines tangent to contract curves at $\bar{q}$ is seven. Since it holds that:

$$|N(D_j) - 2| = |1 - 2| = 1 \leq N(\bar{q}) = 2 \text{ for } j = 1,2,\ldots,7$$

it follows that $\bar{q}$ is the core of this game. Apparently, the degree of symmetry around the core point is larger in this game than in the five-person game illustrated in figure 5.12. This is understandable because the relative significance of a given excess of ideal points coinciding with the core point (an excess of one in the cases of figures 5.12 and 5.13) diminishes as the number of committee members grows, so that one would expect the conditions for core existence to converge to those of the pairwise symmetry theorem when this number grows large.[12]

In the special case of separable and symmetric preferences, it is possible to state a single condition that is both necessary and sufficient for core existence. In that case, distance in the attribute space can be used as an index of utility, possibly after an appropriate linear transformation of the

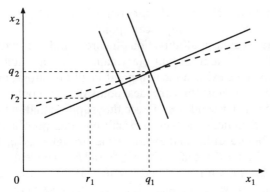

Figure 5.14 The median in all directions in a budgetary game for two goods

axes. This implies that separable and symmetric preference functions induce circular preference sets in a two-dimensional attribute space and (hyper)spherical preference sets in higher-dimensional attribute spaces. This condition is stated in the following theorem (Davis, de Groot and Hinich, 1972):

Median in all directions theorem

> In a budgetary game the core exists if and only if the preference functions of the politicians are separable and symmetric and there exists a point $\bar{q}$ in the attribute space which is located at a median position between the ideal points of all politicians in the committee in all directions. The core consists of point $\bar{q}$ and is unique.

The theorem makes use of the concept of a 'median in all directions'. A point is a median in all directions if every hyperplane through that point (every line in a two-dimensional attribute space) is a median hyperplane (median line). A median hyperplane (line) is a hyperplane (line) that divides the ideal points of all members of the committee in such a way that at least half are on, or to one side, of it and at least half are on, or to the other side, of it. In order to see that a median in all directions is a core point, consider point $\bar{q}$ in figure 5.14 and an arbitrary different point $\bar{r}$.

Since preferences are separable and symmetric, the perpendicular bisector of the line segment between $\bar{q}$ and $\bar{r}$ will divide the politicians' ideal points according to whether they prefer $\bar{q}$ to $\bar{r}$ or $\bar{r}$ to $\bar{q}$. However, since $\bar{q}$ is a median in all directions, the line through $\bar{q}$, which is parallel to the perpendicular bisector, must be a median line. Since half of the ideal points are on the opposite side of this median line from $\bar{r}$, or upon it, and since these ideal points are also on the $\bar{q}$ side of the perpendicular bisector, $\bar{r}$ will not dominate $\bar{q}$. Since this holds for every arbitrary point $\bar{r}$ different from $\bar{q}$, $\bar{q}$ is not dominated and is therefore a unique core point.

It follows from the median in all directions theorem and the pairwise symmetry theorem that if in a given budgetary game with separable and symmetric preferences there exists a median point in all directions, and if that point coincides with no more than one ideal point, then that point must satisfy the pairwise symmetry condition. To see this, suppose that in figure 5.14 $\bar{q}$ is a median in all directions and there is exactly one ideal point at $\bar{r}$ and one at $\bar{q}$. Suppose furthermore that on the median line through $\bar{r}$ and $\bar{q}$, there are k other ideal points at the $\bar{r}$ side of $\bar{q}$, with $k \geq 0$, and h other ideal points at the opposite side from $\bar{r}$, with $h \geq 0$ and $h \neq (k + 1)$. In that case, the pairwise symmetry theorem would not be satisfied at $\bar{q}$, because there would be $(k + 1)$ gradients at $\bar{q}$ pointing in the direction of $\bar{r}$ and $h \neq (k + 1)$ gradients pointing in the opposite direction. However, there would also exist a line through $\bar{q}$, such as the dotted line in figure 5.14, which would differ from the median line through $\bar{r}$ and $\bar{q}$, but which would make a sufficiently small angle with that median line to divide all ideal points in the attribute space in exactly the same way except the ideal points on that median line. Since the $(k + 1)$ ideal point on the median line through $\bar{q}$ and $\bar{r}$ at the $\bar{r}$ side of $\bar{q}$ would fall at one side of this line and the $h \neq (k + 1)$ ideal points at the opposite side from $\bar{r}$ at the other side of this line, this line cannot be a median line. But, since $\bar{q}$ is a median in all directions, this conclusion leads to inconsistency. Hence, it cannot be true that $h \neq (k + 1)$, so that the pairwise symmetry condition must apply. A similar reasoning applies if the number of committee members is even and if there is no ideal point at $\bar{q}$.

If a core exists in an attribute space of two or more dimensions, it is usually very unstable. In general, the slightest change in any preference function will destroy the common point of intersection of the relevant contract curves or the coincidence of this point with the required number of ideal points. Not every core is so unstable. A core that in general will not be destroyed by a slight change in any preference function is called a 'structurally stable core'. The median voter theorem assures that every core in an attribute space of one dimension is structurally stable. In a two-dimensional attribute space a core coinciding with one ideal point in a game with an even number of committee members is structurally stable. Because strict symmetry of ideal points is not required in such a case, a slight change in any preference function will in general not destroy the core. It can be proved that under simple majority rule structurally stable cores can exist only in attribute spaces of one or two dimensions (Schofield, Grofman and Feld, 1988).

The pairwise symmetry theorem makes clear that if the dimensionality of the attribute space is larger than one, the core will usually not exist. On the

Table 5.1. *Minimal quorum values sufficient for the existence of the core*

n	m =	1	2	3	4	5
1		1	1	1	1	1
2		2	2	2	2	2
3		2	3	3	3	3
4		3	3	4	4	4
5		3	4	4	5	5

other hand, it may not be concluded that core existence is never guaranteed in a more-dimensional attribute space. In particular, if the number of committee members is (very) small or if the minimal majority required to approve a proposal is larger than the absolute majority of the committee members, core existence may be guaranteed even in more-dimensional attribute spaces. The relevant condition is stated in the following theorem (Kramer, 1977; Greenberg, 1977):

Quorum theorem

If, according to the voting rule of a committee of n members, the minimal number of votes required to approve a proposal is q, and if the dimensionality of the attribute space is m, then it is a sufficient condition for the existence of a core that $q > nm/(m + 1)$.

The minimum number of votes required to approve a proposal is called the 'quorum' of the voting rule. Table 5.1 shows the values of the quorum sufficient for the existence of a core for some budgetary games of low dimensionality in small committees.

It appears from table 5.1 that the rule of simple majority $(q > n/2)$ guarantees a core in one dimension (column $m = 1$). This is of course consistent with the median voter theorem. Furthermore, in a committee of one or two, where $q > n/2$ implies $q = 1$, respectively $q = 2$, a core is guaranteed regardless of the dimensionality of the attribute space (rows $n = 1$ and $n = 2$). In a 'committee' of one, the core consists of the ideal point of the single member and in a committee of two it consists of the entire contract curve between the ideal points of the members. In a committee of three, where $q > n/2$ implies $q = 2$ or $q = 3$, a core is not guaranteed in an attribute space of two or more dimensions. In a committee of four, on the other hand, where $q > n/2$ implies $q = 3$ or $q = 4$, a core is guaranteed in an attribute space of one or two dimensions but not in one of three or more. The reason that a core in a two-dimensional attribute space is not guaranteed in a committee of three but is in a committee of four is not that in the former case the condition on the quorum for core existence would be more demanding than in the latter ($q > 2$ is no more demanding than $q > 8/3$), but rather that in a committee of three the condition of simple majority ($q > n/2$) is less demanding (namely $q \geq 2$, so that $q \geq n \times 2/3$) than it is in a committee of four (namely $q \geq 3$, so that $q \geq n \times 3/4$). In a committee of five or more members, finally, a core is not guaranteed in an attribute space of two or more dimensions.

The results by Plott, Enelow, Hinich, Slutsky, Kramer and Greenberg raise the question: what happens in a budgetary game if an undominated proposal does not exist? Attention will now be paid to possible ways of approaching this question. Essentially two approaches can be distinguished. The first is to look for other solution concepts. Indeed the game-theoretic literature abounds in solution concepts for n-person, cooperative games, many of which are applicable to budgetary games. For instance solution concepts such as the 'stable set', various types of 'bargaining sets', 'the competitive solution' and the 'uncovered set' have successfully been applied to spatial majority games and can be applied to budgetary games. However, insofar as solutions of these kinds exist in games where the core does not exist, it must necessarily be the case that they contain pay-off vectors which are dominated (recall that the core is the set of undominated pay-off vectors).

Since it seems questionable *a priori* to put much confidence in the stability of solutions that contain dominated pay-off vectors, particularly from an empirical point of view, the question may be asked what the characteristics would be of a solution concept, say T, for which it would hold that every pay-off vector inside T, although dominated by one or more other pay-off vectors inside T, would at least itself dominate all pay-off vectors outside T. The smallest solution satisfying these conditions is known as the 'top cycle'. If it were possible to establish that in general the top cycle set would be a reasonably discriminatory solution concept, an important step forward would have been made. Indeed, a strong argument would then be obtained in support of the hypothesis, often advanced in informal discussions about decision-making in democratic systems, that outcomes are essentially arbitrary and unstable, but that this arbitrariness and instability is restricted to a central region of the distribution of ideal points in the policy space so that extreme outcomes cannot occur.

However, the hope that this could be established has effectively been sent to the bottom by important results achieved by McKelvey, Schofield, Cohen and others (McKelvey, 1976, 1979; Schofield, 1978; Cohen, 1979). The main gist of these results can be summarized as follows. As soon as the dimensionality of the policy space is larger than one, the conditions for the top cycle set to be smaller (more discriminatory) than the entire policy

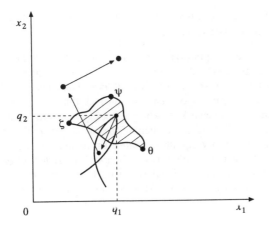

Figure 5.15 Majority rule decision path of a three-person budgetary game for two goods
Source: Variation on a figure in Enelow and Hinich (1984, p. 31).

space, are extremely severe (comparably severe to the conditions for the existence of a core). If the policy space is two-dimensional, the condition for the top cycle set to remain inside the Pareto optimal set is that only pairs of proposals are put to a vote that are 'close' together in the policy space, so that the majority rule decision path is continuous. If this condition is not satisfied, the top cycle set embraces the entire space, also in the two-dimensional case, under almost every circumstance. This is illustrated by the non-continuous majority rule decision path of the three-person budgetary game in figure 5.15.[13]

This leads to the conclusion that the further pursuance of the traditional game-theoretic approach can only yield solution concepts that assign pay-off vectors to the solution of a game, which are not only internally unstable in the sense that they are dominated by other pay-off vectors belonging to the solution concerned but also externally unstable in the sense that they are dominated by pay-off vectors not belonging to the solution.[14] Indeed this is true for all of the solution concepts mentioned above that have been explored in the game-theoretic literature.

Under these circumstances, a second approach to the question of what happens in a budgetary game if the core does not exist seems more promising. Rather than trying to explain the stability that we observe in the real world by the rather subtle considerations that are supposed to motivate politicians according to weaker solution concepts than the core and the top cycle, we may have to shift the entire analytical perspective.

William Riker (1980) has explained the necessity for such change of perspective in a well-known essay, as follows:

Although there are not likely to be equilibria based entirely on tastes, still there are outcomes of social decision processes, those outcomes do embody some people's values, and the outcomes themselves are not wholly random and unexpected. What prevents purely random embodiments of tastes is the fact that decisions are customarily made within the framework of known rules, which are what we commonly call institutions. . . . The outcome, then, of the search for equilibria of tastes is the discovery that, failing such equilibria, there must be some institutional element in the regularities (or actual equilibria) we observe. We are forced back, therefore, to the eclectic stance that political scientists have typically taken. Outcomes are, of course, partially based on tastes because some persons' (not necessarily a majority of people's) tastes are embodied in outcomes. But the ways the tastes and values are brought forward for consideration, eliminated, and finally selected are controlled by the institutions. And institutions may have systematic biases in them so that they regularly produce one kind of outcome rather than another. In this sense, therefore, both institutions and tastes contribute to outcomes.

Clearly the emphasis on institutions in this approach leads away from the study of domination among pay-off vectors given the prevailing decision rules, as the central analytical tool for the study of equilibrium. Instead, the focus turns towards the decision rules themselves; in particular the possibility must be examined that other procedural rules than the ones examined thus far are at work in the real world.

With respect to the study of budgetary decision-making, this change of perspective implies that the empirically relevant procedural rules of the budgetary process have to be dealt with. In particular the rules that govern the access of proposals to the political agenda deserve attention. In chapter 7 the analysis will be pursued in that direction. First, however, it is necessary to turn back to bureaucratic decision-making and in chapter 6 to examine the consequence of political interaction for bureaucratic supply.

Guide to the literature
The theory of spatial majority games as exposed in the present chapter has its roots on the one hand in the general theory of n-person games and on the other hand in treatises on voting. The latter root is older and goes back to the eighteenth-century philosopher Condorcet, who wrote a book which is usually considered as the start of theoretical thinking about the working of voting rules (Condorcet, 'Essai sur l'application de l'analyse à la probabilité des decisions rendues à la pluralité des voix', 1785). The results of Condorcet and other early contributions to voting theory are reviewed in Black, *The Theory of Committees and Elections* (1958), which also contains some reprints from these works. The theory of n-person games developed since the 1950s; von Neumann and Morgenstern are

considered as the founding fathers of game theory (von Neumann and Morgenstern, *Theory of Games and Economic Behavior*, 1953). Early expository books are Luce and Raiffa, *Games and Decisions* (1957); Davis, *Game Theory. A Non-technical Introduction* (1970); and Rapoport, *N-person Game Theory* (1970). These books focus on games in real-valued characteristic function form. Following Aumann, 'A survey of cooperative games without side payments' (1967), the older literature treats games in set-valued characteristic function form as 'games without side-payments'. More modern works on game theory include Owen, *Game Theory* (1982) and Shubik, *Game Theory in the Social Sciences. Concepts and Solutions* (1982). Simple games were first described in Shapley, 'Simple games' (1962).

The analysis of elections in terms of spatial majority games started in the 1960s. In this work, the voting-theoretical and the game-theoretical approaches merged into the theory of spatial majority games as we presently know it. Expository surveys from the 1970s are Davis, Hinich and Ordeshook, 'An expository development of a mathematical model of the electoral process' (1970) and Ordeshook, 'The spatial theory of elections: a review and critique' (1976). An important book from that period is Riker and Ordeshook, *An Introduction to Positive Political Theory* (1973), which treats both electoral and legislative decision-making in terms of spatial majority games. Early treatments of budgetary games in the sense of the presented definition can be found in Buchanan, 'Simple majority voting, game theory and resource use' (1961); Buchanan and Tullock, *The Calculus of Consent* (1962); and Buchanan, *The Demand and Supply of Public Goods* (1968). A modern introduction to the spatial theory of voting is Enelow and Hinich, *The Spatial Theory of Voting* (1984). An essential handbook that not only thoroughly covers the spatial theory of electoral and legislative voting but also many other applications of game theory in political science is Ordeshook, *Game Theory and Political Theory* (1986). A useful survey paper on the spatial theory of legislative voting is Ferejohn and Fiorina, 'Purposive models of legislative behavior' (1975). During the 1980s both the electoral and the legislative branch of the spatial theory of voting developed into more specialized subfields. An important collection of review papers is Enelow and Hinich, *Advances in the Spatial Theory of Voting* (1990).

An early recognition of the median position as an equilibrium point in a spatial model of economic or political competition can be found in Hotelling, 'Stability in competition' (1929). This model is further developed in Smithies, 'Optimal location in spatial competition' (1941). The crucial condition of single-peaked preferences was stated in Black, 'On the rationale of group decision making' (1948) and *The Theory of Elections and Committees* (1958); the median voter theorem is usually attributed to Black. An early voting theoretical exploration of equilibrium in a more-dimensional attribute space is Black and Newing, *Committee Decisions with Complementary Valuation* (1951). A voting-theoretical statement of the pairwise symmetry theorem was provided by Plott, 'A notion of equilibrium and its possibility under majority rule' (1967). An important collection of papers about the stability problem in spatial majority games is Ordeshook and Shepsle, *Political Equilibrium* (1982). Reviews of the main results about core existence are provided in Feld and Grofman, 'Necessary and sufficient conditions for a majority winner in

n-dimensional spatial voting games: an intuitive geometrical approach' (1987) and chapter 5 in Mueller, *Public Choice II* (1989). The quorum theorem was first stated in Kramer, 'A dynamical model of political equilibrium' (1977) and subsequently proved in Greenberg, 'Consistent majority rules over compact sets of alternatives' (1979). A review of results related to the quorum theorem is Schofield, Grofman and Feld, 'The core and the stability of group choice in spatial voting games' (1988).

6   Bureaucratic decision-making

The extended budgetary game

In chapter 4 bureaucratic supply behaviour was considered from the perspective of its effects upon the preferences of the individual politician. It seems reasonable to assume that if the political authority consists of a collective body, the bureaucrat will not only take into account the effects of strategic cost revelation upon individual preferences, but also the effects upon the outcomes of political decision-making. In other words, the bureaucrat will pay attention to interaction among politicians and she will make her strategy choices in view of her expectations. Furthermore, it may be assumed that as soon as decision-making involves more than a single service, not only does politico–bureaucratic interaction become a relevant aspect of the budgetary game, but also interaction among the bureaucrats themselves. That is to say, bureaucrats will take into account the supply behaviour of other bureaucrats in order to optimize their strategies.

The endogenization of bureaucratic strategies implies that bureaucrats enter as fully-fledged players into the budgetary game. In the resulting extended game, the bureaucrats are entirely different kinds of players than the politicians. This distinction concerns both the objectives which motivate each kind of player and the types of 'moves' each kind of player is allowed to make. The objectives and the moves have been discussed in chapters 3 and 4 respectively; it has been assumed that politicians seek the implementation of preferred policies, and that bureaucrats seek some optimal combination of Managerial Discretionary Profit (MDP) and output. Furthermore, the moves of politicians were assumed to consist of votes and those of bureaucrats of transformations of the Apparent Budgetary Cost Function (ABCF), in the sense discussed in chapter 4.

In terms of model V (see p. 89) the endogenization of bureaucratic strategies implies that the ABCF must be removed from the model. Also the bureaucratic maximand, the Total Cost Function (TCF) and the definition of MDP (see model IV, p. 82) have to be inserted again. The resulting model can be written as follows:

Model VII

$$\max u_\xi(\bar{x}, m_\xi) \qquad\qquad \xi = 1,2,\ldots,v \qquad\qquad (1)$$

$$\max u_i(d_i,\, x_i) \qquad\qquad i = 1,2,\ldots,n \qquad\qquad (2)$$

$$\bar{p}_\xi.\bar{x} + m_\xi = g_\xi \qquad\qquad \xi = 1,2,\ldots,v \qquad\qquad (3)$$

$$c_i = c_i(x_i) \qquad\qquad i = 1,2,\ldots,n \qquad\qquad (4)$$

$$D(\bar{x}) = \varnothing \qquad\qquad\qquad\qquad\qquad (5)$$

$$p_{\xi i} \equiv \tau_\xi a_i(x_i)/x_i \qquad\qquad \xi = 1,2,\ldots,v;\, i = 1,2,\ldots,n \qquad (6)$$

$$d_i \equiv a_i(x_i) - c_i(x_i) \qquad\qquad i = 1,2,\ldots,n \qquad\qquad (7)$$

$$D(\bar{x}) \equiv \{\bar{y} \mid u_\xi(\bar{y}) > u_\xi(\bar{x}) \text{ for every } \xi,\, \xi \in S$$
$$\text{and some } S, |S| > |N|/2\} \qquad \xi = 1,2,\ldots,v. \qquad (8)$$

Model VII provides the theoretical background for the analysis of bureaucratic decision-making that will be pursued in this chapter.

A partial approach to bureaucratic decision-making about public goods

Bureaucrats can choose three basic strategies with respect to the shape of the ABCF, given the preferences of the politicians and the TCF. These three strategies will be called (1) the competitive strategy, (2) the public monopoly strategy, and (3) the public monopoly strategy with tax price discrimination.

The competitive strategy (C strategy) consists of an ABCF that coincides with the TCF. The public monopoly strategy (PM strategy) consists of a linear ABCF without a constant term that induces such optimal outputs of the politicians in the committee that the bureaucratic objective function is maximized at the median of those outputs. The public monopoly strategy with price discrimination (PMPD strategy) consists of an ABCF that induces such optimal outputs of the politicians in the committee that the bureaucratic objective function is maximized at either the median or the lowest of those outputs. For reasons that will become clear, the first mentioned variant of the PMPD strategy (maximization at the median output) is called the divisive variant and the last mentioned (maximization at the lowest output) the consensual variant.

It is assumed in all strategies that the same good is supplied to every politician in the committee (no 'benefit share discrimination'). This assumption does not imply that every good yields equal benefits to all politicians. Recall that on pp. 35–6 account was taken of the possibility that different politicians attribute different values to the same good, either for subjective reasons (preferences) or for objective ones (for instance, the distance of the fire station from the home). However, in so far as different evaluations are due to objective reasons, it scarcely seems realistic to assume that in general bureaucrats can influence the relevant circumstances by way of a strategy variable. Hence, there is no need to complicate our models by providing for that possibility. This is an additional reason why the entire concept of benefit shares can be ignored in our analysis (recall p. 36).

The possibility of price discrimination, which distinguishes the PM strategy from the PMPD strategy, refers to price discrimination of the second degree,[1] which concerns different unit prices at different output levels. It may be thought that in the public sector there is usually also price discrimination of the third degree, which concerns different unit prices for different consumers, but this is not the case. The crucial point is that the structure of the tax system is not affected by the supplier of the service (the bureaucrat), but rather by the demanders (the politicians) themselves. Of course, it is conceivable that in a particular situation a bureaucrat can influence the tax shares of politicians, but it scarcely seems realistic to assume that bureaucrats would often avail themselves of this capacity.

In chapter 4 we saw how alternative bureaucratic strategies induced an upward shift of the ideal point and a loss of the individual politician's political surplus, but now the consequences for the resulting committee decisions have to be addressed. In order to examine these consequences, three types of effects deserve particular attention, namely those on (1) the existence of the core, (2) the location of the core and (3) the location of the Pareto optimal set.

The existence of the core is important because it may explain stability. The location of the core is important because it is a measure of output maximization and, in view of the trade-off between output and MDP, of MDP maximization as well. The extension of the Pareto optimal set is important because it is a measure of controversy in the political committee, which may be relevant for what will happen in the absence of a core.

The effects of supply strategies in a budgetary game for one pure public good in a committee of three politicians are illustrated in figure 6.1a and 6.1b. The politician with the median ideal point under a given strategy will

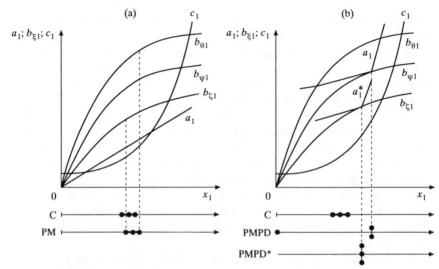

Figure 6.1 Monopolistic supply strategies in a three-person budgetary game for one public good

be called the 'median politician', the politician with the lowest ideal point, the 'extreme low-demand politician' and the politician with the highest ideal point the 'extreme high-demand politician'. Figures 6.1a and 6.1b show the Budget Output Functions (BOFs) of three politicians and the Total Cost Function (TCF) of a single bureaucrat.

Figure 6.1a also shows the ABCF that makes up the PM strategy if the bureaucrat is completely informed about political preferences (no uncertainty margins). Since there is no price discrimination, the ABCF is indicated by a straight line through the origin. As a consequence of the PM strategy the ideal point of the median politician shifts from its position under the C strategy in accordance with the bureaucratic objectives. The particular ABCF shown in figure 6.1a gives a relatively high priority to output. To the extent that this priority (the weight of output in the bureaucratic maximand) is lower, and accordingly the priority of MDP is higher, she will choose a higher unit price for the service which will lead to a steeper ABCF and a smaller upward or even downward shift of the median ideal point. The additional output axes below figure 6.1 show the effects of the C and PM strategies upon the location of the ideal points and the Pareto optimal set. If the committee decides only about a single service, the median ideal point is the core of the budgetary game, so that the core shifts as well. Note, that it is not necessary that the same politician is the median politician over the entire output domain. If not, the bureaucrat still has to choose the price of the service (the slope of the ABCF) in such a way that her objective function is maximized at the induced optimal output for whoever is the median politician at that price.

Figure 6.1b shows the ABCFs that make up the two variants of the PMPD strategy if the bureaucrat is completely informed about political preferences (no uncertainty margins). Both consist of kinked curves, with the kink point just below the BOF curve of the median and extreme low-demand politician respectively. These ABCFs induce a shift of the ideal points of the median and the extreme low-demand politician respectively in comparison to their positions under the C strategy, in accordance with the bureaucratic objectives. The ABCF denoted by a_1 illustrates the divisive variant, the ABCF denoted by a_1* the consensual variant of the PMPD strategy. The additional output axes below figure 6.1 show again the effects of the strategies upon the location of the ideal points and the Pareto optimal set. The divisive variant of the PMPD strategy widens the Pareto optimal set in comparison to the C strategy, and the consensual variant reduces it to a single point. The main reason for the widening of the Pareto optimal set under the divisive variant is that the optimal output for the extreme low-demand politician falls back to zero. In this connection, the term 'widening' refers to distance between opposite boundaries of the Pareto optimal set, not necessarily to the interval or region of the attribute space covered by the Pareto optimal set. Indeed, if an ideal point of a politician falls back to zero, the Pareto optimal set becomes disconnected and may even be reduced to two points (see figure 6.1b). Apparently the divisive variant adds to controversy over the desirable output level in the committee, whereas the consensual variant eliminates controversy (hence the names chosen for the variants). Furthermore, both variants push the core point upwards in comparison to the C strategy. Again, it is not necessary that the same politician is the median or the extreme low-demand politician over the entire output domain. If not, the bureaucrat still has to choose her ABCF in such a way that her objective function is maximized at the induced optimal output for whoever is the median or the extreme low-demand politician at that shape of the ABCF.

Since the results with respect to the existence and location of the core and the extension of the Pareto optimal set illustrated in figure 6.1 are not only dependent on model VI (including the assumed constraints on cost and utility functions), it is useful to be more precise about the necessary conditions in general for these results to apply.

As far as the existence of the core is concerned, the crucial condition is that the committee decides on a single service only. If this is the case, the attribute space is unidimensional. Since it was assumed that all strategies maintain the convexity of the ABCF (see p. 70), it may be concluded that the preference functions of all politicians remain unimodal (single-peaked).

This implies that the median voter theorem applies, and that the core exists. If, on the other hand, the committee decides on more services, a general approach is called for. This will be pursued in the next section.

As far as the location of the core is concerned the following conditions apply. The PM strategy will shift the core upwards or downwards in comparison to its position under the the C strategy, depending on the relative weight of the bureaucratic objectives (output and MDP). In the absence of income effects, the divisive variant of the PMPD strategy will always shift the core upwards or leave it where it is (the latter if the bureaucrat is interested only in MDP). The consensual variant of the PMPD strategy will shift the core either upwards or downwards, depending on the relative weight of the bureaucratic objectives (output and MDP) and the shape of the BOF of the extreme low-demand politician. Furthermore, in order to shift the core downwards under the consensual PMPD strategy, it is necessary that the slope of the ABCF after the kink not only exceeds the slope of the BOF of the extreme low-demand politician – as required to move the ideal point of that politician to the position desired by the bureaucrat – but that it also exceeds the slope of the BOF of the median politician.

As far as the extension of the Pareto optimal set is concerned, the following conditions apply. Under the PM strategy, the Pareto optimal set will shrink or expand in comparison to its extension under the C strategy, depending on the relative size of the shifts of the ideal points of the extreme low-demand politician and the extreme high-demand politician. Under the divisive variant of the PMPD strategy, the optimal output(s) for some politician(s) – not necessarily the (extreme) low-demand politician(s) under the C strategy – will fall back to zero if the total benefits of this (these) politician(s) do not exceed apparent costs under this strategy in the entire output domain. Whether the optimal output for the extreme high-demand politician increases under this strategy depends on the relative weight of output in the bureaucratic maximand. Note, furthermore, that in order for the median and higher than median optimal outputs to converge completely under the divisive PMPD strategy, it is necessary that the slope of the ABCF after the kink not only exceeds the slope of the BOF of the median politician – as required to move the ideal point of that politician to the position desired by the bureaucrat – but that it also exceeds the slopes of the BOFs of all politicians with higher than median optimal outputs. Under the consensual variant of the PMPD strategy, finally, the optimal outputs for all politicians will converge completely and the Pareto optimal set will be reduced to a single point, if the slope of the ABCF after the kink not only exceeds the slope of the BOF of the extreme low-demand politician – as required to move the ideal point of that politician to the position desired by

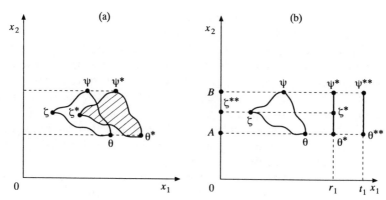

Figure 6.2 Monopolistic supply strategies for a single good in a three-person budgetary game for two public goods

the bureaucrat – but that it also exceeds the slopes of the BOFs of all other politicians in the committee.

A general approach to bureaucratic decision-making about public goods

With respect to bureaucratic behaviour, there are also some important differences between the case in which decision-making involves a single service and the case in which it involves more services simultaneously.

First, the consequences of supply strategies by a single bureaucrat will be considered. Attention must be given again to the existence of the core, the location of the core and the extension of the Pareto optimal set.

The effects of supply strategies for one good in a three-person budgetary game for two pure public goods are illustrated in figure 6.2a and 6.2b. These show the politician's ideal points induced by alternative supply strategies for the first good.

Figure 6.2a shows the effects of the bureaucratic PM strategy in a case where the bureaucrat is more interested in output than in MDP, so that she chooses a unit price of the good which pushes the optimal outputs of the politicians upwards in comparison to their positions under the C strategy. It need not necessarily be assumed that the bureaucrat is completely informed about political benefits. In the case illustrated, the preferences of all politicians are separable, so that the optimal outputs of the second good are not affected by the supply strategies for the first (recall p. 91). The new Pareto optimal set is indicated by the shaded area. Whether this strategy will lead to higher or lower optimal outputs in general, will depend on the same conditions as mentioned in the partial analysis. In contrast to the budgetary game for one good, the game for two or more goods will in general not have a core under the PM strategy for one good nor, for that matter, under the C strategies for all goods.

Figure 6.2b shows the effects of the bureaucratic PMPD strategy. In accordance with the conclusions of the partial analysis, the divisive variant rounds up and pushes up the optimal outputs for a majority of the committee (to output t_1 in figure 6.2b) and the consensual variant rounds up and pushes up the optimal outputs for all committee members (to output r_1 in figure 6.2b). Again, it need not be assumed that the bureaucrat is completely informed about political benefits. In the case illustrated, the politicians have separable preferences.

However, in addition to the effects observed in the partial analysis, it appears that in the situation depicted in figure 6.2b, another important effect occurs. If there are no more than two goods in the budgetary game and if one good is supplied according to the C strategy and the other according the consensual variant of the PMPD strategy, the Pareto optimal set is reduced to a segment of a straight line, parallel to the output axis of the competitively supplied good. Since single-peakedness is maintained in the dimension of this good, the core will exist and be located at the median ideal point in this dimension (indicated by ζ^* in figure 6.2b). In view of the usual absence of a core in a game for more than one service, this effect suggests that consensual PMPD strategies are capable of inducing stability in such games. In general, however, a core cannot be created by a single bureaucrat. In a game for n pure public goods, the Pareto optimal set will be reduced to a segment of a line and the core will consequently exist if $(n - 1)$ goods are supplied according to consensual PMPD strategies. This implies that a single bureaucrat can only create a core in a game for two goods. For these results to apply in general it is necessary that the condition for a complete convergence of optimal outputs as mentioned in the partial analysis is satisfied for the monopolistically supplied good. Furthermore, the output at the core point increases in comparison to the median optimal output under the C strategy, subject to the same conditions as mentioned in the partial analysis.

Figure 6.2b also illustrates what happens if one of the goods is supplied according to the divisive variant of the PMPD strategy. The new Pareto optimal set under this strategy is reduced to two straight line segments (indicated by AB and $\psi^{**}\theta^{**}$ in figure 6.2b). Since in this case the optimal output for the low-demand politician will differ from the optimal output for the median politician, a core will not be induced if $(n - 1)$ or fewer bureaucrats opt for such a strategy. Furthermore the Pareto optimal set will widen and become disconnected, subject to the same conditions as mentioned in the partial analysis. This raises the question whether divisive PMPD strategies cause instability in general. In order to answer this

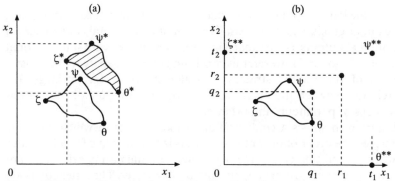

Figure 6.3 Monopolistic supply strategies for all goods in a three-person budgetary game for two public goods

question, it is necessary to examine the case where all goods are supplied according to the same strategies. This case is illustrated in figure 6.3a and 6.3b.

Figure 6.3a shows the effects of the PM strategies in a case where all bureaucrats are more interested in output than in MDP, so that they choose unit prices for the services which push the politician's optimal outputs upwards in comparison to their positions under the C strategy. Again, it need not be assumed that the bureaucrat is completely informed about political benefits. The new Pareto optimal set is indicated by the shaded area. Whether this strategy will lead to higher or lower optimal outputs in general, will depend, by service, on the same conditions as mentioned in the partial analysis. Under PM strategies for all goods, the budgetary game for two or more pure public goods will in general not have a core. Note, furthermore, that this strategy sometimes pushes up the optimal output of the extreme low-demand politician – as it does in figure 6.3a – but that it does not necessarily do so. If the extreme low-demand politician is influential, the PM strategy may therefore result in a lower output than the C strategy. In this light, one may question the entire rationale of the strategy in games for two or more public goods. Since in such games a median politician for a good has no more influence on outcomes than any other politician, there is no reason for the bureaucrat to opt for the PM strategy to begin with. However, if price discrimination is impossible, the bureaucrat still has to set some price for her service. It may be argued that under these conditions she will adjust her ABCF to the preferences of the politician that she considers particularly influential. If she is strongly risk averse, she may also focus upon the extreme low-demand politician in the committee.

Figure 6.3b shows the effects of PMPD strategies. Under the consensual variant the Pareto optimal set is reduced to a single point $(\bar{r})$. In a game for n pure public goods a core will exist if the conditions for total convergence of the optimal outputs as mentioned in the partial analysis are satisfied for at least $(n - 1)$ goods. However, this conclusion does not apply to the divisive variant of the PMPD strategy. For the effects of this strategy, the correlation between the distributions of optimal outputs of the various services is of paramount importance.

Figure 6.3b shows a configuration of ideal points in which, under C strategies, the order of the optimal outputs is not the same for all services. A weaker condition is that the high demand minimal majority does not consist of the same group of politicians for all services. The latter condition will be called the condition of 'heterogeneous preferences'. The opposite condition, which requires that the high-demand minimal majority consists of the same group of politicians for all services, will be called the condition of 'homogeneous preferences'. Although it follows from these definitions that under random distributions of ideal points by service, heterogeneous preferences are more frequent than homogeneous preferences, it may not be concluded that homogeneous preferences are a highly exceptional phenomenon. In reality, many public goods are inferior goods in the sense that they are higher valued by low-income earners than by high-income earners. In so far as this factor dominates other factors that determine political preferences, it may induce homogeneous preferences for some groups of services.

It appears from figure 6.3b that under heterogeneous preferences, the divisive variant of the PMPD strategy does not induce stability. There will be no core and, in accordance with the conclusions from the partial analysis, the Pareto optimal set will widen and become disconnected, rather than shrink. The new Pareto optimal set in figure 6.3b consists of the points $(t_1, t_2), (t_1, 0)$ and $(0, t_2)$. In general this widening will occur if the condition for widening the Pareto optimal set as mentioned in the partial analysis is satisfied for each of the public goods in the budgetary game.

It appears from the present analysis that the divisive variant of the PMPD strategy is a risky strategy for the bureaucrat. If preferences are heterogeneous, there is no core and many things can happen. For one thing, since this strategy creates alienated minorities (the politicians who prefer a zero output of some good), the possibility of a coalition of such minorities arises. This might lead to the adoption of a proposal for zero outputs of both services. Note, that this proposal dominates proposal (t_1, t_2). Only under homogeneous preferences may the divisive variant of the PMPD strategy induce a core. If, for instance, the ideal point of politician θ under the C strategy was located at $\bar{q}$ rather than where it is indicated in figure 6.3b, then the minimal high-demand majority would consist of the politicians θ and ψ for both goods and the divisive PMPD strategy would induce a core. In general, the divisive variant of the PMPD strategy induces a core if the conditions for complete convergence of the median and higher than median optimal outputs as mentioned in the partial analysis are satisfied for each public good in the game and if, moreover, the preferences of politicians are homogeneous for all goods. It follows from these conditions that under homogeneous preferences the divisive variant of the PMPD strategy also induces a core if all or some of the other bureaucrats follow the consensual rather than the divisive variant of the PMPD strategy (which also leads to complete convergence of median and higher optimal outputs).

Up to this point, bureaucratic strategies were considered in relation to political preferences. However, in the extended budgetary game described by model VI, the strategies of bureaucrats must not only be considered in relation to the reactions of politicians but also in relation to the reactions of rival bureaucrats. In order to trace the consequences of these possibilities, let us see what happens in the model when bureaucratic strategies are interdependent.

Bureaucratic interaction proceeds in two stages in model VI. In the first stage, bureaucrats choose a strategy. In the second stage, they reveal an ABCF, given the strategy choice.

In the first stage, bureaucrats can particularly influence the realization of each other's objectives by opting for strategies that contribute to stability in the political sphere. As we have seen PMPD strategies are capable in principle of inducing a core in a budgetary game that does not have a core under other strategies. Whether this characteristic will affect the choice of strategies depends upon bureaucratic expectations about what will happen in the absence of a core. This question can be answered only when the institutions of the budgetary process are taken into account. That theme will be taken up in chapter 7, but at this point it can already be mentioned that some institutions may not induce a unique, certain outcome but rather a set of possible outcomes from which in reality one will be selected on the basis of chance or political bargaining skills. Moreover, it seems likely that the institutions that are characteristic for the budgetary process in representative government are actually of this kind. This does not imply, however, that anything can happen. Under these conditions the analysis of interaction must be based upon a realistic assumption about bureaucratic expectations. Such an assumption is that only combinations of outputs in the partial Pareto optimal sets for the separate services qualify as possible outcomes of political decision-making. Although this is not a very specific assumption, it permits some interesting inferences about bureaucratic interaction.

First, it implies that the consensual variant of the PMPD strategy is a so-called 'maximin strategy', namely a strategy that maximizes the minimal utility that the bureaucrat can expect from the game. This is the case regardless of core existence and hence regardless of whether other bureaucrats follow the same strategy. This strategy is consequently an attractive option for the risk averse bureaucrat.

Secondly, it follows from the assumption mentioned that the divisive variant of the PMPD strategy is not an attractive option for the risk averse bureaucrat. A cautious bureaucrat will opt for this strategy only if a core exists, so that she can be sure that the optimal output of the median politician will be the outcome of political decision-making. This implies that she will opt for this strategy only if (a) all other bureaucrats in the budgetary game choose PMPD strategies – either consensual or divisive – as well, and (b) if political preferences are homogeneous. In this light, it seems plausible that in budgetary games for more than a single service, divisive PMPD strategies will occur only in the case of collusion of at least $n - 1$ of the bureaucrats.

In the second stage of bureaucratic interaction, bureaucrats reveal an ABCF. The easiest way to analyse ABCF revelation in this stage is through the examination of 'reaction functions'. A reaction function describes how a bureaucrat will adjust her ABCF to the ABCFs of other bureaucrats in order to influence the optimal output of the pivotal politician for her service in the committee. The 'pivotal politician' for a service is the politician whose preferences are decisive for the strategy choice of the bureaucrat who supplies it. In the case of the PM strategy and the divisive variant of the PMPD strategy the median politician is pivotal, in the case of the consensual variant of the PMPD strategy, the extreme low-demand politician is pivotal. In particular, the reaction function specifies the optimal output of a service for the pivotal politician that the bureaucrat supplying that service will induce at a given output of another service.

In a budgetary game for two goods, the reaction function characterizes a reaction curve in the attribute space. Figure 6.4a illustrates the reaction curves of the bureaucrats for the case of separable preferences of the pivotal politician. Since in this case the induced optimal output of a service is independent of the output of the other service, the reaction curve of each bureaucrat is a straight line parallel to the output axis of the service supplied by the other bureaucrat.

In order to keep the figure as simple as possible it is supposed that the same politician (θ) is pivotal for both services.

Figure 6.4a shows the ideal point and the individually beneficial set of this politician under the C strategy. Since the preferences of the politician are separable, the individually beneficial set is a circle. The line character-

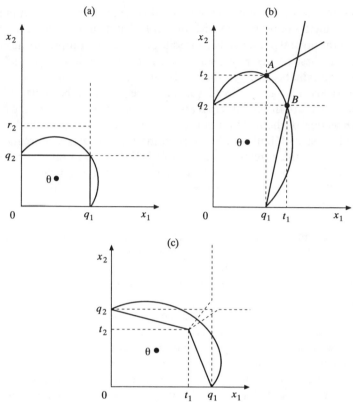

Figure 6.4 Reaction curves of bureaucrats according to given supply strategies in a budgetary game for two public goods

ized by $x_1 = q_1$ is the reaction curve of the bureaucrat supplying the first service (the first bureaucrat) and the line characterized by $x_2 = q_2$ is the reaction curve of the other (second) bureaucrat. In the particular case illustrated in figure 6.4a it is assumed that the bureaucrats opt for PMPD strategies and that they maximize output only (according to the strictly Niskanean maximand). In this case, the reaction curve of each bureaucrat coincides with the curve that indicates the maximal acceptable outputs of the service that she supplies at given outputs of the other service. The maximal acceptable output is the output that yields an equal political surplus (or an equal political deficit) to the pivotal politician as the zero output.

If the bureaucrats follow PM strategies or maximize MDP next to output, the reaction curves will indicate somewhat smaller than maximal acceptable outputs at given outputs of the other service.

Each reaction curve consists of an attainable part and an unattainable part. The unattainable part consists of points that do not qualify as an ideal point of the pivotal politician because she prefers a zero output of one of the services at these points. For instance, output combination (q_1,r_2) in figure 6.4a is unattainable because the politician will prefer combination $(q_1,0)$ which yields a larger political surplus. The unattainable parts of the reaction curves of the bureaucrats are dotted in figure 6.4a. Since the point of intersection of the reaction curves of the bureaucrats is located in the attainable part of both curves, this point $(\bar{q})$ indicates a bureaucratic equilibrium. If the bureaucrats maximize MDP next to output, or if they follow PM strategies, the reaction curves will indicate somewhat smaller outputs than the reaction curves in figure 6.4a so that their point of intersection will be located somewhat closer to the ideal point of the politician.

If there are more than two goods in the budgetary game the boundary of the individually beneficial set of the pivotal politician under the C strategy becomes a (hyper)sphere, but the preceding analysis applies to the interaction between any pair of bureaucrats, given the outputs supplied by all other bureaucrats.

Figure 6.4b illustrates the case that the preferences of a pivotal politician are not separable, and that the services are complementary goods. Figure 6.4b shows again the ideal point and the individually benefical set of a politician who is pivotal for both services. An example of a utility function that in general yields non-separable preferences is a quadratic utility function. Such a utility function induces an elliptical individually beneficial set as shown in figure 6.4b. A quadratic utility function also implies that the curves which indicate the maximal acceptable outputs of a service at given outputs of the other service are straight lines.

In the case of complementary goods the bureaucrats' reaction curves consist of three parts. In the interval from 0 to q_2 the reaction curve of the first bureaucrat indicates the optimal output/MDP combination according to the bureaucratic maximand. In figure 6.4b it is assumed again that the bureaucrat opts for a PMPD strategy and that she maximizes output only, so that her reaction curve coincides in this interval with the curve that indicates the maximal acceptable outputs of the service that she supplies at given outputs of the other service. If the bureaucrat follows the PM strategy or maximizes MDP alongside output, the reaction curve will indicate somewhat smaller than maximal acceptable outputs in this interval. In the interval between q_2 and t_2 the reaction curve follows the boundary of the individually beneficial set of the politician. In this interval, the reaction curve does not any longer indicate the optimal output/MDP combination according to the bureaucratic maximand, given the strategy choice, because this would lead to output combinations that would be rejected by the politician in favour of the combination of zero outputs. In the interval above t_2, finally, the reaction curve remains at output q_1. This is the case because such high outputs of the second service will be rejected by the politician regardless of the shape of the ABCF of the first bureaucrat, so that this bureaucrat can adjust her ABCF to a zero output of the second service. The latter part of the reaction curve is again the unattainable part (as indicated by the dotted line). Analogously, the reaction curve of the second bureaucrat indicates the optimal output/MDP combination of the bureaucrat in the interval from 0 to q_1, it follows the boundary of the individually beneficial set in the interval from q_1 to t_1 and it remains at output q_2 in the interval above q_1. The latter interval is again the unattainable part. It appears from figure 6.4b that the attainable parts of both reaction functions coincide at a part of the upper boundary of the individually beneficial set (segment AB). This implies that in the case of complementary goods the bureaucratic equilibrium is not unique. Rather, there is a set of equilibrium points. Which point will actually be reached depends upon the initial situation and the course of the mutual adjustment process.

If the bureaucrats maximize MDP alongside output or if they follow PM strategies, the reaction curves will indicate somewhat smaller outputs than the reaction curves in figure 6.4b, so that they either intersect in their first interval, in which case there is a unique equilibrium, or reach the boundary of the individually beneficial set at higher given outputs, so that the second interval of both curves in which they coincide is smaller than in figure 6.4b.

If there are more than two goods in the budgetary game, the boundary of the individually beneficial set becomes a convex surface – a (hyper)ellipsoid in the case of quadratical preferences – but the preceding analysis applies to the interaction between any pair of bureaucrats, given the outputs supplied by all other bureaucrats.

Figure 6.4c illustrates the case where the preferences of a pivotal politician are not separable and where the services are substitutes. Figure 6.4c shows again the ideal point and the individually beneficial set of a politician who is pivotal for both services. The individually beneficial set is again an ellipse and the curves that indicate the maximal acceptable outputs of a service at given outputs of the other service are again straight lines.

In the case of substitutes the reaction curves consist also of three parts. In the interval from 0 to t_2 the reaction curve of the first bureaucrat indicates the optimal output/MDP combination of the first bureaucrat. In figure 6.4c it is assumed again that the bureaucrat opts for a PMPD strategy and that she maximizes output only, so that her reaction curve coincides in this interval with the curve that indicates the maximal acceptable outputs of the service that she supplies at given outputs of the other service. If the bureaucrat follows a PM strategy or maximizes MDP alongside output, the reaction curve will indicate somewhat smaller than maximal acceptable outputs in this interval. In the interval from t_2 to q_2 the reaction curve increases again in the dimension of the first service. The reason is that at a given output of the second service higher than t_2, the first bureaucrat can opt for an output higher than t_1. In that case, the politician will forgo one of the services entirely so that the first bureaucrat only has to make sure that her service is maintained. To that end she must make sure that for each output combination (x_1,x_2) offered, the politician prefers $(x_1,0)$ to $(0,x_2)$. In the interval above q_2, finally, the reaction curve remains at q_1. This is the case because such high outputs of the second service will be rejected by the politician, regardless of the shape of the ABCF of the first service, so that the bureaucrat can adjust her ABCF to a zero output of the second service. Both the second and the third part of the reaction curve are unattainable (as indicated by the dotted lines), because in these intervals the politician will forgo the second service. Analogously, the reaction curve of the second bureaucrat indicates the optimal output/MDP combination according to the bureaucratic maximand in the interval from 0 to t_1, it increases again in the dimension of the second service in the interval from t_1 to q_1 and it remains at q_2 above q_1. In the second interval it must hold that for each output combination (x_1,x_2) satisfying this reaction function, the politician prefers $(0,x_2)$ to $(x_1,0)$, so that the politician will forgo the first service and maintain the second. The point of intersection of the reaction curves $(\bar{t})$ indicates a bureaucratic equilibrium. This point can only be approached from the upper side (from point $\bar{q}$ downwards) in a process in which the politician bids down the budget by eliciting a better offer (an ABCF that yields a positive optimal political surplus at some output) from each bureaucrat in turn.

If the services are substitutes it is also possible that there is an equilibrium in which one of the services is not supplied at all. In figure 6.4c this would be the case when the boundary of the individually beneficial set was rotated slightly clockwise so that the attainable part of the reaction curve of the second bureaucrat intersected the output axis of the first service at a lower output than q_1. In that case, the second bureaucrat would have no effective counteroffer against an offer of q_1 by the first bureaucrat. In that case, a corner solution would be attained at $(q_1,0)$.

If the bureaucrats maximize MDP alongside output, of if they follow PM strategies, the reaction curves will indicate somewhat smaller outputs than in figure 6.4c, so that their point of intersection will be located somewhat closer to the politician's ideal point and so that the second interval of both curves will start at lower output levels of both services. There may also be a corner solution in that case if the attainable part of both curves does not intersect.

If there are more than two goods in the budgetary game, the boundary of the politician's individually beneficial set becomes again a convex surface – a (hyper)ellipsoid in the case of quadratic preferences – but the preceding analysis applies to the interaction between every pair of bureaucrats, given the outputs supplied by all other bureaucrats. However, the politician will make use of the substitutability of the services by bidding down the output of each service by use of the first most similar substitute. If there are many close substitutes in the game, this might result in an outcome that approaches the outcome under the competitive bureaucratic strategy (which is located at the politician's ideal point). This solution would also be reached if the politicians purchased the services in a competitive external market.

The preceding exposition is based on the assumption that the same politician is pivotal for all services. If there are different pivotal politicians for different services, figures become messy but the reasoning remains the same. If preferences are separable and the goods are public, the reaction curves of every pair of bureaucrats will intersect so that an equilibrium will be assured. If the goods are complementary, the reaction curves of every pair of bureaucrats will intersect or coincide along the boundary of the collectively beneficial set of the pivotal politicians for both goods rather than along that of the individually beneficial set of the single pivotal politician. This will again assure a multiple equilibrium. If the goods are substitutes, there may again be an internal equilibrium at the point where the reaction curves intersect each other, or a corner solution where one of the services is not supplied.

Summarizing the results of the analysis so far, it may be concluded that the results of the general analysis of bureaucratic decision-making are quite similar to those of the partial analysis: optimal output levels are pushed up and rounded up. However, in two respects the general approach leads to a different conclusion. First, the core does not exist if more than a single public good is involved, so that the stability-enhancing effects of bureaucratic strategies become of foremost importance. As it turns out, PMPD strategies are capable of inducing stability, but as far as the divisive variant is concerned, homogeneous preferences are a necessary condition.

Secondly, in a game for two or more goods, bureaucratic interaction becomes of paramount importance. Bureaucratic interaction concerns the choice of strategies and the choice of ABCFs given the strategy choice. As far as the choice of strategies is concerned the consensual variant of the PMPD strategy is a maximin strategy that will be followed in particular by risk averse bureaucrats. The divisive variant of the PMPD strategy is a risky strategy unless (a) it is followed by all bureaucrats, and (b) preferences in the political committee are homogeneous. Only if the latter conditions are satisfied will a core exist and the divisive variant guarantee certainty of better results from the bureaucratic perspective. As far as the choice of ABCFs is concerned a unique bureaucratic equilibrium will generally exist if the preferences of the pivotal politician are separable, or if the goods are substitutes. If the goods are complements, there will generally be a set of bureaucratic equilibria.

Before pursuing the analysis in the direction of games for private and group goods, it seems useful to dwell for a while upon the empirical significance of these results.

The argument developed in this section constitutes the basic explanation of stability in collective decision-making about public goods that the model presented yields. Of course, the value of this explanation has to be assessed in the light of empirical evidence. However, as usual, the intuition behind these hypotheses comes from casual observation and practical experience. An observation that has particularly inspired the construction of the model in this respect concerns the tendency that bureaucratic supply strongly depoliticizes collective decision-making and enhances the illusion that there is a unique 'reasonable' service level that everybody, or at least the 'responsible' majority, is willing to accept. In practice, this tendency materializes in the documents that actually reach the conference tables of political authorities. In the executive budget process, for instance, these documents result from preliminary negotiations that have taken place between officials of public agencies and officials of budget bureaux. These negotiations concentrate on a few budget–output alternatives (points of the ABCF curve) closely centred around last year's decision. As mentioned before, bureaucrats typically reveal strongly kinked ABCFs in such negotiations. Since budget bureau officials and their political superiors do not want to be overruled, they acquiesce in the proposals of agencies if they feel that these are politically acceptable. For this purpose they estimate the preferences (BOFs). Of course, they know that the proposals submitted to the political authority often do not embody efficient budget–output combinations. As argued in chapter 4, budget bureaux are generally aware of the inefficiencies in the programmes under scrutiny. They know, too, that as far as cost estimates are concerned, the numbers of the responsible agency will ultimately prevail. By and large a budget bureau will only insist upon the submission of more than a single proposal to the political authority, or if necessary submit an alternative proposal itself, if it feels that such a step may lead to a different decision. If the services under review exhibit strong public good characteristics this will be the case only if bureaucrats have misjudged the politician's BOFs. For the vast majority of services with strong public good characteristics, this implies that political authorities will not be confronted with more than a single budget–output alternative.

Similar considerations apply to the legislative stage of decision-making. In national governments like the UK and the Netherlands where Parliament does not have its own budgetary office, it is fairly difficult for the members of the House or Chamber to get factually accurate alternatives for the executive proposals on the political agenda in the first place.

In the US federal government, the Congressional Budget Office is capable of providing such information, but the staff of this office operate under the same constraints as their colleagues in the executive budget bureau. This situation provides public agencies with the opportunity to use cost information as a means to advance stability in the legislative arena as well.

Bureaucratic decision-making about private and group goods

Bureaucrats who are supplying private or group goods can in principle choose the same strategies as bureaucrats who are supplying public goods. However, in the case of private and group goods, the PM strategy, as well as the consensual and the divisive variant of the PMPD strategy may closely resemble the C strategy. In particular, these strategies are identical to the C strategy if the extreme low-demand or median politician does not benefit at all from the good, or benefits only from type I externalities (recall pp. 57–8), and they are similar to that strategy if the extreme low-demand or median politician only benefits from type II externalities. In these cases PM and PMPD strategies do not make sense. Only in the cases of majority private or group goods may the median politician, or even the extreme low-demand politician, be a consumer. In those cases, the analysis presented on pp. 134–51 with respect to the effects of strategies on outcomes and with respect to bureaucratic interaction is fully applicable. Otherwise, the bureaucrat may consider a third variant of the PMPD strategy, which differs from the consensual variant in that only the consumers of the service are taken into account (not the politicians who do not benefit or benefit only from externalities). In particular, this variant consists of an ABCF that induces such optimal outputs for the consumers of the good in the committee that the bureaucratic objective function is maximized at the lowest of those outputs. We shall call this variant of the PMPD strategy simply the 'third variant'. According to this variant the extreme low-demand consumer is the pivotal politician. In this section, the effects of this variant will be examined in comparison to the C strategy. It will turn out that this variant is illustrative of all other variants involving the strategic supply of private or group goods.

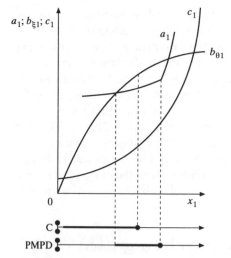

Figure 6.5 Monopolistic supply strategy in a three-person budgetary game for one private or group good

The effects of the third variant of the PMPD strategy in a three-person budgetary game for one private or group good are illustrated in figure 6.5. Politician θ is the consumer of the good and politicians ψ and ζ do not benefit. Figure 6.5 shows the TCF of the service and the BOF of politician θ. The BOFs of politicians ψ and ζ coincide with the output axis (no externalities). Figure 6.5 also shows the ABCF that makes up the third variant of the PMPD strategy. In order to avoid a degenerate case, it is supposed that the bureaucrat is not completely informed about political preferences (so that there is an uncertainty margin). This ABCF induces a shift of the ideal point of politician θ in comparison to its position under the C strategy in accordance with the bureaucratic objectives. The additional output axes below figure 6.5 again show the effects of the strategies upon the location of the ideal points.

When attention is again paid to the existence and location of the core and the extension of the Pareto optimal set, it appears that the core under the third variant of the PMPD strategy exists and remains where it was under the C strategy, namely in the origin, and that the Pareto optimal set consists of the origin and an interval below the optimal output of the pivotal politician.

The situation is different, however, in the general approach. Now it turns out that goods which do not benefit a majority of the politicians can be purchased beyound the optimal output level of non-consumers as part of a package deal that also includes outputs of private goods in favour of other

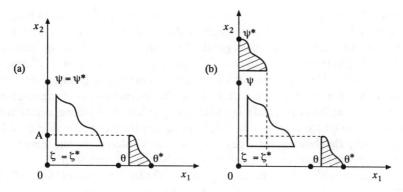

Figure 6.6 Monopolistic supply strategies for a single good in a three-person budgetary game for two private or group goods

politicians. For this purpose, the consumers of different services must enter into coalitions of minorities. This phenomenon is known as 'log-rolling'. In the context of the model presented, log-rolling is a perfectly rational phenomenon that offers the only possible explanation for the public provision of private or group goods that benefit less than half of the politicians in the decisive committee. In view of the fact that in the modern welfare state usually more than half of the governmental budget at the national level is spent on minority private and group goods, it seems plausible that log-rolling is a very common phenomenon.

Figure 6.6 illustrates the consequences of the third variant of the PMPD strategy in a three-person budgetary game for two private or group goods in comparison with the consequences of the C strategy.

It is supposed that the first good benefits political agent θ and the second good political agent ψ. Agent ζ is supposed to benefit from neither good. Figure 6.6a shows the shift of the ideal points and the Pareto optimal set as a consequence of a move from the C strategy to the PMPD strategy by the supplier of the first good, when the second good is supplied according to the C strategy. It appears that the optimal output for politician θ increases and those for politicians ψ and ζ remain where they were (at zero). Furthermore, the contract curve of politicians θ and ψ turns partially into the segment of the output axis of the second good between point A and the optimal output of politician ψ, due to the convex shape of the preference sets of politician ψ and to the fact that for any given output of the second good, the zero output of the first good will be an almost optimal output for politician θ (the best alternative apart from outputs in the neighbourhood of her optimal output).

Turning again to the existence and location of the core and the extension of the Pareto optimal set, the following observations can be made. Whereas a core did not exist under C strategies, it does under the third variant of the PMPD strategy for the first good. The core is located in the origin. Accordingly, the proposal to cease all public provision dominates all other proposals. This implies that in a game for two private or group goods, an individual bureaucrat can create a core in the origin. Just as in the game for public goods, however, PMPD strategies by at least $n - 1$ bureaucrats are required to create a core in the origin in a game for more than two goods. However, the bureaucrat does not have any interest in the resulting stability, because it concerns stability at the zero output level!

Figure 6.6a also show the consequences of the third variant of the PMPD strategy for the Pareto optimal set. Since the contract curves of the coalitions $\{\theta,\psi\}$ and $\{\zeta,\psi\}$ partially coincide under this strategy, the Pareto optimal set consists of the interval of the output axis of the second good between zero and the optimal output of politician ψ, plus an area in the neighbourhood of the ideal point of the pivotal politician (the shaded area in figure 6.6a).

Let us now see what happens if all bureaucrats turn to the the third variant of the PMPD strategy. This case is illustrated in figure 6.6b. The ideal points of politicians ψ and θ are pushed up along the respective output axes. The core exists and is in the origin and the Pareto optimal set would consist of the union of three disconnected areas, namely two areas in the neigbourhood of the ideal points of politicians θ and ψ and the origin (the shaded area plus the origin in figure 6.6b).

It is also interesting to see how bureaucratic interaction works out in the case of private or group goods. The preceding analysis makes clear that the risk involved in the third variant of the PMPD strategy is large. Although the optimal outputs for the consumers increase, the probability that these consumers will enter a coalition with the consumers of other goods in order to maintain or even increase output levels decreases. By taking away political surplus from a consumer, the incentive to make concessions on other goods in order to maintain or increase output is reduced. Whereas the chance that all bureaucrats choose this strategy – so that a core exists and all outputs are reduced to zero – is extremely small, the chance that this strategy will improve results for an individual bureaucrat if other bureaucrats choose C strategies is not much larger. Furthermore, it appears from the preceding analysis that a bureaucrat not only worsens the prospects for herself by choosing this strategy, but also for all other bureaucrats who supply private or group goods to a minority of the committee of politicians. By eliminating the political surplus of her own clients in the committee, she hampers the kind of log-rolling agreements among the politicians that also help to maintain the output levels of other services. Clearly, such behaviour will not be appreciated by colleague bureaucrats, which yields an additional reason to hypothesize that PMPD strategies are unlikely in budgetary games for private or group goods.

Summarizing these results, one can say that in contrast to the conclusions concerning the supply of public goods, PMPD strategies with respect to private and group goods are scarcely attractive from the bureaucrat's perspective. Because positive outputs of services that benefit only a minority of the politicians in the decisive committee are dependent on log-rolling coalitions, the bureaucrat supplying such services will not easily engage in supply strategies that undermine the very viability of such coalitions. Since similar reasoning as was developed in the present section for PMPD strategies can be developed for every supply strategy that diminishes the utility of consumers among politicians, this finding suggests that bureaucrats who supply services to a minority of politicians have a strong incentive to choose C strategies and accordingly supply their services at cost price.

Guide to the literature
In the second half of *Bureaucracy and Representative Government* (1971), Niskanen offers a first discussion of the interaction of a single bureaucrat and a committee of politicians. The particular institutional structure that he assumes consists of a 'review committee', that has to approve the budget–output combination proposed by the bureaucrat and a legislative assembly that has to endorse the budget–output combination approved by the review committee. The preferences of the members of the review committee are identical, but those of the members of the legislature deviate. The legislature decides by majority rule and the preferences of the median politician are supposed to be decisive. If the review committee consists of high-demand politicians – which in Niskanen's view is usually the case in reality – this structure implies that the review committee has no independent role (a 'stylized farce'). According to Niskanen, the bureaucrat will then adjust her strategy to the preferences of the median politician in the legislature (the divisive variant of the PMPD strategy in our terminology). Hettich has rightly observed in 'Bureaucrats and public goods' (1975) that this structure implies that the service can be undersupplied rather than oversupplied, even if the bureaucrat is a pure budget (or output) maximizer. This will particularly be the case if the median politician in the legislature is a low-demander. A more detailed examination of the interaction between a single bureaucrat and a committee of politicians is provided in Mackay and Weaver, 'Monopoly bureaux and fiscal outcomes' (1978) and Denzau and Mackay, 'Benefit and tax share discrimination by a monopoly bureau' (1980). These papers consider not only bureaucratic price discrimination of the second degree, but also of the third degree (tax and benefit share discrimination), which has been left out of consideration in this chapter. Price discrimination of the third degree is also considered in Mackay and Weaver, 'On the mutuality of interests between bureaux and high demand review committees: a perverse result' (1979) and Munger, 'On the

mutuality of interest between bureaux and high demand review committees: the case of joint production' (1984). In these papers, benefit share discrimination takes the specific form of 'commodity-bundling', which amounts to the manipulation of the mix of services in a multi-service bureau. It is shown in these papers that if a review committee of high-demand politicians rather than the bureaucrat decides about the service mix, its role is more than a stylized farce.

Bureaucratic interaction with second degree price discrimination has been examined in Mackay and Weaver, 'Agenda control by budget maximizers in a multi-bureau setting' (1981) and in McGuire, Coiner and Spancake, 'Budget maximizing agencies and efficiency in government' (1979). In the former paper political decision-making proceeds by service, so that equilibria outside the individually beneficial set of the pivotal politician are possible. McGuire, Coiner and Spancake have considered a model with a single politician. In this model, political decision-making is simultaneous, so that equilibria outside the individually beneficial set of the politician are impossible.

7 Institutions

Agenda rules

In chapter 6 it appeared that bureaucratic supply induced a good deal of stability in the model of the budgetary game as it was presented in the opening section. As far as public goods are concerned, the model is able, in principle, to explain stability, provided that bureaucratic price discrimination is possible.

The stability question remains to be answered for the cases in which bureaucratic supply does not induce stability. This is the purpose of the present chapter. One must then think of services with unevenly distributed benefits such as minority private and group goods, and of public goods in situations where price discrimination is not possible.

In the initial analysis of political decision-making, it was mentioned that budgetary games generally lack cores or other stable solutions, so that attention has to be focused on the institutions of the budgetary process. Institutions are, of course, not an invention of economic theory. Indeed, the importance of rules that lead to the selection of a small group of 'feasible' proposals before any political decision-making in the proper sense starts, has since long been recognized in the organizational process branch of budgetary theory: recall, for instance, the notion of 'taking the base for granted' as a major ingredient of the organizational process perspective on budgetary decision-making. In this light, the recent upswing of interest in the institutional aspects of collective decision-making among economists can be interpreted as a late recognition that the organizational process theorists have been looking at the crucial factors all along. However, this interpretation must be qualified in two respects.

First, institutions as such are not a recently discovered domain of economic investigation. Indeed, from the economic point of view institutions are nothing else than decision rules, and hence belong to the traditional subject matter of public choice analysis. What seems to be new, however, is the direction of theory development. Until quite recently, research efforts focused on the discovery of solution concepts.

Assumptions in the sphere of procedural rules were chosen in such a way that plausibility in empirical applications was assured. Now, however, analysts are making attempts to construct models in which the plausibility of the solution concept can be taken for granted – for instance, because it can be proved that the core exists – and which can be used to discover procedural rules, particularly agenda rules. This may be a fruitful approach, especially when the lack of institutional structure that typically character-izes traditional models would require highly artificial solution concepts in order to induce stable results.

Secondly, the economic view of institutions remains quite different from that of organizational process theory. This stems from the considerable methodological differences between both disciplines, as discussed in chapter 1. Economists keep searching for explanations that are compatible with the paradigm of rationality. In relation to the study of agenda rules, this implies two things:

1. That the influence of agenda rules on collective decisions is supposed to be exclusively dependent on the impact of these results upon the behaviour of rational actors (actors whose behaviour can be described by utility functions expressing individual objectives)
2. That agenda rules are supposed to be the outcome of a rational choice process themselves, that is to say that they are supposed to be consistent with rational behaviour in the situation of constitutional choice.

The second requirement is even more important for the study of procedural rules on the basis of given solution concepts than for the study of solution concepts on the basis of given procedural rules. In the former approach, constitutional and postconstitutional analysis are involved in the same endeavour, namely the discovery of procedural decision rules. In this endeavour results of both kinds of analysis can either lend support to or contradict each other. If, for instance, a certain assumption about an agenda rule could explain some empirically observed decisions, such an assumption would nevertheless remain suspect when the agenda rule itself would be inexplicable as a constitutional choice. Under such circumstan-ces, it might be advisable to look for other agenda rules that could induce the same outcomes.

Conversely, there is little reason to use results from constitutional analysis in the study of solution concepts on the basis of given procedural rules, since in the latter approach the existence of the rules is simply taken for granted. If procedural rules are easily observable in reality, such as majority rule, such practice seems reasonable. Inconsistency with the results of constitutional analysis can in that case only be used to refute the empirical relevance of the constitutional analysis.

With respect to the assumptions about agenda rules to be explored in this chapter, we shall require the following. First, these assumptions must be specific enough to allow the derivation of hypotheses that can be subjected to empirical testing. Secondly, these assumptions must describe agenda rules that are understandable as a constitutional choice. However, the latter requirement will not be taken to imply complete deducibility from a set of specific assumptions about the conditions of constitutional choice. Apart from the fact that such a strict requirement would lead us too far into the domain of constitutional analysis, there is no need for it. In each case a sketch of constitutional aspects will suffice. In particular, decision costs, risk and 'net social value' (expected political surplus) are important criteria in this respect.

The modelling of agenda rules

Many contributions in the field of institutions build on the notion of a 'structure induced equilibrium' which was proposed by Shepsle (1979) as a solution concept for a spatial majority game based on a unified theory of agenda rules. Although Shepsle's model is beset by some problems – and for that reason will be modified in this chapter – it provides a useful starting point for the discussion.

The solution concept of 'structure induced equilibrium' can be explained as follows.

The starting point is a spatial majority game, not necessarily a budgetary game. If preference sets are convex, the dominant set with respect to a given proposal $\bar{q}$, $D(\bar{q})$, will generally be non-empty. From the fundamental disequilibrium results that have been proved for such games, it follows indeed that for many such games, the core is empty so that $D(\bar{x}) \neq \emptyset$ for every proposal $\bar{x}$ in the attribute space.[1]

Now, assume that there is an agenda rule that limits the set of proposals that any given coalition of players can put to a vote against a given status quo proposal and that can be described by the set-valued function $G_S(\bar{x})$, where S represents the given coalition and $\bar{x}$ the given status quo proposal. According to Shepsle and Weingast (1981a) the set $G_S(\bar{x})$, to be called the 'admissible set', captures 'the idea that some institutions single out different roles for institutional actors, and that the behavioural discretion of these roles may be dependent on the prevailing state'. As an example, the authors cite a single individual with full agenda power $(G_{\{\xi\}}(\bar{x}) = E$ for every $\bar{x}$, $\bar{x} \in E$ and $G_S(\bar{x}) = \emptyset$ for every $\bar{x}$, $\bar{x} \in E$ and every $S \neq \{\xi\})$, where E is the entire

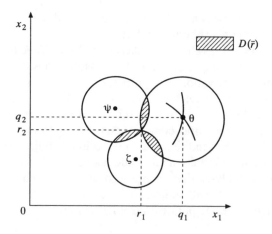

Figure 7.1 SI solution in a three-person simple spatial majority game with full agenda power of a single player

policy space and ξ the individual with full agenda power), or a subcommittee with full agenda power ($G_S(\bar{x}) = E$ for every $\bar{x}$, $\bar{x} \in E$ and $G_T(\bar{x}) = \varnothing$ for every $\bar{x}$, $\bar{x} \in E$ and every T, $T \neq S$ where S is the subcommittee).

Define $P_S(\bar{x})$ as the subset of $G_S(\bar{x})$ which contains all elements of $G_S(\bar{x})$ which are strictly preferred by all members of S to $\bar{x}$. So:

$$P_S(\bar{x}) = \{\bar{y} \mid \bar{y} \in G_S(\bar{x}); u_\xi(\bar{y}) > u_\xi(\bar{x}) \text{ for every } \xi, \xi \in S\}.$$

Define, furthermore, a proposal $\bar{x}$ as 'vulnerable' if there is a proposal $\bar{y}$, such that:

$$\bar{y} \in P_S(\bar{x}) \text{ for some } S, S \subseteq N \tag{1}$$

$$\bar{y} \in D(\bar{x}). \tag{2}$$

A 'structure induced equilibrium' can now be defined as an invulnerable proposal. In the words of Shepsle and Weingast (1981a), 'a proposal $\bar{x}$ is a structure induced equilibrium if and only if those proposals that defeat $\bar{x}$ either can be proposed only by those who do not prefer to do so, or cannot be proposed at all'.

The set of structure induced equilibrium proposals, to be called the structure induced solution (SI solution), can be illustrated by pursuing the example of an individual with full agenda power mentioned above (see figure 7.1).

Figure 7.1 shows the ideal points of the players in a committee of three players, in a two-dimensional policy space. The indifference curves through $\bar{q}$ and $\bar{r}$ are also indicated. The former proposal ($\bar{q}$) coincides with the ideal point of player θ, who holds full agenda power. The latter proposal ($\bar{r}$) is an arbitrary proposal that does not coincide with θ's ideal point. The figure makes clear that $\bar{r}$ is a vulnerable proposal in the sense of the given definition and that $\bar{q}$ is invulnerable. Vulnerability of $\bar{r}$ follows from the fact that $D(\bar{r})$ is non-empty (the shaded region) and intersects with $P_{\{\theta\}}(\bar{r})$. Note that in this case $P_{\{\theta\}}(\bar{r})$ is nothing else than the preference set of θ with respect to $\bar{r}$.

In general it holds that $D(\bar{r})$ is non-empty unless $\bar{r}$ is a core proposal (recall that the core is the set of undominated proposals), but additional conditions are necessary for the existence of a non-empty intersection of $D(\bar{r})$ and $P_S(\bar{r})$. Obviously, one of these conditions is that $P_S(\bar{r})$ is non-empty itself. Since θ's preference set with respect to her own ideal point is empty by definition, it follows that $\bar{q}$ is a structure induced equilibrium, although it is not a core proposal (that is to say, although $D(\bar{q})$ is non-empty, see the indifference curves of ψ and ζ through $\bar{q}$).

The example makes clear that in the case of the full agenda power of a single player, the SI solution includes at least the core – if the core exists – and the ideal point of the player with full agenda power. Since the latter point will always exist, the SI solution will always exist under this condition.

The SI solution certainly embodies a valuable attempt at a solution concept based on a general and unified theory of agenda-setting. Nevertheless, it raises some problems. The first problem is that it requires so-called 'myopic expectations' on the part of all coalitions S for which in a given status quo $\bar{x}$, $G_S(\bar{x})$ is non-empty (Hinich, 1986). This can be explained as follows. Call any coalition S which is allowed to put a proposal to a vote against a given status quo proposal $\bar{x}$, an agenda-setter. It follows from the definition of vulnerability that an agenda-setter will not put forward a proposal $\bar{y}$ against a status quo proposal $\bar{x}$, if it prefers $\bar{x}$ to $\bar{y}$. However, it may be the case that $\bar{y}$ is vulnerable and that if $\bar{y}$ were put to a vote against a third proposal $\bar{z}$, this would lead to the adoption of $\bar{z}$, which the agenda-setter does prefer to $\bar{x}$. It seems very doubtful that an agenda-setter would refrain from proposing $\bar{y}$, if it expected that $\bar{y}$ would subsequently be defeated by a proposal that it preferred to $\bar{x}$. Indeed, it would do so only if its expectations were limited to the proximate vote ('myopic expectations').

This problem can be illustrated by the example of a player with full agenda power (see figure 7.2).

If $\{\theta\}$ is the agenda-setter in the three-person spatial majority game illustrated in figure 7.2, proposal $\bar{q}$ is a special structure induced equilibrium ('special' because it is neither a core proposal nor coincides with the agenda-setter's ideal point).

This follows from the fact that $D(\bar{q})$, indicated by the shaded region, does not intersect with $P_{\{\theta\}}(\bar{q})$. This implies that there are no proposals that $\{\theta\}$ is prepared to propose and that simultaneously dominate $\bar{q}$. Hence $\bar{q}$ is

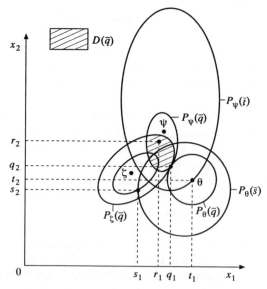

Figure 7.2 Special SI solution in a three-person spatial majority game with full agenda power of a single player

invulnerable and included in the SI solution. However, if $\{\theta\}$ has more foresight than only the proximate vote, she will for instance propose $\bar{r}$, which from her perspective is worse than $\bar{q}$ – namely outside $P_{\{\theta\}}(\bar{q})$ – and subsequently $\bar{s}$, and then her own ideal point $\bar{t}$.

Since the assumption of myopic expectations on the part of agenda-setters is a far-reaching and implausible assumption, its necessity provides a strong reason to modify the concept of the SI solution in such a way that it can be omitted.

A second problem raised by the SI solution concerns the plausibility of the restriction of agenda-setting competence as such. This restriction forbids players who are excluded from the agenda-setting coalition from putting forward proposals or amendments of their own liking. The existence of such restrictions is usually hard to prove in empirical applications. At least as far as budgetary decision-making is concerned, the political agenda tends to be open to all kinds of minorities.

A third problem attached to the SI solution is that it requires perfect information about the preferences of committee members on the part of the agenda-setting coalition. Enelow and Hinich (1987) have shown that benefits from agenda manipulation rapidly evaporate as soon as uncertainty about the location of the ideal points and about the shape of the preference sets is introduced (see also Hinich, 1986).

In order to solve the above-mentioned problems with the SI solution, the definition of 'vulnerability' has to be altered slightly. In particular, it is proposed to omit the constraint on agenda-setting behaviour, as expressed by the set $P_S(\bar{x})$. The coalition index in the function $G_S(\bar{x})$, that expresses the set of admissible proposals against a given status quo proposal, can then be omitted as well. Accordingly, this function, to be called the 'agenda function' of the committee, can be denoted by $G(\bar{x})$.

A proposal $\bar{x}$ may now simply be considered as vulnerable if there is a proposal $\bar{y}$, such that:

$$\bar{y} \in G(\bar{x}) \tag{1}$$

$$\bar{y} \in D(\bar{x}). \tag{2}$$

A proposal which is not vulnerable can be considered as an equilibrium proposal. A proposal $\bar{x}$ satisfies this condition if $G(\bar{x}) \cap D(\bar{x}) = \varnothing$. In order to indicate the distinction from the SI solution, a proposal that satisfies the present definition will be called an 'agenda induced equilibrium' and the corresponding solution concept the agenda induced solution (AI solution).

The proposed solution concept represents a generalization as well as a simplification of the SI solution. It is a generalization because constraints on agenda-setting behaviour can be brought back via the agenda function, for instance by stipulating that a proposal $\bar{y}$ is only admissible against a given status quo proposal $\bar{x}$ if, apart from other requirements, described by the restriction $y \in G^*(\bar{x})$, it is preferred by a particular agenda-setting coalition (S) to the given status quo proposal:

$$G(\bar{x}) = \{\bar{y} \mid \bar{y} \in G^*(\bar{x}); u_\xi(\bar{y}) > u_\xi(\bar{x}) \text{ for every } \xi, \xi \in S\}.$$

Of course, one must be aware of the problems concerning myopic expectations and informational requirements which arise from the re-introduction of constraints on agenda-setting behaviour in this way.

The AI solution also amounts to a simplification of the SI solution, because the set of admissible proposals is specified directly via the agenda function.

How can the AI solution be applied to the budgetary game? Up to this point the institutional features of collective decision-making have been discussed in the context of the spatial majority game in general, but the application to the budgetary game is straightforward. Since the AI solution is the core of the reduced game that follows from the removal of inadmissible proposals, the condition for the AI solution can simply be substituted for the core condition. The resulting model VIII is presented below (see particularly (5) and (6); the other expressions of the model are identical to those of model VII).

Model VIII

$$\max u_\xi(\bar{x}, m_\xi) \qquad\qquad \xi = 1, 2, \ldots, v \tag{1}$$

$$\max u_i(d_i,x_i) \qquad\qquad i = 1,2,\ldots,n \qquad\qquad (2)$$

$$\bar{p}_\xi.\bar{x} + m_\xi = g_\xi \qquad\qquad \xi = 1,2,\ldots,v \qquad\qquad (3)$$

$$c_i = c_i(x_i) \qquad\qquad i = 1,2,\ldots,n \qquad\qquad (4)$$

$$G = G(\bar{x}) \qquad\qquad (5)$$

$$D(\bar{x}) \cap G(\bar{x}) = \varnothing \qquad\qquad (6)$$

$$p_{\xi i} \equiv \tau_\xi a_i(x_i)/x_i \qquad\qquad \xi = 1,2,\ldots,v;\ i = 1,2,\ldots,n \qquad (7)$$

$$d_i \equiv a_i(x_i) - c_i(x_i) \qquad\qquad i = 1,2,\ldots,n \qquad\qquad (8)$$

$$D(\bar{x}) \equiv \{\bar{y} \,|\, u_\xi(\bar{y}) > u_\xi(\bar{x}) \text{ for every } \xi,\ \xi \in S$$
$$\text{and some } S, |S| > |N|/2\} \qquad \xi = 1,2,\ldots,v. \qquad (9)$$

The next two sections of the chapter will deal with the exploration of two agenda rules that play an important role in the budgetary process in representative government.

These agenda rules are (1) the germaneness rule, and (2) the rule of non-intervention. The rules will be described by specification of the agenda function and their consequences will be examined in the context of model VIII. Since the outcomes arising from both rules are quite different, further thought about empirical relevance is called for.

The germaneness rule

The germaneness rule is often seen as the single most important stability-enhancing factor in political decision-making. However, this claim is hard to justify. It will be argued in this section that although the effect of the germaneness rule on collective decisions is straightforward and easy to understand, its empirical relevance cannot easily be established.

The basic idea of the germaneness rule was firstly stated in Shepsle's (1979) paper about structure induced equilibrium. The rule supposes that the agenda of a committee is partitioned into 'domains of responsibility' or 'jurisdictions'. Each jurisdiction is defined by a set of dimensions of the policy space. The rule prescribes that in each jurisdiction only those proposals are admissible that change the status quo proposal in the dimensions belonging to the jurisdiction. All proposals with respect to other dimensions are out of order (not germane), and may not be taken into consideration. Although the germaneness rule may be often combined with constraints on agenda-setting competence, in that there is a specific politician or group of politicians in the committee with exclusive competence for each jurisdiction, both aspects are logically distinct. In his (1979) paper about the structure induced equilibrium Shepsle remarks that:

The idea of jurisdiction is quite independent of division-of-labor structural arrangements. The formal agenda of an ordinary business meeting, with its separate categories of activity – old business, new business, officer's reports, etc. – suggests a separation into jurisdictions without a structural division-of-labor. While a matter of new business may not be brought up (i.e. is out of order) during the session on old business and vice versa, the entire membership of the organization participates in both deliberations. (Shepsle, 1979, p. 31)

Of course, restrictive agenda-setting competence can be assumed in addition to a jurisdictional partition, but at present no such assumption is made.

From a formal point of view, the presence of jurisdictional partitions in the budgetary process is quite obvious. As mentioned on pp. 29–30, budgetary decisions are scattered over a large number of separate laws, such as entitlement laws, fiscal laws, and appropriation laws.

In many governments, the budget for each fiscal year is authorized in dozens of different laws. Furthermore, most of these laws contain large numbers of spending authorizations for different public agencies. According to usual rules of order, these laws and spending authorizations are decided one by one. This holds true for representative assemblies as well as for executive bodies such as cabinets.

In fact the presence of the germaneness rule has been recognized implicitly throughout the entire discussion in the previous chapters. Each time the *ceteris paribus* assumption with respect to 'other services' was made, and the analysis thereby limited to a smaller number of services than the complete set of n services funded by the total budget, it was in fact assumed that the status quo was maintained as far as those other services were concerned. In the case of the one- and two-dimensional analyses, it was in fact assumed that the politician(s) only had to decide about one or two services and that these decisions could be taken in complete separation from decisions about other services.

The germaneness rule can be described by the following agenda function:

$$G(\bar{x}) = \{\bar{y} \mid y_i = x_i \text{ for every } i, i \notin J\}.$$

The set J is the set of services that determines the jurisdiction. The function implies that the admissible set against the status quo proposal exclusively consists of proposals that deviate from the status quo proposal in the outputs of services that belong to J. All output levels of services that

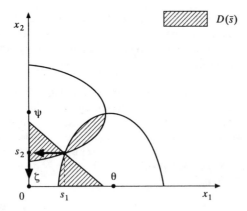

Figure 7.3 The decision path induced by the germaneness rule and simple jurisdictions in a three-person budgetary game for two private or group goods

are not included in J must be held constant. In the specific case of simple jurisdictions, the set J will contain only one service.

The effect of the germaneness rule is very much dependent on the number of services in each jurisdiction. The main distinction is that between simple jurisdictions which contain only a single service and plural jurisdictions which contain more services. Usually, the purpose of a jurisdictional partition is the creation of simple jurisdictions. In such jurisdictions, coordinated voting achieves nothing. The core of the budgetary game in a simple jurisdiction is the ideal point of the median voter in the dimension defining the jurisdiction, which is the origin in the case of minority private or group goods. This is illustrated in figure 7.3 for the case of a budgetary game for two private goods.

Point $\bar{s}$ indicates the status quo proposal. The first jurisdiction is simple and contains only the first private good. In this jurisdiction proposals with respect to the second good cannot be put forward. Of course, this leads to the approval of the core proposal $(0,s_2)$. When this decision is taken, $(0,s_2)$ becomes the status quo proposal in the next jurisdiction. If this jurisdiction only contains the second good the next proposal to be approved will be the zero proposal for that good, and the origin will indicate the total result of both decisions. The shaded region indicates the dominant set with respect to the first status quo proposal.

Obviously, the effect of a jurisdictional partition depends upon the possibility of vote coordination across jurisdictional boundaries. Whereas within every jurisdiction repeated voting can always be avoided by approval of only a single equilibrium proposal by the grand coalition –

supposing that such a proposal exists – the partition of the agenda into jurisdictions implies that in every jurisdiction a separate decision must be made, and hence a vote must be taken, before proposals in a next jurisdiction can be decided upon. Vote coordination across jurisdictional boundaries therefore requires agreements about actual individual voting behaviour, so-called 'vote trades'.[2] Although vote trades in this sense are somewhat more visible than other coordinated votes, effective suppression of vote trading remains a difficult matter. Before giving further attention to the probability of an effective ban on vote trading in the budgetary process, it is necessary to look more closely into the basic claim that the germaneness rule leads to stable equilibrium outcomes, provided that vote trading can be prevented.

The main problem with the germaneness rule is that in order to be effective it requires myopic expectations on the part of the committee members. In other words, the existence of the corresponding AI solution not only depends upon an effective ban on cross-jurisdictional vote trading, but also upon a complete absence of individual foresight that would transcend the jurisdictional boundary.

The general problem can be illustrated by an example of a three-person budgetary game for two public goods. Suppose that the ideal points of the politicians do not coincide (because price discrimination is impossible) and that these points are located in the attribute space as indicated in figure 7.4.

Politicians ψ and ζ have separable preferences; politician θ does not. It is assumed that all preferences are symmetric about the ideal points (for instance, because of quadratic preference functions politicians ψ and ζ hold circular indifference curves, agent θ elliptical ones).

If the outputs of both services are decided within the same jurisdiction, there is no core and anything can happen. If both outputs decided in separate jurisdictions and if cross-jurisdictional vote trading can be prevented, the final outcome of the decision process depends on the order of decision-making.

If $\bar{s}$ is the initial status quo proposal and if the first dimension is decided first, $\bar{r}$ will be the equilibrium outcome (proposal (r_1,s_2) will be approved in the first jurisdiction and proposal (r_1,r_2) in the second jurisdiction). If, on the other hand, starting from the same status quo proposal, the second dimension is decided first, $\bar{q}$ becomes the equilibrium outcome (proposal (s_1,q_2) will be approved in the first jurisdiction, and proposal (q_1,q_2) in the second jurisdiction). Note that, due to the non-separable preferences of politician θ, neither outcome coincides with the median point in the direction of both dimensions (indicated in figure 7.4 by the letter D).

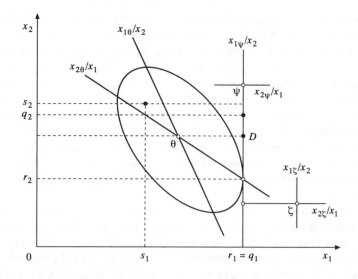

Figure 7.4 The AI solution according to the germaneness rule and simple jurisdictions in a three-person budgetary game for two public goods

The question now arises whether politician θ would really let the order of decision-making determine her voting behaviour, if she knew that both dimensions had to be decided anyhow. If politician θ anticipated the voting behaviour of all other politicians (also with respect to dimensions to be decided in future jurisdictions) she might as well vote for r_2 in the second dimension, even if that dimension were decided first. Only under the assumption of 'myopic expectations', or expectations not reaching further than the present jurisdiction, would she do otherwise. Still, it may not be concluded that if all politicians vote 'sophisticatedly', $\bar{r}$ is the equilibrium outcome. Indeed, under that condition, the expected outcome in the next jurisdiction will be anticipated by agents ψ and ζ as well.

In order to keep track of the equilibrium outcome of sophisticated voting it is sensible to make use of the so-called 'lines of optima' or 'ridge lines' of the politicians, which indicate the optimal outputs for a certain service at given outputs for the other services.

Both the ridge lines for politician θ, indicated by $x_{1\theta}/x_2$ and $x_{2\theta}/x_1$ and the ridge lines for politicians ψ and ζ, indicated analogously, are shown in figure 7.4.

In order to determine the final equilibrium outcome after both services have been decided in simple jurisdictions by sophisticated voting, it is necessary to construct the 'median ridge line' for each service.

This curve indicates the outputs that will be decided for a certain service

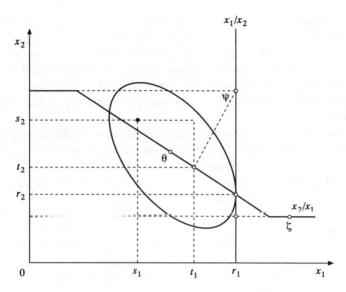

Figure 7.5 Ridge lines and median ridge line in a three-person budgetary game for two public goods

by majority voting, conditional upon alternative outputs for the other service. It consists of (segments of) the median ridge line(s) of the median politician(s). It may occur that the same politician remains the median politician for a certain service in the entire output domain for all outputs of the other service, but in the case of non-separable preferences this need not necessarily be the case.

The median ridge lines are indicated in figure 7.5, which is based on exactly the same pattern of preferences as figure 7.4. The median ridge line for the first service, indicated by x_1/x_2, coincides with the ridge line of politician ψ for that dimension $(x_1/x_2 = x_{1\psi}/x_2)$, whereas the median ridge line for the second dimension, indicated by x_2/x_1, consists of three different segments.

In order to see how the politicians will vote in each jurisdiction, the optimal points on the ridge lines must be determined.

Suppose, for instance, that in figure 7.5 the first service is decided in the first jurisdiction. All politicians know in this case that the final equilibrium point will be somewhere upon the median ridge line for the second dimension (x_2/x_1). With respect to the first service each politician will thus opt for the output indicated by the x_1 coordinate of her most preferred point upon that median ridge line. Because of the circular indifference curves of politician ψ, her induced optimal point follows from dropping a perpendicular onto the median ridge line. This induced optimal point is indicated in figure 7.5 by the unshaded point $\bar{t}$ on the median ridge line x_2/x_1.

Note that formally s_2 will be maintained for the second dimension during decision-making about the first dimension, but since sophisticated politicians anticipate that a point along x_2/x_1 will become the final outcome for the second dimension, they will ignore this fact. It follows that $\bar{t}$ is the equilibrium outcome if the first dimension is decided first (proposal (t_1,s_2) will be approved in the first jurisdiction and proposal (t_1,t_2) in the second jurisdiction).

Suppose, next, that the second service is decided first. Politicians will now induce their optimal points along the vertical median ridge line x_1/x_2. The resulting optimal points are indicated in figure 7.5 by the unshaded points on the median ridge line x_1/x_2. In this case voting in the first jurisdiction will formally occur along the line $x_1 = s_1$, but again politicians will anticipate what will happen in the next jurisdiction and actually vote along the median ridge line x_1/x_2. It follows that $\bar{r}$ will result as the final equilibrium outcome (proposal (s_1,r_2) will be approved in the first jurisdiction and proposal (r_1,r_2) in the second jurisdiction). Apparently the voting order becomes relevant again, if not only politician θ, but all politicians have perfect foresight!

Of course, this is an important conclusion but it does not *per se* contradict the alleged key characteristic of the germaneness rule, namely that if the agenda is partitioned into simple jurisdictions, a unique equilibrium outcome will result. Although in the present example sophisticated voting leads to a different outcome than myopic expectations – namely $\bar{t}$ or $\bar{r}$ depending on voting order, instead of $\bar{r}$ or $\bar{q}$ – both suppositions lead to a unique equilibrium.

It has been shown, however, that in general the alleged key characteristic does not prevail (Kramer, 1972; Denzau and Mackay, 1981). Whereas myopic expectations automatically lead to unique equilibria because optimal points are induced along straight status quo lines, securing single-peaked preference curves, perfect foresight might lead to multi-peaked preference curves. Under the latter condition the median output need not necessarily emerge as a voting equilibrium (core solution) even in a simple jurisdiction! This can be shown by an example resulting from an upward shift of the ideal points of politicians ψ and ζ from their positions in figure 7.4 and 7.5, namely as shown in figure 7.6a (the former positions of these ideal points are indicated by ψ^* and ζ^*).

Again politicians ψ and ζ are supposed to hold separable preferences and politician θ is supposed to hold inseparable preferences. Accordingly, the median ridge line for the second service consists of different segments, as shown in figure 7.6.

If the second service is decided first, the optimal points are induced along the median ridge line for the first service – as shown by the unshaded points

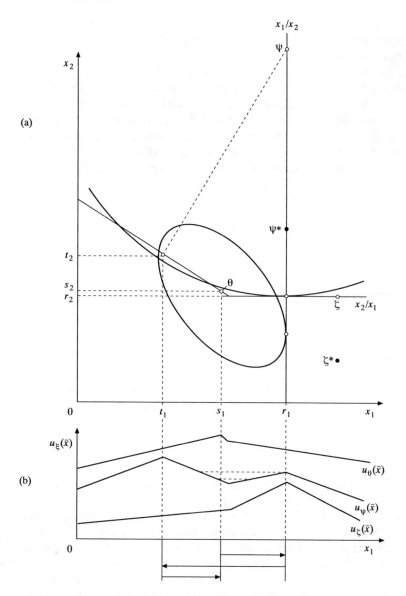

Figure 7.6 Ridge lines and median ridge line in a three-person budgetary game for two public goods leading to a double-peaked preference curve

on x_1/x_2 – which results in the equilibrium outcome $\bar{r}$. (The status quo proposal is omitted from figure 7.6 because it does not play a role under sophisticated voting.)

If, on the other hand, the first service is decided first, optimal points must be induced along the kinked median ridge line for the second service. This results in induced optimal points, as indicated by the unshaded points on x_2/x_1. The induced optimal point of politician θ is now her own ideal point ($\bar{s}$) and the induced optimal point of politician ψ is $\bar{t}$; the induced optimal point of ζ is her own ideal point. Since $\bar{s}$ is the median of these three points along the second dimension, it is the equilibrium proposal. Look, however, at what happens if in the first jurisdiction politician ζ or politician ψ proposes r_1 against s_1. Since $\bar{r}$, just like $\bar{s}$, is on the median ridge line x_2/x_1 and since $\bar{r}$ is preferred by both ζ and ψ, r_1 will defeat s_1! But if θ or ψ subsequently proposes t_1, t_1 will defeat r_1. And if θ or ζ then proposes s_1, the cycle is closed. The reason for the cycle is of course that the induction of preferences along the kinked median ridge line for the second dimension leads to multi-peaked preferences for the first dimension.[3] The corresponding preference functions are shown in figure 7.6b.

The importance of this result should not be underestimated. It means that, contrary to common belief, the splitting up of a political agenda into simple jurisdictions does not necessarily induce a unique equilibrium as soon as politicians stretch their time horizon even to a small degree beyond the current jurisdiction. Furthermore, it appears that this result is completely independent of the possibility of vote trading. In other words, even if vote trading could effectively be prevented, the germaneness rule could only lead to a unique solution under the extreme assumption of myopic expectations. This result seems indeed rather critical for the empirical relevance of the AI solution based on this particular agenda rule.

An interesting attempt to save the AI solution induced by the germaneness rule was made by Enelow and Hinich (Enelow and Hinich, 1983b, 1983c; Enelow, 1984). These authors relaxed the perfect foresight condition a little by the introduction of uncertainty. They assumed that politicians are treating decisions in future jurisdictions as random variables with known probability distributions. Under certain assumptions about the density functions of these variables, the authors were able to deduce a unique equilibrium, coinciding with the mean of the multivariate density function of the random variables.

The conclusion of the preceding argument is that the germaneness rule may contribute to stability, but does not guarantee it. In particular, this agenda rule will induce stability in an otherwise unstable budgetary game only if vote-trading can effectively be prevented and if, moreover, politicians lack any specific information as to the preferences of fellow politicians with respect to services that are still to be decided. It follows also from this argument that if the latter conditions are satisfied in a budgetary game for private or group goods that benefit only a minority of the committee, public provision of these services will be abolished.

Empirical data about actual decisions are needed in order to establish the occurrence of such decisions and thereby the potential empirical relevance of the AI solution induced by the germaneness rule. Meanwhile, it may be useful to take a closer look at the budgetary process from the specific perspective of this particular agenda rule, in order to get an idea of where effective jurisdictional agenda partitions may be found.

It has been mentioned already that budgetary decisions are scattered over a large number of laws and that each law typically authorizes a number of services. Although prevailing rules of order in political committees usually prescribe that each service must be decided in a separate jurisdiction, in practice jurisdictional partitions are hard to maintain and in many cases deliberately removed. It may, for instance, be argued that a large part of the procedural innovation in the budgetary process that has been realized or attempted in central governments during the postwar period in the executive as well as in the legislative stage of decision-making has been aimed at the removal of jurisdictional parti- tions. Policies in this sphere are aimed at 'improvement of budgetary control'. In this connection, 'better control' means that the need for warships can be weighed against the need for subsidized kindergartens and that both of these needs can be weighed against the additional burden from an increased excise duty on spirits or a decreased income tax allowance on mortgage interest. Of course, budgetary control also implies that substantive laws can be adjusted from year to year in the light of budgetary priorities.

Apart from the formalized attempts at the improvement of control, there is much informal coordination between separate decisions which is hard to detect or to suppress. Politicians may conclude agreements about their voting behaviour in different jurisdictions. As long as these agreements are voluntarily adhered to, formal agenda partitions are rather irrelevant and impossible to enforce. A long lapse of time between separate decisions may be one of the few effective barriers against vote trading.

The impossibility of effective enforcement of the germaneness rule raises the question whether this rule should be incorporated in an empirical model at all. It might be argued that even if the kind of far-reaching retrenchment decisions that this rule predicts were actually observed, the deeper cause of such outcomes should be sought in bad political manoeuvring on the part of the beneficiaries of the services in question, rather than in the presence of the rule *per se*. In such cases, the beneficiaries would apparently have tolerated decisions being taken in isolation from decisions about other services. The limits of economic modelling are touched on here. Incidental deviations from rational behaviour belong to the domain of psychology rather than to that of economics.

The latter consideration also bears upon the constitutional aspects of the germaneness rule. The character of the rule is somewhat paradoxical in this respect. The germaneness rule in principle selects a unique invulnerable proposal; hence one would expect that it scores high on limitation of risk and decision costs. If the rule could effectively be enforced, these characteristics would probably apply. Since this is not the case, however, the impending enforcement of the rule is perceived as extremely risky and high (decision) costs are incurred by potential beneficiaries of services in order to avert such a threat. Of course, these effects cannot be attributed to the germaneness rule itself. They are rather due to uncertainty about whether, and when, it is effectively enforced.

Something similar is true of the net social value of the corresponding AI solution. In principle, expected political surplus should be rather high because, if effectively applied and enforced, the germaneness rule prevents all public provision of private and group goods that benefit only a minority of the politicians in the decisive committee(s). As soon as the effective prevention of vote trading becomes incidental and unpredictable, however, it is not clear how expected political surplus of the rule could be determined in advance. Politicians who believe that the rule might be applied discriminately to their disadvantage are likely to oppose it.

The rule of non-intervention

The agenda rule of non-intervention restricts the set of admissible proposals against the status quo proposal to the proposals either to increase outputs, without increasing the output of any service further than wanted by at least some member of the committee, or to decrease outputs unanimously. This rule implies that a politician can never propose changing the output of the favourite service of another politician (the service for which that politician favours the prevailing or a higher output) against her wishes. Hence the rule is called 'the rule of non-intervention'. It will be argued in this section that the rule of non-intervention leads to a specific form of coordinated voting which has been encountered already in chapter 6, and which is known as 'log-rolling'. The latter phenomenon is a well-known theme in the public choice literature that has aroused much controversy, particularly with respect to its normative characteristics. These matters will be touched upon below, but in the context of the present

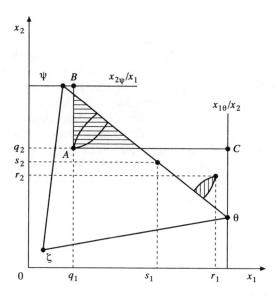

Figure 7.7 The AI solution according to the rule of non-intervention in a three-person budgetary game for two goods

discussion it seems appropriate to develop the argument from the starting point of the rule of non-intervention.

The agenda function that describes the rule of non-intervention and the definition of the Pareto superior set that it makes use of, can be written as follows:

$$G(\bar{x}) = \{\bar{y} \mid \bar{y} \ge \bar{x}; \{\bar{z} \mid \bar{x} \le \bar{z} \le \bar{y}\} \cap S(\bar{y}) = \varnothing\}$$
$$\cup \{\bar{y} \mid \bar{y} \le \bar{x}; \bar{y} \epsilon S(\bar{x})\} \tag{5}$$

$$S(\bar{x}) \equiv \{\bar{y} \mid u_\xi(\bar{y}) > u_\xi(\bar{x}) \text{ for every } \xi, \ \xi \epsilon N\} \quad \xi = 1,2,\dots,v. \tag{10}$$

Equation (5) is the specific function form of (5) of model VIII that expresses the rule of non-intervention.[4] The definition of the Pareto superior set (recall p. 109) has to be added as equation (10) to model VIII. All other expressions of model VIII remain unchanged.

The proposed agenda function works out differently if the dimensionality of the attribute space is equal to or smaller than the number of politicians making up a minimal majority of the committee (that is, equal to or smaller than $|N|/2 + 1$) than when it larger than that. The case that it is equal to or smaller is illustrated in figure 7.7.

Figure 7.7 shows an attribute space of two publicly provided services. The politician's ideal points are indicated as θ, ψ and ζ. For the sake of clarity, the loci of the ideal points have been chosen wide apart: the case of minority private or group goods with externalities. Furthermore in figure 7.7 (not in the model) it is assumed that the politicians have separable preferences so that the contract curves are straight lines and the ridge lines are straight lines parallel to the coordinate axes. The AI solution of the game illustrated in figure 7.7 is the contract curve of politicians θ and ψ.

In order to see this, consider first a point below the contract curve and on or below the ridge line of politician θ for the first service and on or below the ridge line of politician ψ for the second service ('below' in the sense of all coordinates smaller than those of some point on the line). Such a point is $\bar{q}$. The admissible set with respect to $\bar{q}$ consists of the horizontally shaded region and the two line segments through $\bar{q}$ that are parallel to the coordinate axes (indicated in figure 7.7 by AB and AC). Each point in this region indicates combinations of equal or larger outputs, but no further increases than wanted by at least some member of the committee (no 'Pareto inferior' increases). This condition corresponds to the first part of the admissible set: $\{\bar{y} | \bar{y} \geq \bar{x}; \{\bar{z} | \bar{x} \leq \bar{z} \leq \bar{y}\} \cap S(\bar{y}) = \varnothing\}$. It states that a proposal $\bar{y}$ can only be admissible with respect to a given proposal $\bar{x}$ if there is no proposal between $\bar{x}$ and $\bar{y}$ (a proposal for outputs equal to or larger than $\bar{x}$ and equal to or smaller than $\bar{y}$) that is Pareto superior to it. The second part of the admissible set with respect to $\bar{q}$: $\{\bar{y} | \bar{y} \leq \bar{x}; \bar{y} \in S(\bar{x})\}$, is empty. Proposal $\bar{q}$ is vulnerable because the intersection of the admissible set and the dominant set with respect to $\bar{q}$ is not empty. This applies to every proposal $\bar{q}$ that satisfies the stated conditions. Note, that with respect to a point upon the ridge line of politician θ for the first service indicating a smaller than optimal output of the second service, the admissible set consists of the segment of that ridge line between that point and the ideal point of θ. Analogously, the admissible set with respect to a point upon the ridge line of politician ψ for the second service indicating a smaller than optimal output for the first service consists of the segment of that ridge line between that point and the ideal point of ψ.

Consider now a point above the contract curve of ψ and θ or above the ridge line of politician θ for the first service or above the ridge line of politician ψ for the second service ('above' in the sense of all coordinates larger than those of some point on the line). Such a point is $\bar{r}$. The admissible set with respect to $\bar{r}$ is the vertically shaded region. The first part of the admissible set consists now exclusively of point $\bar{r}$ itself because point $\bar{r}$ is Pareto superior to every point, indicating an increase of any output. In this case, the second part of the admissible set is not empty. It consists of all points that (a) indicate combinations of outputs that are equal to or smaller than $\bar{r}$, and (b) are Pareto superior to $\bar{r}$. Note, furthermore, that proposal $\bar{r}$ is vulnerable because the intersection of the admissible set and the dominant set with respect to it is not empty. Again this applies to every proposal that satisfies the stated conditions.

Consider finally a point upon the contract curve of θ and ψ. Such a point is $\bar{s}$. The proposal indicated by $\bar{s}$ is invulnerable because the intersection of the first part of the admissible set with respect to $\bar{s}$ (consisting of $\bar{s}$ itself) and the dominant set with respect to $\bar{s}$ is empty, and the second part of the admissible set (indicating Pareto superior smaller outputs) is empty as well. Since this holds for all points of the contract curve of θ and ψ, and not for any other point in the attribute space, the AI solution induced by the rule of non-intervention consists of this particular contract curve (including the ideal points of θ and ψ).

In a three-person budgetary game for two goods it is not always the case that the AI solution for the rule of non-intervention consists of the entire contract curve of two politicians. It can easily be seen that if the ideal point of politician ζ in figure 7.7 were located at $\bar{q}$, the AI solution would consist only of the part of the contract curve of politicians θ and ψ between points D and E. In the extreme case that the ideal point of politician ζ coincided with that of politician ψ, the AI solution would consist of the coinciding ideal points (which would, of course, also be a core point).

The result illustrated in figure 7.7 does not carry over to committees that decide over a number of services that is larger than the minimal number of politicians that make up a majority of the committee. Unfortunately this case cannot readily be illustrated by geometric means. In order to provide some visual support, however, figure 7.8 shows a three-dimensional attribute space of a three-person game in perspective.

In figure 7.8 the politician's ideal points are located on the coordinate axes (the case of minority private or group goods without externalities). For the sake of simplicity, it is furthermore assumed in figure 7.8 (not in the model) that the politician's preference functions are symmetric and separable, so that the indifference surfaces are spherical and the Pareto optimal set is a flat triangle ($\Delta \theta\psi\zeta$ in figure 7.8). Politician θ is the consumer of the first good, politician ψ of the second good and politician ζ of the third good. Starting from a status quo proposal in or below the Pareto optimal set, it is now possible to attain points above it.

Suppose, for instance, that point $\bar{s}$ in figure 7.8 indicates the status quo proposal and that politicians θ and ψ conclude a voting agreement with respect to the first and second good in order to overrule the status quo proposal. Since the projection of $\bar{s}$ upon the subspace spanned by the coordinates of the first and good (the x_1,x_2 plane), which is point $(s_1,s_2,0)$, is located below the contract curve of θ and ψ, both politicians can gain, even if the output of the third good is not touched. Figure 7.8 shows the indifference curves of θ and ψ through $(s_1,s_2,0)$ in the x_1,x_2 plane. Since for a

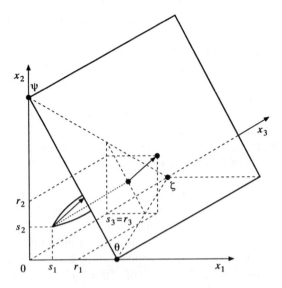

Figure 7.8 Vulnerable proposals according to the rule of non-intervention in a three-person budgetary game for three private or group goods

given output of the third good, output combination (r_1,r_2) is better for coalition $\{\theta,\psi\}$ than output combination (s_1,s_2), proposal $\bar{r}$ is in the dominant set with respect to proposal $\bar{s}$. Furthermore $\bar{r} \geq \bar{s}$, because $r_1 > s_1$, $r_2 > s_2$, and $r_3 = s_3$, so that $\bar{r}$ is also in the admissible set with respect to $\bar{s}$. Hence $\bar{r}$ will defeat $\bar{s}$, so that $\bar{s}$ is vulnerable and not an equilibrium proposal. Note that θ and ψ would gain even more if they were allowed to propose $(r_1,r_2,0)$ against $\bar{s}$ or against $\bar{r}$, but the agenda rule forbids such proposals: $(r_1 r_2,0)$ cannot be proposed against $\bar{s}$ because it contains a mixture of increases and decreases of outputs, and it cannot be proposed against $\bar{r}$ because it contains decreases that are not Pareto superior.

Once proposal $\bar{r}$ is attained, coalition $\{\theta,\psi\}$ cannot make further advantageous proposals to increase outputs. This is the case because $\bar{r}$ is located in the surface (plane in the present case) through the contract curve of the minimal winning coalition $\{\theta,\psi\}$ that is parallel to the coordinate axis of the excluded politician ζ. This surface will be called the 'extended contract set' of the coalition $\{\theta,\psi\}$.[5] Once a point in this surface is attained, further increases of outputs of the first and second good are not attractive to θ and ψ, if the output of the third good cannot simultaneously be decreased. However, there may be other winning coalitions than $\{\theta,\psi\}$ that are allowed and willing to propose further increases of outputs. Since the projection of $\bar{r}$ upon the

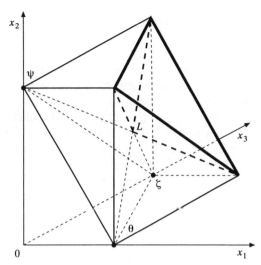

Figure 7.9 The universalistic set in a three-person budgetary game for three private or group goods

subspace spanned by the coordinates of the second and third good (the x_2,x_3 plane), which is point $(0,r_2,r_3)$, is located below the contract curve of ψ and ζ, the latter politicians can gain, by proposing further increases of the outputs of the second and third good, even if the output of the first good is not touched. Note, however, that the projection of $\bar{r}$ upon the subspace spanned by the coordinates of the first and third good (the x_1,x_3 plane), which is point $(r_1,0,r_3)$, is located above the contract curve of θ and ζ, so that the latter politicians cannot gain by proposing further increases of the first and third good, while not touching the output of the second good.

While checking for vulnerability of proposals for output increases it is sufficient to examine admissible proposals that minimal winning coalitions will approve. This is so because if all members of a larger coalition gain, all members of the minimal coalitions included in it must gain. This implies that a status quo proposal is vulnerable to proposals for output increases as long it is characterized by a point below any extended contract set of a minimal winning coalition. However, under the conditions of model VIII, a point will finally be reached which is not below the extended contract set of any minimal winning coalition. Such a proposal is invulnerable to all proposals for further increases of outputs. For the configuration of ideal points of figure 7.8, the set of all proposals that are invulnerable to proposals for increases of outputs is indicated in figure 7.9 as the sides of the boldly drawn trilateral pyramid with its top at L, which floats upside down above the Pareto optimal set.

Notice that points inside this pyramid cannot be reached if the decision-making process starts below it, because between every such point and every status quo point below it there exists a Pareto superior point in the extended contract set of a minimal winning coalition. In other words, a point inside the pyramid could be reached only if one or more outputs were further increased than was wanted by all members of the committee. Such proposals are inadmissible under the first part of the agenda function.

Note also that points above the extended contract sets of the maximal losing coalitions (the one-person coalitions in a three-person budgetary game) cannot be reached if the decision-making process starts below it. In the example illustrated in figure 7.9 the extended contract sets of the maximal losing coalitions are the planes through the ideal points of the politicians perpendicular to the coordinate axes. A point above the contract set of a maximal losing coalition cannot be reached because between every such point and every status quo point below it there exists a Pareto superior point in the extended contract set of the maximal losing coalition. In other words, a point above the extended contract set of a maximal losing coalition could be reached only if one or more outputs were further increased than was wanted by all members of the committee. Such proposals are inadmissible under the first part of the agenda rule.

If the second part of the agenda function is also taken into account (Pareto superior decreases of outputs), it appears that no AI solution exists. This appears from the fact that for each point in the sides of the pyramid there exists a point in the Pareto optimal set that is Pareto superior to it. This follows immediately from the definition of the Pareto-optimal set. The conclusion is that under the rule of non-intervention, the decision path will wander back and forth between the sides of the pyramid with top L and the Pareto optimal set without attaining an equilibrium point. Since the agenda function does not impede discontinuous decision paths ('jumps' in the attribute space), even points below the Pareto optimal set can be attained. In order to finish the process, some kind of stop rule has to be inserted, for instance the rule that no more than two rounds of decision-making are allowed per annual budget.

Although it follows from the preceding example that in general no AI solution exists if the number of services is larger than the minimal number of politicians that make up a majority of the committee, it also appears that not everything can happen. In particular, it appears that under the rule of non-intervention there exists a limited set of possible outcomes. This set set consists of the proposals that do not exceed (in the sense of all outputs smaller or equal) any proposal included in the extended contract set of any maximal losing coalition or some minimal winning coalition. For reasons that will become clear, this set will be called the universalistic set.

The universalistic set has two outstanding properties: (1) it is attractive, in the sense that every status quo proposal in the attribute space that it does not include is defeated by some proposal that it does include, and (2) it is retentive, in the sense that no status quo proposal that it includes is defeated by any proposal in the attribute space that it does not include. The universalistic set is attractive because it includes the Pareto optimal set and because by the definition of the Pareto optimal set, for every point in the attribute space there exists a point in the Pareto optimal set, which is Pareto superior to it, and hence is included in the admissible set and the dominant set with respect to it. The universalistic set is retentive because, for the reasons already discussed, there is no status quo proposal inside the set which is vulnerable to a proposal outside it. Note, also, that the projection of the universalistic set upon the separate coordinates is included in the partial Pareto optimal sets for the separate services (this might explain bureaucratic consensual PMPD strategies; recall pp. 143–4).

Attention will now be paid to (1) the relation between the universalistic set and the concept of 'log-rolling', and (2) the empirical relevance of the universalistic set for the outcomes of the budgetary process.

The explanation of the relation between the universalistic set and the concept of log-rolling is complicated by the fact that in the existing literature log-rolling is usually treated in terms of abstract game theory, rather than in terms of spatial game theory. The main difference between these approaches is that in abstract game theory the assumption of quasi-concave utility functions is lacking, so that there is no reason for ordering the choice alternative according to a limited number of spatial dimensions. The prevalence of the abstract approach is probably due to the presumption that with respect to log-rolling the spatial approach has few intuitive advantages because it requires at least three-dimensional analysis. This presumption, however, is not true for all kinds of analysis.

The analytical advantages of the spatial representation of log-rolling behaviour were first recognized by Tullock (1970c, 1981). It seems therefore appropriate to build on Tullock's work in the following attempt to establish the relation between log-rolling and the particular kind of coordinated voting that is induced by the rule of non-intervention.

Tullock distinguishes two kinds of log-rolling. The first kind, which he calls 'implicit log-rolling', is simply vote coordination in a single majority coalition, directed at larger outputs of the favourite services of the coalition members. This will lead to the approval of an output combination in the contract set of the coalition. As Tullock has observed there is no reason to presume that 'implicit log-rolling' in this sense will result in stable outcomes if coalitions are allowed to combine their proposals for increases of outputs with proposals for decreases of other outputs. However, if coalitions concern themselves only with increases of outputs and if, moreover, they do not increase outputs further than wanted by at least some member of the committee, repeated log-rolling in this sense will finally result in a stable outcome in the upper bound of the universalistic set (in the specific example of the budgetary game illustrated in figure 7.9: the sides of the pyramid with top L).

The second kind of log-rolling, which Tullock calls 'explicit log-rolling', differs from other coordinated voting in that it involves 'individual bargains' between pairs of committee members, directed at larger outputs of the favourite services of these members[6] (1981, p. 192). In this negotiation process, each member has to organize sufficient support for her own favourite service. Since every deal to support the output of somebody else's favourite service costs money, each member will attempt to keep the number of deals as small as possible. This implies that every member will conclude no more deals than necessary to acquire the support of a minimal winning majority for the desired output of her own favourite service. Furthermore, since each member has to organize the winning majority for the desired output of her own favourite service, everybody is competing with everybody else for support. Consequently, each member is able to bid down the output of the favourite services of her potential supporters to the level these supporters could also get in other minimal winning majorities. In turn, each potential supporter is able to bid down the output of the favourite service of each member who attempts to organize her own winning majority. In terms of the spatial model, the result of this negotiation process will be an equilibrium combination of outputs, which will be included in the extended contract sets of all minimal winning coalitions. This outcome can be called the 'log-rolling equilibrium'. A crucial condition for the stability of this outcome is that in a given status quo, committee members can only conclude deals about increases of outputs. In the specific example of the game illustrated in figure 7.9, the equilibrium combination of outputs is indicated by point L.

It should be noted that in a committee of three politicians the log-rolling equilibrium is somewhat harder to attain than in a committee of four or more members, because in a committee of three every 'individual bargain' between a pair of members is sufficient for both members to attain a minimal majority. Therefore the chance is high that an exclusive two-member coalition will be formed which holds down the output of the service favoured by the third member. However, in a three-person committee, a member who fears to be excluded from a potential coalition can also lower her 'price' (the increase of output of her own favourite service) in order to defend herself. Therefore, the intersection of the extended contract sets of the two-person coalitions will be the only stable proposal in the three-person game as well.

It appears from these descriptions that 'implicit' log-rolling is basically a less sophisticated form of 'explicit' log-rolling in which the individual members of a single minimal winning majority bargain only with one another, but omit to bargain with the excluded members. Since every member of the minimal winning majority is necessary for a deal, each member holds 'monopoly power' over her vote, and the result is an outcome somewhere in the extended contract set of the minimal winning coalition, which may be located above or below the extended contract set of a different minimal winning coalition.

With respect to the relation between the agenda rule of non-intervention and the voting strategies of implicit and explicit log-rolling, the following conclusions can be drawn:

1. There is a direct relation between the agenda rule and log-rolling because under the agenda rule, only log-rolling coalitions (coalitions that engage in implicit log-rolling or whose members engage in explicit log-rolling) can realize output increases. This implies that the agenda rule can be considered as an explanation of log-rolling.

2. Log-rolling (implicit and explicit) results in stable outcomes only if proposals for decreases of outputs as well as further increases of output than wanted by at least some members of the committee are prohibited. This is exactly what the first part of the agenda rule guarantees. The resulting stable outcomes are located in the upper bound of the universalistic set.[7] The set of possible outcomes consists of the entire upper bound in the case of implicit log-rolling and of the point of intersection of all extended contract sets of minimal winning majorities in the case of explicit log-rolling.

As yet, no empirical studies can be reported in which the universalistic set has been tested as a separate hypothesis about possible outcomes of a budgetary game. Since the proposed formulation of the agenda rule of non-intervention, from which the universalistic set is derived, is primarily inspired by considerations of empirical plausibility, it may instead be useful to pay attention to some of these considerations.

In the empirically oriented literature log-rolling practices are often treated under the heading of 'universalism' (hence the term 'universalistic set'). It is often alleged or suggested that universalism in this sense is an outstanding characteristic of budgetary processes in some political systems but not in others. Traditionally, American governments are considered as particularly amenable to universalistic decision-making. A connected idea is that in the presence of strong party discipline, log-rolling practices are less common. Parties would always be reluctant to endorse policies that were based upon minority interests, rather than on ideological views about the 'general interest'. This would *a fortiori* hold in a two-party system such as British central government.

It seems, however, that this argument puts too much emphasis upon the visible aspect of the bargaining process. Since legislative assemblies, in contrast to cabinets, are working in relative openness, log-rolling practices tend to be more visible in systems that accord a strong position in budgetary matters to the representative assembly. In Britain, Parliament does not hold such a position, but this does not mean that there is no log-rolling in that country. Without careful empirical research it is impossible to tell how important log-rolling is in an actual government and an actual decision-making body.

The empirical literature about log-rolling often focuses on policies involving the geographical distribution of services. In principle, however, log-rolling can be used for decision-making about every kind of policy with unevenly by distributed benefits. It seems probable that in most governments of the western world a vast majority of the issues figuring on the agendas of political authorities involve policies with unevenly distributed benefits. Most of these issues concern either minority group goods (roads, harbours, irrigation projects, etc.) or private goods consumed by minorities (public housing, public transport, art subsidies, social security, industrial subsidies, tax expenditures, etc.). Although direct observation of the bargaining process is sometimes not possible in view of the prevailing secrecy in executive political authorities, it is still possible to draw conclusions about the occurrence of log-rolling by looking at realized outcomes.

Although universalism is often treated as a typical characteristic of American politics, the 'rule of non-intervention' is usually considered as a typical ingredient of cabinet decision-making in European parliamentary systems. In the preceding discussion it was argued that both phenomena are closely related. If this reasoning is correct, the divergence between the emphasis on the strategic side of the coin (the log-rolling deals) in the literature about American goverments, and on the institutional side of the coin (the agenda rule in cabinet meetings) in the literature about European governments, may have to be explained by differences in the observability of the phenomena concerned, rather than by the different nature of the phenomena themselves.

Finally, the agenda rule of non-intervention has to be considered from the constitutional point of view. Again, in this respect, a distinction must be made between risk, costs of decision-making and net social value.

Since risk is determined by the differences in net benefits between bad and good outcomes, the rule of non-intervention is an attractive rule for risk averse politicians. This follows from the fact that the rule tends to spread benefits evenly. Committee members can always negotiate for larger outputs of their favourite services, and decreases of outputs can be approved only by general consent. Since there is no equilibrium, every outcome is provisional and every politician can start new negotiations to overrule an unwanted status quo at every moment that prevailing procedural rules allow her to do so.

On the other hand, costs of decision-making will in general be considerable. Since the universalistic set is relatively large, much depends upon the bargaining skills of the committee members; every increase of output involves the choice of a proposal in the dominant set with respect to the status quo proposal by a majority coalition, which implies a division of the gains among the coalition members. Given the frequency of such increases, much time and energy will be invested in the associated bargaining processes.

The spatial model sheds light upon the well-known dispute about the net social value of the log-rolling equilibrium. To begin with, it should be noted that the entire universalistic set, including the log-rolling equilibrium, is quite spectacularly non-Pareto optimal. Nevertheless, it may be the case that from the point of view of constitutional choice, the net social value of some subset of the universalistic solution exceeds that of some subset of the Pareto optimal set. Comparisons in this respect have particularly focused upon the log-rolling equilibrium, which is a element of the universalistic set, and on the contract sets of the minimal winning coalitions, which are subsets of the Pareto optimal set. Proposals in the contract sets of minimal winning coalitions are obviously highly advantageous to the members of such coalitions, but since they are similarly disadvantageous to the excluded committee members, and since in the situation of constitutional choice the probability of all minimal winning coalitions is equal, the resulting net social value may be lower than that of the log-rolling equilibrium (recall that net social value is the expected value of political surplus).

In order to determine the net social value of the union of the contract sets of the minimal winning coalitions, one needs an assumption about the probability of each proposal in each contract set. One assumption might be that the proposals in each contract set are equally likely. Another assumption might be that every coalition will split the gains evenly. The latter assumption is the one that Tullock made in his seminal papers about log-rolling (1970c, 1981). For the game illustrated in figure 7.9 this assumption would imply that the result of the formation of each minimal winning coalition of two politicians would be the adoption of the proposal indicated by the mid-point of the contract curve between their ideal points.[8]

It is certainly possible that the net social value of the log-rolling equilibrium exceeds the net social value following from either of the assumptions mentioned. Tullock has in particular shown that the net social value of the log-rolling equilibrium may exceed the net social value of the union of the contract sets of the minimal winning coalitions, provided that each minimal winning coalition is equally likely and that the coalitions split the gains evenly.

However, as it turns out, Tullock's result is not very robust. In this respect the net social value of the outcomes presumably induced by the formation of a single minimal winning coalition is decisive. A sufficient condition for Tullock's result to hold is that the balance of benefits over costs of every output approved by any minimal winning coalition is positive, that is to say that the total costs of every such output borne by all committee members together are smaller than the total benefits received by the beneficiaries. This condition is intuitively plausible. If a single minimal winning coalition is formed, only the members of that coalition get the outputs of their favourite services increased, whereas in the log-rolling equilibrium all committee members do. If each increase of output yields a positive balance of benefits over costs, the approval of increases of outputs for all goods will have a larger net social value than the approval of increases for only a minimal majority of goods. If, on the other hand, a sufficient number of increases yields a negative balance of benefits over costs, the net social value of the outcomes induced by the formation of a single minimal winning coalition will exceed the net social value of the log-rolling equilibrium because fewer socially harmful increases of outputs are better than more. [9] The condition for the superiority of the log-rolling equilibrium to the formation of a single minimal winning coalition amounts to a far-reaching qualification of the argument in support of the desirability of log-rolling as originally put forward by Buchanan and Tullock (Buchanan and Tullock, 1965; Tullock, 1970c; the condition is acknowledged in Tullock, 1981).[10]

As noted before, the log-rolling equilibrium is included in the unversalistic set, but it cannot be considered as representative for that set. This raises the question of what can be said about the net social value of the universalistic set as a whole. In order to answer this question, it does not seem appropriate to focus on a comparison with a specific alternative set of proposals. In particular, there is no reason to compare the universalistic set with the set of proposals in the contract sets of minimal winning coalitions, because the latter set does not correspond to any plausible solution concept of a budgetary game with or without an agenda rule. However, it is still possible to formulate a minimal criterion that a set of possible outcomes associated with an agenda rule has to satisfy, in order to represent a desirable institution. This criterion is that the net social value of the set of possible outcomes is positive. Applied to the universalistic set this criterion requires that the 'representative' proposal in the set be included in the collectively beneficial set of the committee as a whole. In order to determine whether this is the case, something must be known about the likelihood of separate proposals in the set.

As argued before, the likelihood of separate proposals is quite diverse and depends among other things on the bargaining skills of the committee members and the working of the stop rule. To the extent that the bargaining skills are distributed more evenly, outcomes will be located more centrally in and above the Pareto optimal set. If the working of the stop rule is such that increases and decreases of outputs are not decided in the same round of budgetary decision-making, 'upward rounds' will generally result in worse outcomes from the perspective of net social value than 'downwards rounds'. Given these effects of external factors, it makes little sense to define a 'representative' proposal. This implies that it becomes very hard to establish the net social value of the universalistic set. The problem of finding an appropriate measure to evaluate the consequences of universalism not only confronts the economic analyst but also the observer who relies on more intuitive forms of reasoning. This might explain the paradox that the agenda rule of non-intervention is accepted as a normal procedural rule for budgetary committees everywhere in the western world, in spite of the fact that in actual cases it can inflict enormous losses of social welfare on society.

Guide to the literature
The idea of discovering institutions by 'retroduction' from observed outcomes has been developed in Fiorina and Shepsle, 'Equilibrium, disequilibrium and the general possibility of a science of politics' (1982). Shepsle has explored possible causes of the relative stability of institutions, in 'Institutional equilibrium and equilibrium of institutions' (1986a). Ferejohn, Fiorina and Weisberg have argued in 'Toward a theory of legislative decision' (1978), that 'institution-free' equilibria such as the core and other game-theoretic solution concepts should not be dismissed lightheartedly because the working of institutions is inherently liable to counteraction by vote coordination. A similar argument has been put forward by Ordeshook in his comment, 'Political disequilibrium and scientific inquiry' (1980), on Riker's paper, 'Implications from the disequilibrium of majority rule for the study of institutions'.

A survey paper about institutions from a public choice perspective is Ostrom, 'An agenda for the study of institutions' (1986).

The basic papers about structure induced equilibrium are Shepsle, 'Institutional arrangements and equilibrium in multidimensional voting models' (1979) and Shepsle and Weingast, 'Structure induced equilibrium and legislative choice' (1981a). Survey papers about structure induced equilibrium and agenda rules are,

Shepsle, 'The positive theory of legislative institutions: an enrichment of social choice and spatial models' (1986b), and Krehbiel, 'Spatial models of legislative choice' (1988). McCubbins and Schwarz have argued in *The Politics of Flatland* (1985) that many legislative institutions are aimed at the creation of simple jurisdictions in which the germaneness rule guarantees equilibrium. In the area of the budgetary process, one such institution is the separation of the decision about the totals (of expenditures and revenues) from the decision about the division of the totals over the separate expenditure and revenue categories. According to Ferejohn and Krehbiel, 'The budget process and the size of the budget' (1987), this separation is the main rationale of the budget resolutions procedure that has been superimposed upon the appropriations procedure in the US Congress by the 1974 Congressional Budget Act. Earlier papers in which the jurisdictional separation of decision-making about totals and about division of totals was considered include Mackay and Weaver, 'On the mutuality of interests between bureaus and high demand review committees: a perverse result' (1979), and Benson, 'Logrolling and high demand committee review' (1983). The latter paper acknowledges that vote coordination across jurisdictional boundaries can counteract the working of simple jurisdictions. Kramer, 'Sophisticated voting over multidimensional choice spaces' (1972), has shown that even if decision-making proceeds in simple jurisdictions without vote coordination across jurisdictional boundaries, inseparable preferences can lead to cycles. The same result is stated in terms of conditions on 'foresight' (perfect or myopic) by Denzau and Mackay, 'Structure induced equilibrium and perfect foresight expectations' (1981).

There is a large literature on explicit log-rolling and vote trading. For a survey see Miller, 'Logrolling, vote trading and the paradox of voting: a game theoretic overview' (1977b). A systematic treatment is also provided in chapter 9 of Ordeshook, *Game Theory and Political Theory* (1986). The spatial representation of log-rolling is developed in Tullock, 'A simple algebraic logrolling model' (1970c) and 'Why so much stability?' (1981). Explanations of the stability of log-rolling outcomes are discussed in: Bernholz, 'On the stability of logrolling outcomes in stochastic games' (1978), and Enelow, 'The stability of logrolling: an expectations approach' (1986). The thesis that log-rolling practices are less common in the UK than in the USA was stated by Pennock, 'The pork barrel and majority rule: a note' (1970). This was a reaction to the idea put forward by Barry in his book, *Political Argument* (1965) that log-rolling practices are associated with a political culture of unanimous decision-making ('universalism') which prevailed in the USA, but not in the UK. Pennock rightly observes that log-rolling has a larger impact under majority than under unanimity rule (in both cases, it allows positive outputs of the favourite services of minorities, but in the latter case outcomes cannot exceed the Pareto optimal set). For an empirical study about log-rolling practices in the US Congress, see Ferejohn, *Pork Barrel Politics. Rivers and Harbors Legislation 1947–1968* (1974). For a lively account from the perspective of an insider, Stockman, *The Triumph of Politics* (1986). The relative advantages of implicit versus explicit log-rolling from the perspective of net social value have been emphasized by Coleman, 'The possibility of a social welfare function' (1966; with comments by Park and Mueller and a reply by Coleman, 1967); Tullock, 'Problems of majority voting' (1959; with comment by Downs and a reply by Tullock, 1961); and Buchanan, 'Simple majority voting, game theory and resource use' (1961). Riker and Brams have rejected the main arguments in favour of log-rolling in 'The paradox of vote-trading' (1973; with comments by Tullock and Bernholz and reply by Brams and Riker, 1974). For an account of the discussion see chapter 5 in Mueller, *Public Choice II* (1989). The condition for the superiority of explicit to implicit log-rolling from the point of view of net social value was stated by Weingast, 'A rational choice perspective on Congressional norms' (1979) and restated in terms of a spatial model by Brennan in an appendix to Tullock's paper 'Why so much stability?' (1981).

8   Ways to reform

The deficiencies of the budget mechanism

The integrated models of public demand and supply treated in chapters 6 and 7 make it possibly to identify a number of deficiencies of the budget mechanism. It should be kept in mind, however, that the models do not offer a complete explanation of the budgetary process in any specific government, but rather purport to explain elements of the process that are relevant to many different governments. Other partial aspects, that may be equally important in some specific government, are not treated.

An example of an element that has not been treated is the interaction between the representative assembly and the supreme executive authority. It was mentioned in chapter 2 that in the parliamentary and presidential systems of representative government both political authorities have to approve of budgetary decisions. The question arises as to what happens when both authorities have arrived at different (potential) decisions. In practice, this is a highly important element of the budgetary process that has to be studied on the basis of government-specific models because the competence rules that govern the relations between both political authorities vary strongly between governments. It was mentioned in chapter 2 that the executive authority has a much stronger position *vis-à-vis* the representative assembly in the parliamentary than in the presidential system. In the presidential system, much depends upon the expiration term of budgetary decisions. If this term is unlimited, the position of the President is much stronger than if annual authorizations are required. In fact, the usefulness of the executive veto right is limited if the consequence of vetoing a substantive law, fiscal law or appropriation law is that an expenditure or revenue item, or a whole category of expenditures, is completely abolished. As far as appropriations laws are concerned, this effect can be moderated by introduction of a line item veto which makes it possible to veto separate expenditure items instead of an entire law, but in that case there is also no possibility for reduction instead of complete cancellation of an appropriation.[1] If on the other hand the effect of a veto is that the previously prevailing law remains intact, the impact of the veto is much less severe and the usefulness of the veto right, and thereby the influence of the President, is much larger. This is the case with fiscal legislation and some entitlement legislation in the US federal government.

Elements of budgetary processes that have not been treated can also have consequences for the allocative and productive efficiency of outcomes. These consequences may be equally important as the consequences of the elements that have been treated. With this caveat in mind, the main deficiencies of the budget mechanism that follow from the models of legislative demand and agency supply can be summarized:

1. Public agencies produce services inefficiently, due to bureaucratic misrepresentation of total costs (public monopoly strategies with or without price discrimination)
2. Public services that have the character of public goods or of majority private or group goods are produced in too large quantities, due to bureaucratic misrepresentation of marginal costs (public monopoly strategies with price discrimination)
3. Public services that have the character of minority private or group goods are produced in too large quantities due to coalitions of minorities in political authorities connected with the agenda rule of non-intervention.

Each of these deficiencies works in the direction of too large expenditures, including tax expenditures. In combination, they may explain a substantial part of the growth of government that has taken place in the western world during the twentieth century.[2]

Apart from these main deficiencies, the models reveal various other, more subtle, imperfections of the budget mechanism. One can think, for instance, of the fact that under bureaucratic public monopoly strategies the output of a public good only reacts to the preferences of the median politician and not to those of low-demand and high-demand politicians. One can think also of the fact that the output of a minority private good does not react to the preferences of the beneficiaries of externalities. These imperfections are less serious than the main deficiencies mentioned because the resulting deviations from Pareto optimal outcomes are smaller and less biased in a specific direction. The latter does not apply to the imperfections originating in the lack of representativeness of political authorities for the subjects of government. Recall in this connection our discussion on pp. 41–2 of the interest group democracy. The latter problem, however, cannot be attributed to the budget mechanism, and should better be conceived as a deficiency of the 'electoral mechanism'.

In the next sections of this chapter some ideas about institutional reform that might improve the working of the budget mechanism with respect to the main deficiencies will be discussed. These reforms are concerned with 'financial management' and 'privatization'. Financial management is directed at the improvement of information available to political authorities. Improvement of information strengthens the bargaining position of political authorities in the internal market and thus diminishes the opportunities for misrepresentation of total and marginal costs by agency administrators. Privatization is directed at the termination of public demand or supply for a service. This will enhance the opportunities for production and consumption of these services in the private sector of the economy, which may subsequently lead to better allocative and distributive results.

Financial management

Since the second half of the 1960s, interest in the financial management of government has increased considerably. Whereas in the first two decades after the Second World War most governments in the western world were engrossed in policy development, during the late 1960s the awareness gradually emerged that prevailing tools of management had grown obsolete. 'Financial management' is conceived here as the systematic collection, registration and promulgation of data about outputs, costs and benefits that are useful to political authorities. The increased interest in financial management has inspired the development and implementation of new informational procedures. These procedures consist of competence rules that enable budget bureaux or special staff units to collect, register and promulgate the relevant data. Many of these procedures originated in the USA, sometimes at the level of state or local government. After implementation in the US federal government, various of these procedures have aroused world-wide interest. In this way the procedures of the Planning–Programming–Budgeting System (PPBS), of Management By Objectives (MBO) and of Zero-Base-Budgeting (ZBB) have gained a large following among central as well as regional and local governments.

Informational procedures originate in the practice of budgetary decision-making. Often the implementation of a specific procedure is connected with the emergence of a new style of public management which is advocated by new political leaders. Against this background, informational procedures should not merely be judged on the basis of their contribution to productive and allocative efficiency. Nevertheless, it can be observed that all the procedures mentioned have principal aims in this sphere, possibly alongside other objectives. In view of the models presented, the improvement of information available to political authorities may contribute to productive and allocative efficiency in two different ways:

1. Information about benefits and apparent costs will enable political authorities to improve their estimates of optimal output levels, given the conditions of supply.
2. Information about real (minimal) costs will enable political authorities to put more pressure upon public agencies to decrease apparent costs. For this purpose, it is not necessary that additional measures should change the structure of the internal market, for instance by breaking the monopolistic position of the agency, or even by establishing effective control by the political authority over the production process (so that the relation between both parties is transformed into a principal–agent one). Even in a monopolistic internal market political authorities do not acquiesce permanently in substantial discrepancies between apparent and real costs. Reliable information about such discrepancies induces active searching for substitute services. If successful, such searching can be accounted for within the structure of the models by a fall in demand for the services of the agencies resulting in a downward shift of Budget Output Functions (BOF). Even if not successful, an increase in bureaucratic uncertainty margins seems likely. Both effects will lead in turn to an improvement of productive and allocative efficiency.

In view of the important role of information in the model of bureaucratic supply, it may be interesting to look at the consequences of some exemplary procedures in relation to the deficiencies of the budget mechanism. For that purpose, a certain ordering of these procedures is needed. Such an ordering is presented in table 8.1.

A few comments on table 8.1 are in order. The first need that arises in a government if policy grows more complex and if the number of services increases, is the need for cost–price data. Such a need reflects the fact that political authorities are losing sight of prevailing output levels and of the division of expenditures over separate services. If output information per service is lacking, the validity of request estimates cannot be judged. Whereas the regular budget specifies expenditures and revenues and (physical) inputs and outputs to be purchased and sold in external markets, a performance budget specifies outputs to be purchased in the internal market (recall p. 23). This information enables political authorities to estimate the Apparent Budgetary Cost Function (ABCF) more accurately than would be possible on the basis of personal observation and past experience alone.

A next phase in the development of financial management occurs when the need for additional information about the benefits of services arises.

Table 8.1. *Survey of informational procedures*

Informational procedure	Type of data
1 Performance budgeting	Total apparent costs
2 Programme budgeting	Total apparent costs
Examples:	Total benefits
a Planning–Programming–Budgeting System (PPBS)	
b Management By Objectives (MBO)	
c Zero-Base-Budgeting (ZBB)	
d Programme Analysis and Review (PAR)	
e Reconsideration procedure	
3 Cost budgeting	Real (minimal) costs
Examples:	
a Productivity analysis	
b Efficiency scrutinies	
c Financial management initiative	

Informational procedures that were implemented in the US federal government between 1965 and 1977 by subsequent administrations were PPBS, MBO and ZBB (see table 8.1). Although there are important differences between these procedures with respect to the organization of data collection and the presentation of results, the basic ideas are quite similar. Accordingly, it seems sensible to order these procedures under the common heading of 'programme budgeting'. Basic characteristics of programme budgeting are:

1. Identification and operational specification of objectives that have to be realized in the medium term ('planning')
2. Specification of the outputs of services to be produced in the budget year in order to realize the objectives ('programming')
3. Calculation of the production costs of the services in the budget year, possibly followed by an adjustment of outputs or objectives in order to meet deficit or revenue constraints ('budgeting').

Akin to these American procedures are the British PAR procedure that was in force between 1970 and 1979 in the UK central government, and the Dutch Reconsideration procedure that was implemented in the central government of the Netherlands in 1981 and is still in use.

An important difference between these European procedures and their American precursors is that the former are selective in that planning and output data need not be collected for all publicly funded services as part of the regular budget process, but rather for a limited, annually designated, group of services, as part of a separate annual process that is linked to the budget process.

From an economic point of view it can be observed that programme budgeting goes one step further than performance budgeting. Programme budgeting focuses upon the generation of information about the effectiveness of services in relation to the formal objectives that have been established for them. Although these formal objectives need not coincide with the individual objectives of the members of political authorities, this information helps them to understand the effects of the services and to determine the individual benefits that the services yield to them. Such information may lead in principle to an increase as well as to a decrease of estimated individual benefits of given outputs in comparison to a situation in which the consequences of output proposals have to be judged on the basis of personal observation and experience. Nevertheless, data of this type tend to be perceived as dangerous by agency administrators. In view of the models presented, this tendency is quite explicable. In contrast to performance data, data about effects influence the value of services to members of political authorities. Whereas performance data enable political authorities to improve estimates of apparent costs, data about effects enable them to improve estimates of individual benefits.[3] Agency administrators are suspicious about the latter type of information because they cannot influence it. In spite of the monopolistic structure of the internal market, output and Managerial Discretionary Profit (MDP) will collapse if demand for the services collapses.

From a normative point of view, information about effects is of course to be welcomed: although productive efficiency will not be affected – at least not directly[4] – allocative efficiency will increase when members of political authorities improve their estimates about benefits.

The third type of information that strengthens the position of political authorities in the internal market is information about the efficiency of the public production process, that is to say about the real (minimal) costs of outputs. Of course, productive efficiency has always been an important criterion for the evaluation of public performance. In fact, this criterion has played a major role in the administrative science literature since the beginning of the century. However, a more economically oriented approach towards the measurement of public production did not arise until the 1970s. In that period numerous initiatives were taken in the USA for the systematic measurement of productivity in public organizations. The states and organizations of local governments took the lead in this respect, and similar initiatives soon emerged in Europe. The Thatcher Cabinet in the UK was particularly active in this respect. In 1979 a scrutiny procedure was implemented in the UK central government. This procedure provided for the annual conduct of a select number of productivity studies under the supervision of the 'Efficiency Unit', which was set up under the direct responsibility of the Prime Minister. The conclusions and recommendations of the studies were submitted to the ministers primarily responsible, but also to the Treasury, and could subsequently play an important role in the budgetary process. An even more ambitious procedure, known as the Financial Management Initiative, was set up in UK central government in 1982, as an integral part of the regular budgetary process. The Financial Management Initiative required from departments and agencies that they submit detailed productivity data in addition to regular budget requests. Procedures of productivity evaluation, just as those of effectiveness evaluation, share a few basic characteristics, which justify their subsumption under a common heading. The characteristics of 'cost budgeting' are the following:

1. The definition of services on the basis of quality criteria
2. The investigation of production processes and the collection of quantitative data about productivity; investigations may be carried out on a cross-sectional basis (by comparison of data for similar agencies in the same period) or on a longitudinal basis (by comparison of data for the same agency in similar periods)
3. The estimation of efficient budget output ratios.

Information about productivity sheds light on the difference between apparent and real (minimal) costs. Obviously, such information is extremely important to political authorities. If enough information becomes available to estimate both total and marginal costs over a sufficiently large interval of output, political authorities will not only adjust their views about appropriate funding levels per unit of output, but also those about optimal outputs (recall that at the optimal output of a politician marginal benefits equal marginal costs). Although reliable cost information does not necessarily affect bureaucratic dominance in the internal market, it may be expected that in the long run such information will still have an impact upon productive and allocative efficiency. As argued above, it seems plausible that political authorities start searching for substitute services when the existence of substantial productive inefficiency is discovered. Even if appropriate substitutes have not yet been found, the mere presumption that search activities are taking place may increase the margin of uncertainty of bureaucrats and thus induce a downward shift of the Apparent Budgetary Cost Function (ABCF). Another consequence may be that political authorities cut budgets while expressing the expectation that outputs ought not to be affected, or take the initiative towards institutional reform, for instance, through the privatization of the production or consumption of the service in question.

Privatization

Until the beginning of the 1980s the discussion about institutional reform focused upon financial management; efforts in the sphere of privatization were often seen as motivated by ideological rather than rational considerations. It is symptomatic in this respect that whereas plans for the reform of financial management have always enjoyed a lively interest among politicians of widely diverging ideological persuasions, the interest in privatization has usually been limited to the parties at the right side of the political spectrum.

This state of affairs should possibly be attributed to the fact that until quite recently insight into the deficiencies of the budget mechanism was poorly developed. Whereas a great deal of economic thought has been devoted to the discovery and analysis of market failure, the capacity of the budget mechanism to increase social welfare has always been taken for granted. Only the recent advances in public choice theory seem to have provided the cause of privatization with an intellectual foundation that may prove to be a match for the assorted doctrines of market failure that have swamped the economic literature in the past. Basically, this foundation amounts to the thesis that although the market mechanism may not perform optimally in areas like excludable and non-excludable public goods, external effects, natural monopoly and income distribution, there is no *a priori* reason to presume that the budget mechanism would do any better. The models treated in this book lend some support to this thesis. Under these circumstances, constitutional design has to be based upon a careful comparative analysis of alternative institutional arrangements.

The question arises as to what can be said on the basis of the models presented about the desirability of privatization.

Privatization is a kind of institutional reform by which an economic activity is transferred from the public to the private sector of the economy. There are four different types of privatization:
1. Privatization of production, which can be divided into:
   a diversion
   b contracting out;
2. Privatization of consumption, which can be divided into:
   a abolition of subsidies
   b abolition of public contributions in the narrow sense.
Privatization of production is the transfer of a productive activity from

the public production sector to the private production sector. Whereas diversion embraces the entire production chain, contracting out is limited to the lower part of it; diversion implies that the public production sector terminates its supply of a service in external markets.

Examples of services that may be diverted are public transport, public education, public lotteries and public utilities like telecomms, electricity, and water. Contracting out implies that the public production sector terminates its demand for certain production factors (labour and capital) and initiates a demand for certain intermediary products in external markets. Examples of services that may be contracted out are catering services, construction, technical design, professional consultancy, and weapon systems.

Privatization of consumption is the transfer of a consumptive activity from the public consumption sector to the private consumption sector.

Privatization of consumption is realized by the elimination of the public share in the funding of a service. Abolition of a subsidy implies that the public consumption sector terminates its demand for a service in the internal market so that the production sector has to terminate its demand of that service in external markets.[5] Examples of services that may be provided without subsidies are health services, housing, and cultural services. Abolition of a public contribution in the narrow sense implies that the public consumption sector terminates its demand for a service in the internal market so that the public production sector has to reduce its supply of that service (or find a new demand for it). Examples of services that may be provided without public contribution are public transport, postal services, public parks.

Privatization has been defined above as a kind of institutional reform. In view of the above-mentioned specifications, one may wonder what the 'institutional' aspect of a change in public demand or supply behaviour is. In particular, the question arises why a mere decrease of public demand or supply should be considered as a budgetary decision and the complete termination of demand or supply as an institutional reform.

Admittedly, different conceptualizations are conceivable on this point. A consideration that supports the above-mentioned distinction is that political authorities tend to reason in a different way about the decision to initiate or terminate the demand or supply of a service than about the decrease or increase of existing levels of input or output. In general, political authorities are aware that the question whether the production or consumption of a service is a task of government has a wider significance than the question what the levels of input or output should be, and that the former question cannot be answered on the basis of preferences for the service only.

Before turning to the effects of privatization upon the various deficiencies of the budget mechanism, it is useful to pay attention to some forms of internal reorganization within the public production sector that should be distinguished from privatization in the proper sense.

As appears from the preceding exposition, both contracting out and diversion lead to a task reduction in the public production sector. The question arises what happens to the (parts of) agencies whose tasks are being transferred. One likely solution is that the agencies are transferred as well, so that they can continue their activities in the private sector. Although this solution is often pursued, it should be emphasized that the transfer of an agency to the private sector is an organizational sequel of privatization, rather than its essence.

Transfer of an agency to the private sector usually involves two steps, (1) the incorporation of the agency in a legally independent household, and (2) the sale of the stock of the incorporated agency. Sometimes agencies are already incorporated at the time of the privatization decision, so that only step (2) has to be taken in order to effect the transfer.

Incorporation of an agency (step (1)) may also be pursued for its own sake, that is to say without the intention to sell stock. This possibility has attracted much interest because of the policy of the British Cabinet in the late 1980s to put a large part of the production sector of central governments into incorporated public agencies ('new-style' agencies).

It should be emphasized that incorporation and full privatization are essentially different kinds of institutional reform. Incorporation does not affect the size of the public production sector nor the turnover in external or internal markets. The legal construction of the incorporated agencies, which may be based upon civil or public law, is irrelevant in this respect. The incentives that determine the supply behaviour of the agency are decisive.[6] Even if an incorporated agency is allowed to make a profit, public ownership implies that this profit is not at the free disposal of the agency administrator. Under these circumstances, it is virtually impossible to suppress the maximization of output and managerial discretionary profit (MDP) as objectives of supply behaviour, and thus remove the main causes of inefficiency and misallocation. It should not be inferred, however, that incorporation is valueless. In the first place, it is an indispensable intermediate stage on the way to privatization. This stage is necessary in order to prepare an agency for survival in the private sector. Usually this preparation requires a rather fundamental turnaround of company culture, which may take several years. In the second place, incorporation offers large advantages from the point of view of financial management. Since incorporated agencies have an independent financial administration, these advantages are comparable to those of performance budgeting: data about output, average apparent costs and profit will become available as a matter of course and will strengthen the position of political authorities in the internal market.

If the portents are not deceptive, incorporation will become a major trend in public administration in the years to come. However, in view of the fundamental differences from full privatization, the effects of both forms of reorganization may not be equivalent. The discussion below will focus upon full privatization.

Let us now see what can be said about privatization from the perspective of the deficiencies of the budget mechanism. The model of agency supply predicts that the effects of diversion upon productive and allocative efficiency are dependent upon the structure of the external market where the agency sells its service. Usually this market is not fully competitive (in the sense that the agency competes with private suppliers) and free from political intervention. Often the production of excludable services has become a public activity in the first place because there are externalities that have induced partial public funding and/or because the agency is a natural monopoly. Diversion will often be accompanied by a change in the public funding share – so that the subsidy per unit of service after the privatization will be smaller than the public contribution before the privatization – or by accession of new suppliers to the market. However, these accidental changes should be distinguished from the diversion decision in the proper sense. Let us therefore suppose that the public funding share and/or the monopolistic market structure are maintained after the diversion of a service.

In that situation, a change will still occur: since a private monopoly, in contrast to a public monopoly, maximizes profit, both productive and allocative efficiency are affected. Productive efficiency will improve because a profit maximizing private monopoly produces at real (minimal) costs. Allocative efficiency will change, but not necessarily improve. Although the objectives of profit maximization and of MDP maximization work out identically on allocation, different outcomes are still to be expected by virtue of the fact that a public monopolist may seek output maximization as well. It might thus be hypothesized that the tendency to oversupply that characterizes public agencies vanishes after diversion. It is not certain, however, that a public monopoly that produces for an external market will affect oversupply, even if the output objective is relatively important in comparison to the MDP objective. This is the case because external markets usually do not allow price discrimination, so that all units of the service have to be sold at the same price (for instance, transport services, museums, access to public parks). As we have seen on p. 86, this leads to market prices above marginal costs and to undersupply of the service if the monopolist maximizes only profit. In the case of public monopoly the output objective and the MDP objective work in opposite directions: the first in that of oversupply, the latter in that of undersupply. After the diversion the output objective is eliminated, so that allocative efficiency may worsen (recall the discussion about public monopoly without price discrimination on pp. 85–8).

Contracting out is a form of vertical diversification. Of course, the structure of the external market that connects the divided parts of the production chain is decisive for the consequences that may be expected. If there is free competition in this market, services can in principle be purchased at minimal cost. However, since the public consumption sector is dependent for its supply upon the public production sector, agency administrators are capable, in principle, of maintaining their Apparent Budgetary Cost Functions (ABCFs) in the internal market. Furthermore, as we have seen in chapter 4, they can use a part of MDP to provide patronage to clients in the private production sector by paying higher prices for the services that are contracted out than necessary in view of market circumstances. The extent to which such practices are feasible depends upon the transparency of the relevant external market. In this respect, contracting out is comparable to cost budgeting. A wide discrepancy between purchasing price and market price – consequently, between apparent costs and real (minimal) costs of public services – if generally perceived, weakens the bargaining position of the agency in the internal market. This may lead to active searching for a substitute service on the part of political authorities, and finally to a collapse of demand.

In this light, it may be expected that contracting out will improve the productive and allocative efficiency of public production.

In contrast to the privatization of production, the privatization of consumption does not affect productive efficiency. This is the case because the abolition of a subsidy or public contribution does not change the incentives within the agency or firm that produces the service. It remains to be seen how the privatization of consumption affects allocative efficiency.

The abolition of a subsidy or public contribution induces the substitution of an external market for the internal market. Again, the nature of the service and the structure of the external market (the market in which the public agency or subsidized private firm sells its service) are decisive for the allocational consequences of privatization. If this market is competitive, and if the service is a minority private good, allocational efficiency will improve. This follows from the hypothesis that subsidies and public contributions for these services are too high as a consequence of coalitions of minorities. If the external market is monopolistic, oversupply may turn into undersupply. This is particularly plausible if a subsidy is abolished, because a private monopoly maximizes profit. If a public contribution to a public agency is abolished, the resulting degree of undersupply or oversupply depends upon the relative salience of MDP and output maximization as bureaucratic objectives. The reasoning with respect to the allocative effect of diversion applies to this case.

Usually publicly funded excludable services are not purely private goods. If there are substantial externalities – public education, public housing, public health, etc. – the desirability of complete abolition of a subsidy or other public contribution may not be obvious. Optimal allocation would require that the sum of the marginal benefits from the external effects would equal the total subsidy or public contribution at the equilibrium output. Unfortunately the budget mechanism does not induce this output. If the services benefit only a minority of the electorate, the budget mechanism rather tends to induce oversupply, due to coalitions of minorities. Under this condition, complete abolition of a subsidy or public contribution may be preferable.

If the service is an excludable group good or public good – public transport, public broadcasting, trunk road, etc. – distortions due to uniform pricing are a complicating factor (all consumers pay the same price regardless of individual benefits). In principle, such distortions work against the abolition of subsidies and public contributions, but the welfare loss resulting from uniform pricing has to be weighed against the welfare loss induced by oversupply in the internal market.

The main consequences of the four types of privatization are summarized in table 8.2. A plus sign indicates that on the basis of the models presented an improvement may be expected, a minus sign indicates the opposite, and a zero indicates that probably no change will occur.

In view of the fact that the presence of (natural) monopoly has often been considered as a justification for public provision of excludable services, diversion is distinguished according to the structure of the external market. With respect to the other forms of privatization, it seems appropriate to consider competition in the external market as the standard condition. It appears from table 8.1 that the privatization of production can be important for productive as well as allocative efficiency.

The privatization of consumption improves allocative efficiency, provided that externalities are relatively small and that the relevant external markets are reasonably competitive.

Of course, these conclusions are not spectacular in themselves. But then, the present analysis should not be judged on the basis of its conclusions but on the basis of its method. The essence of this method is that alternative institutional arrangements have to be evaluated on the basis of explicit empirical hypotheses about their consequences. For that purpose, appropriate models of the budgetary process are an indispensable precondition.

Table 8.2. *The consequences of privatization for productive and allocative efficiency*

Type of privatization	Productive efficiency	Allocative efficiency
1 Diversion		
a competitive external market	+	+
b monopolistic external market	+	+ or −
2 Contracting out (competitive external market)	+	+
3 Abolition of subsidy (competitive external market)		
a service without externalities	0	+
b service with externalities	0	+ or −
4 Abolition of public contribution (competitive external market)		
a service without externalities	0	+
b service with externalities	0	+ or −

The public choice perspective reconsidered

In chapter 1 of this book, public choice theory was identified as an important theoretical perspective for the positive analysis of the budgetary process. It was furthermore noted that the results of public choice analysis are often relevant for policy development, especially as far as policy concerning institutions is concerned. At the end of our discussion it seems useful to look back at these statements and to reconsider them in the light of the ideas, arguments and models that have been described and discussed in chapters 2–7.

It has hopefully become clear that, apart from other aspects, public choice theory is a relatively 'rich' perspective. It allows the student of the budgetary process to build a great variety of models and, by choosing among possible features for those models, to capture quite precisely those aspects of reality that are crucial for explanation and prediction.

The models presented in this book were mostly based on existing ideas. This applies, for instance, to the separate models of legislative demand and agency supply, and to certain extensions of the former model concerning agenda rules and of the latter model concerning bureaucratic interaction. However, in addition to the exposition of these elementary models, some more integrated models were presented and analysed. These exercises gave rise in most cases to a restatement of familiar results in a more general context, but in some cases to new results, for instance about supply induced equilibrium and the universalistic solution and about the (in)stability and allocative (in)efficiency of the associated budgetary outcomes. The new results have not yet been used to formulate and test specific empirical hypotheses. Although in some cases existing empirical work casts a certain light on the plausiblity of these results, additional efforts, specifically designed to test concrete hypotheses, are called for. Empirical work in this area might also offer new insights in the relation between the micro- and macro-level of political and administrative behaviour. One of the perennial arguments against public choice theory is that it has little to say about the characteristics of macro-behaviour. Provided that in the budgetary process the strategies and decisions of individual bureaucrats and politicians, and the collective decisions of separate political committees can be considered as the micro-level of behaviour, and the final decisions of a government as the macro-level of behaviour, it would contribute to the general confidence in public choice theory if we could avail ourselves of reliable empirical results connecting both levels of behaviour in this particular area. As in more traditional areas of public choice research, such as electoral behaviour and political participation, it seems also possible to integrate insights from other theoretical perspectives into this research. As far as the budgetary process is concerned, one has to think in the first place of the organizational process perspective that has yielded a large body of knowledge especially at the macro-level: upwards and downwards trends in expenditures and revenues, the distribution of expenditures over programmes and agencies, the development of the deficit, etc.

As far as the policy relevance of public choice analysis is concerned, it is useful to distinguish between two aspects of the policy-making process: (1) the diagnosis of the problems caused by existing policies, and (2) the development of new policies that can contribute to the solution of these problems. With respect to diagnosis it appears that the public choice perspective shares with the traditional public finance perspective the emphasis on allocative and productive efficiency. Like public finance, public choice analysis makes use of welfare theory. For instance, the three major deficiencies of the budget mechanism that were identified at the beginning of this chapter were all deficiencies in the sense of deviations from efficient allocation and efficient production. It should be noted, though, that the emphasis on efficiency as a normative criterion is not inherent in the methodology of public choice analysis *per se*. In this respect, there seems to be a subtle distinction between the role of welfare theory in public choice analysis on the one hand and in traditional public finance on the other. Whereas public finance is nothing other than the application of welfare theory to budgetary and institutional policy, public choice theory is in the first place a positive theory of the budgetary process. In principle, public choice theory can be used to assess the effectiveness of proposals in relation to any problem that someone would consider as important. In other words, public choice analysis tends to focus on efficiency problems because these problems are generally considered as the most fundamental problems for budgetary policy, but nothing precludes the use of public choice models for the assessment of proposals in relation to any other kind of problem.

The more fundamental difference between the public choice perspective and the traditional public finance perspective is concerned with the ways in which policies can contribute to the solution of problems. In this respect, the public choice perspective tends to generate more sceptical conclusions about the opportunities for change and reform than the public finance perspective. This is due to the use of positive models of the decision-making process. One cannot at the same time put confidence in the explanatory and predictive value of a positive model and accept that actors can be persuaded to endorse policies that are inconsistent with the motivational assumptions that the model has specified for them. This applies to budgetary proposals that have to be decided within a given institutional framework, but also to proposals for institutional reform, provided that actors can predict, with more or less certainty, the consequences of the proposed reform for subsequent budgetary decisions. In this light, it is understandable that the tendency towards scepticism that is characteristic for public choice analysis is shared by perspectives that start from other positive theories.

It is interesting to observe, for instance, that Wildavsky in the last chapter of his book *The New Politics of the Budgetary Process* (1988) expresses great doubts about almost every remedy that has been proposed in the last decades to cure the problems of the budgetary process in the American federal government, including volume budgeting (implying automatic compensation for inflation), multi-year budgeting, all forms of programme budgeting (the Planning–Programming–Budgeting System, Zero-Base-Budgeting, etc.), capital budgeting (implying separate budgets for running capital expenditures and running expenditures), top-down budgeting as required by the Gramm–Rudman–Hollings legislation, and introduction of a Presidential line item veto. Obviously, these remedies have not only been directed at problems of allocative and productive efficiency but, as argued already, the policy relevance of positive theory is by definition not limited to efficiency problems.

In Wildavsky's view, many governments in the western world are facing problems connected with the breakdown of the norms of classical budgeting, such as comprehensiveness, annuity and balance. Most remedies come down to attempts at resurrection of these norms through binding legislation. However, such legislation remains ineffective because it does not affect the basic cause of the breakdown of budgetary norms, which is, in Wildavsky's view, the withering away of social and political consensus

about the tasks of government. If there is political conflict about what
government ought to do, and consequently about fundamental budgetary
priorities, it is not to be expected that political authorities will easily submit
to norms or procedures that are directed at the containment and orderly
settlement of disputes within a narrow procedural framework. That does
not mean that such norms and procedures cannot be enacted by temporary
majorities, but it is a general characteristic of norms and procedures that
they tend to cause trouble during implementation if they are resisted by a
substantial proportion of the people to whom they apply. Translated into
public choice terminology, if politicians have different preferences for
publicly provided services, it is not to be expected that they will agree about
institutions if they can predict the effects of those institutions upon future
budgetary decisions. Unless, that is, that these institutions can be shown to
induce Pareto superior effects. The latter point, which remains under-
examined in Wildavsky's work, is crucial for the policy relevance of public
choice analysis. Indeed, by the use of the analytical apparatus of micro-
economics, public choice analysis provides insight into the welfare
theoretical characteristics of budgetary and institutional proposals as a
matter of course, and this might point the way to improvements that
arguments starting from other perspectives have overlooked.

It is the author's impression that until very recently public choice
arguments had hardly penetrated either official policy documents or the
policy oriented literature concerning the budgetary process. In this respect,
there in a reciprocity between research and policy development. On the one
hand, theoretical results will eventually affect the policy debate and on the
other the use of theoretical results in the policy debate will enhance
scientific and academic interest. A necessary precondition for both is the
dissemination of relevant knowledge. Hopefully the present volume can
contribute to that purpose.

Guide to the literature

Survey papers about 'government failure' on the basis of public choice
models are Hanusch, 'Inefficiencies in the public sector: aspects of demand and
supply' (1983); Peacock, 'On the anatomy of collective failure' (1980); Rowley,
'Market "failure" and government "failure"' (1978); Recktenwald, 'The public waste
syndrome: a comprehensive theory of government failures' (1984), 'Potential welfare
losses in the public sector. Anatomy of the nature and causes' (1983); Wolf, 'A theory
of non-market failure: framework for implementation analysis' (1979), 'Non-market
failure revisited: the anatomy and physiology of government deficiencies' (1983). See
also the book by Wolf, *Markets or Governments: Choosing Between Imperfect
Alternatives* (1988). A critical comment on the public choice literature about

government failures from a traditional public finance perspective is Musgrave, 'Leviathan cometh – or does he?' (1981).

There is a very large literature about the various procedures of programme budgeting. Only a few important contributions will be mentioned. About PPBS, Harper, Kramer and Rouse, 'Implementation and use of PBB in sixteen federal agencies' (1969); Hitch and McKean, *The Economics of Defense in the Nuclear Age* (1960); Hovey, *The Planning Programming Budgeting Approach to Government Decision Making* (1968); McKean, *Efficiency in Government Through Systems Analysis, With Emphasis on Water Resource Development* (1958); Merewitz and Sosnick, *The Budget's New Clothes* (1971); Novick, *Program Budgeting* (1965), *The Origin and History of Program Budgeting* (1968); Schick, 'The road to PPB: the stages of budget reform' (1966), 'Systems politics and systems budgeting' (1969), 'A death in the bureaucracy: the demise of federal PPB' (1973); Schulze, *The Politics and Economics of Public Spending* (1968); Wildavsky, 'The political economy of efficiency. cost-benefit analysis, systems-analysis and program-budgeting' (1966). For a public choice perspective on PPBS see Peacock, 'New methods of appraising government expenditure: an economic analysis' (1972). About MBO, Brady, 'MBO goes to work in the public sector' (1973); Drucker, *The Practice of Management* (1954), *Managing for Results* (1964), 'What results should you expect? A users' guide to MBO' (1976); McCaffery, 'MBO and the federal budgetary process' (1976); Sherwood and Page, 'MBO and public management' (1976); Rose, 'Implementation and evaporation: the record of MBO' (1977). About ZBB, Draper and Pitsvada, 'ZBB. Looking back after ten years' (1981), 'Congress and executive branch budget reform: the House Appropriations Committee and Zero-Base-Budgeting' (1980); Lauth, 'Zero Base Budgeting in Georgia State Government: myth and reality' (1978); Pyhrr, 'Zero-Base-Budgeting' (1970), *Zero-Base-Budgeting* (1973), 'The zero-base approach to government budgeting' (1977); Schick, 'The road from ZBB' (1978); Taylor, 'Introduction to Zero-Base-Budgeting' (1977). About PAR, Gray and Jenkins, 'Policy analysis in British central government: the experience of PAR' (1982); Fletcher, 'From PPBS to PAR in the Empire State' (1972); Heclo and Wildavsky, *The Private Government of Public Money: Community and Policy Inside British Political Administration* (1974). About the Reconsideration Procedure, Kraan, 'Towards more flexibility of government expenditure: some recent developments in the Netherlands' (1984); van Nispen tot Pannerden, *Het Dossier Heroverweging* (1993).

Some surveys about the economic approach to productivity analysis in the USA are Fisk, 'Public sector productivity and relative efficiency: the state of the art in the USA' (1984); Hatry, 'The status of productivity measurement in the public sector' (1981), 'Current state of the art of local government productivity improvement and potential federal roles' (1980); Scott Fosler, 'Local government productivity: political and administrative potential' (1980). For the British scrutiny procedure see Beesley, 'The Rayner scrutinies' (1983). For the Financial Management Initiative, see Lukierman, 'Public expenditure. Who really controls it and how?' (1988).

The literature about privatization is also very large. Some important contributions from a theoretical perspective are Arrow, 'The organization of economic activity: issues pertinent to the choice of market versus non-market allocation' (1983); Deacon, 'The expenditure effects of alternative supply institutions' (1979); Pack, 'The determinants of the choice between public and private production of a publicly funded service reconsidered' (1990). An extensive treatment of the various forms of privatization from a microeconomic perspective is Vickers and Yarrow, *Privatization: An Economic Analysis* (1988). More practically oriented are Savas, *Privatization of the Public Sector: How to Shrink Government?* (1982), *Privatization: The Key to a Better Government* (1987). Incorporation of agencies was launched in the UK in the 'Next Steps' programme, which is described in Treasury, Efficiency Unit, *Improving Management in Government: The Next Steps* (1988); see also National Audit Office, *The Next Steps Initiative. Report by the Comptroller General* (1989); Treasury, Efficiency Unit, *Making the Most of Next Steps* (1991).

Mathematical appendix

Numerical example for model I

$$u_\theta = m_\theta(x_1 + \alpha_1) \tag{1}$$

$$p_1 x_{\theta 1} + m_\theta = g_\theta. \tag{2}$$

The political maximand is a generalized Cobb–Douglas utility function.

The quasi-concavity of the utility function can be checked by evaluation of the determinant $|B|$ which consists of the Hessian determinant bordered by the first derivatives.[1] So:

$$|B| = \begin{vmatrix} 0 & \dfrac{du_\theta}{dm_\theta} & \dfrac{du_\theta}{dx_1} \\[2mm] \dfrac{du_\theta}{dm_\theta} & \dfrac{d^2 u_\theta}{dm_\theta^2} & \dfrac{d^2 u_\theta}{dm_\theta x_1} \\[2mm] \dfrac{du_\theta}{dx_1} & \dfrac{d^2 u_\theta}{dx_1 dm_\theta} & \dfrac{d^2 u_\theta}{dx_1^2} \end{vmatrix}.$$

The principal minors of this determinant are:

$$|B_1| = \begin{vmatrix} 0 & (x_1 + \alpha_1) \\[2mm] (x_1 + \alpha_1) & 0 \end{vmatrix} = -(x_1 + \alpha)$$

$$|B_2| = \begin{vmatrix} 0 & (x_1 + \alpha_1) & m_\theta \\[2mm] (x_1 + \alpha_1) & 0 & 1 \\[2mm] m_\theta & 1 & 0 \end{vmatrix} = 2m_\theta(x_1 + \alpha_1).$$

If m_θ, $\alpha_1 > 0$ and $x_1 \geq 0$, it follows that $|B_1| < 0$ and $|B_2| > 0$, so the utility function is quasi-concave. The indifference curves are rectangular hyperbolas with centre: $(-\alpha_1, 0)$, asymptotes: $m_\theta = 0$ and $x_1 = -\alpha_1$ and m_θ intercept: $\alpha_1^{-1} u_\theta$. The parameter α_1 characterizes the 'dispensability' of the good, not to be confused with its marginal expenditure share. Since after translation of the m_θ axis, the utility function is homogeneous, it induces a linear expansion path and a constant marginal expenditure share.

The marginal expenditure share could be made explicit by inserting a second parameter in the utility function, for instance as follows:

$$u_\theta = m_\theta^{1 - \beta_{\theta 1}}(x_1 + \alpha_1)^{\beta_{\theta 1}};$$

this is a proper Cobb–Douglas utility function that induces a marginal expenditure share of the public good of $\beta_{\theta 1}$.

Note that there is no dispensability parameter in the utility function for net private income. Implicitly the dispensability parameter for net private income is zero (the function can be written as $u_\theta = (m_\theta + 0)(x_1 + \alpha_1)$).

Since the utility of net private income ('money') represents the utility of 'all other goods', this feature of the utility function reflects the fact that although every single good is dispensable, all goods together are not dispensable. Accordingly, the indifference curves do not intersect with the x_1 axis while they do intersect with the m_θ axis.

The ordinary ('Marshallian') demand function follows from maximizing the utility function subject to the income constraint and expressing the price of the public good in terms of its quantity. The Lagrangean maximand is:

$$Z = m_\theta x_1 + \alpha_1 m_\theta + \lambda(p_{\theta 1} x_1 + m_\theta - g_\theta).$$

The first order condition is:

$$\begin{bmatrix} 1 & p_{\theta 1} & 0 \\ 0 & 1 & 1 \\ 1 & 0 & p_{\theta 1} \end{bmatrix} \begin{bmatrix} m_\theta \\ x_1 \\ \lambda \end{bmatrix} = \begin{bmatrix} g_\theta \\ -\alpha \\ 0 \end{bmatrix}.$$

The determinant of the coefficient matrix is:

$$\begin{vmatrix} 1 & p_{\theta 1} & 0 \\ 0 & 1 & 1 \\ 1 & 0 & p_{\theta 1} \end{vmatrix} = 2p_{\theta 1}.$$

By Cramer's rule it follows:

$$m_\theta = \frac{1}{2p_{\theta 1}} \begin{vmatrix} g_\theta & p_{\theta 1} & 0 \\ -\alpha & 1 & 1 \\ 0 & 0 & p_{\theta 1} \end{vmatrix} = \frac{g_\theta p_{\theta 1} + \alpha_1 p_{\theta 1}{}^2}{2p_{\theta 1}} = \frac{g_\theta + \alpha_1 p_{\theta 1}}{2} \quad (3)$$

$$x_1 = \frac{1}{2p_{\theta 1}} \begin{vmatrix} 1 & g_\theta & 0 \\ 1 & -\alpha & 1 \\ 1 & 0 & p_{\theta 1} \end{vmatrix} = \frac{g_\theta - \alpha_1 p_{\theta 1}}{2p_{\theta 1}}. \quad (4)$$

From (4):

$$p_{\theta 1} \equiv p_{\theta 1(ord)} = \frac{g_\theta}{2x_1 + \alpha_1}. \quad (5)$$

This is the equation of the ordinary individual demand curve. Furthermore:

$$p_{\theta 1} x_1 = \frac{g_\theta - \alpha_1 p_{\theta 1}}{2}$$

so that the constant marginal expenditure share of the public good is:

$$\frac{d(p_{\theta 1} x_1)}{dg_\theta} = \frac{1}{2}.$$

The compensated individual demand function measures the absolute value of the slope of the indifference curve which is reached in the optimal situation.

The optimal utility level follows from inserting the optimal values of the endogenous variables in the utility function.

Hence:

$$u_\theta = \left(\frac{g_\theta + \alpha_1 p_{\theta 1}}{2}\right)\left(\frac{g_\theta - \alpha_1 p_{\theta 1}}{2p_{\theta 1}}\right) + \alpha_1\left(\frac{g_\theta + \alpha_1 p_{\theta 1}}{2}\right).$$

Expansion and rearrangement yields:

$$u_\theta = \frac{(g_\theta + \alpha_1 p_{\theta 1})^2}{4p_{\theta 1}}. \quad (6)$$

The equation of the corresponding indifference curve is:

$$\frac{(g_\theta + \alpha_1 p_{\theta 1})^2}{4 p_{\theta 1}} = m_\theta (x + \alpha_1).$$

Hence:

$$m_\theta = \frac{(g_\theta + \alpha_1 p_{\theta 1})^2}{4 p_{\theta 1}(x_1 + \alpha_1)}. \qquad (7)$$

The slope of an indifference curve at a given point follows from setting the total differential of the utility function equal to zero:

$$du_\theta = \frac{\delta u_\theta}{\delta m_\theta} dm_\theta + \frac{\delta u_\theta}{\delta x_1} dx_1 = 0.$$

So:

$$\frac{dm_\theta}{dx_1} = - \frac{\dfrac{\delta u_\theta}{\delta x_1}}{\dfrac{\delta u_\theta}{\delta m_\theta}} = \frac{-m_\theta}{x_1 + \alpha_1}. \qquad (8)$$

The slope of the indifference curve which is reached in the optimal situation follows from inserting (7) in (8).

Taking the absolute value yields the following equation for the individual compensated demand curve:

$$p_{\theta 1 (comp)} = \left| - \frac{(g_\theta + \alpha_1 p_{\theta 1})^2}{4 p_{\theta 1}(x_1 + \alpha_1)^1} \right| = \frac{(g_\theta + \alpha_1 p_{\theta 1})^2}{4 p_{\theta 1}(x_1 + \alpha_1)^2}. \qquad (9)$$

The ordinary Marginal Evaluation Function (MEF) measures the absolute value of the slope of the indifference curves along the income constraint. Accordingly, the ordinary MEF follows from insertion of $m_\theta = g_\theta - p_{\theta 1} x_1$ in (8):

$$e'_{\theta 1 (ord)} = \left| - \frac{g_\theta - p_{\theta 1} x_1}{x_1 + \alpha_1} \right| = \frac{g_\theta - p_{\theta 1} x_1}{x_1 + \alpha_1}. \qquad (10)$$

The Compensated Marginal Evaluation Function (CMEF) measures the absolute value of the slope of the indifference curve through the point that indicates a given initial situation s_1. Accordingly, the CMEF follows from insertion of

$$m_\theta = \frac{(g_\theta - p_{\theta 1} s_1)(x_1 + \alpha_1)}{(x_1 + \alpha_1)} \text{ in (8):}$$

$$e'_{\theta 1 (\text{comp})} | (s_1) = \left| -\frac{(g_\theta - p_{\theta 1} s_1)(s_1 + \alpha_1)}{(x_1 + \alpha_1)^2} \right| = \frac{(g_\theta - p_{\theta 1} s_1)(s_1 + \alpha_1)}{(x_1 + \alpha_1)^2}.$$

Figure MA.1a shows the ordinary and compensated individual demand and evaluation functions for a numerical example in which the parameters and exogenous variables take the following values:

$$\alpha_1 = 1$$
$$p_{\theta 1} = 2$$
$$g_\theta = 10$$
$$s_1 = 2$$

The corresponding functions are:

$$p_{\theta (\text{ord})} = \frac{10}{2x_1 + 1}$$

$$p_{\theta 1 (\text{comp})} \equiv e'_{\theta 1 (\text{comp})} | (2) = \frac{18}{(x_1 + 1)^2}$$

$$e'_{\theta 1 (\text{ord})} = \frac{10 - 2x_1}{x_1 + 1}.$$

The optimal values of m_θ and x_1 follow from (3) and (4). These values are $m_\theta = 6$ and $x_1 = 2$.

The Preference Function (PF) follows from inserting the income constraint in the political maximand:

$$u_\theta = (x_1 + \alpha_1)(g_\theta - p_{\theta 1} x_1)$$
$$= -p_{\theta 1} x_1^2 + (g_\theta - \alpha_1 p_{\theta 1}) x_1 + \alpha_1 g_\theta.$$

The curve of this PF is a parabola with vertex at

$$\left(\frac{g_\theta - \alpha_1 p_{\theta 1}}{2 p_{\theta 1}}, \frac{(g_\theta + \alpha_1 p_{\theta 1})^2}{4 p_{\theta 1}} \right)$$

and u_θ intercept of $\alpha_1 g_\theta$.

Figure MA.2 shows the PF for a numerical example in which the parameters and exogenous variables take the same values as used in figure MA.1 (so $\alpha_1 = 1$, $p_{\theta 1} = 2$, $g_\theta = 10$).

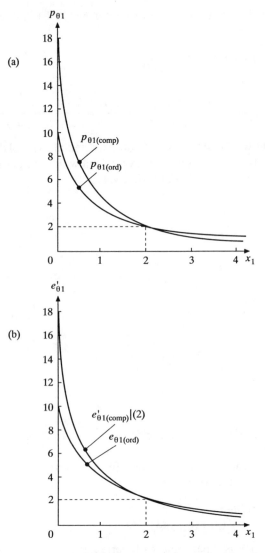

Figure MA.1 Ordinary and compensated demand and evaluation functions of the numerical example for model I

The corresponding PF is:

$$u_\theta = -2x_1^2 + 8x_1 + 10.$$

The curve of the Total Evaluation Function (TEF) is a shifted mirror image of the indifference curve through the point $(0, g_\theta)$.

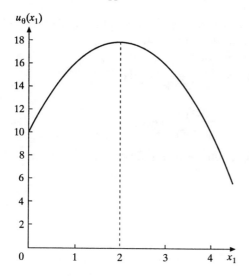

Figure MA.2 Preference function of the numerical example for model I

The axis of symmetry is perpendicular to the m_θ axis and the shift takes place in the negative direction of that axis over a distance of g_θ.

The equation of the indifference curve through the point $(0,g_\theta)$ is:

$$m_\theta = \frac{u(0,g_\theta)}{x_1 + \alpha_1}.$$

Hence, the TEF is:

$$e_{\theta 1} = \frac{-u_\theta(0,g_\theta)}{x_1 + \alpha_1} + g_\theta. \tag{11}$$

Furthermore, from (1):

$$u_\theta(x_1,m_\theta) = m_\theta(x_1 + \alpha_1).$$

Hence:

$$u_\theta(0,g_\theta) = \alpha_1 g_\theta. \tag{12}$$

Inserting (12) in (11) yields:

$$e_{\theta 1} = \frac{g_\theta x_1}{x_1 + \alpha_1}. \tag{13}$$

Note that the TEF equals the definite integral of the CMEF for initial situation (0) from 0 to the argument output:

$$\int_0^{x^1} e'_{\theta 1(comp)} |(0)dx_1 = \int_0^{x^1} \frac{\alpha_1 g_\theta}{(x_1 + \alpha_1)^2} dx$$

$$= \frac{g_\theta x_1}{x_1 + \alpha_1} = e_{\theta 1}.$$

The budget output function (BOF) follows from division by the politician's tax share:

$$b_{\theta 1} = \frac{g_\theta x_1}{\tau_\theta (x_1 + \alpha_1)}. \tag{14}$$

Figure MA.3 shows the BOF for a numerical example in which $\tau_\theta = 1/5$ and the other parameters and exogenous variables take the same values as used in figures MA.1 and MA.2 (so $\alpha_1 = 2$, $p_{\theta 1} = 2$, $g_\theta = 10$). The corresponding function is:

$$b_{\theta 1} = \frac{50x_1}{x_1 + 1}.$$

Numerical example for model II

$$u_1 = m_\theta(x_1 + \alpha_1)(x_2 + \alpha_2) \tag{1}$$

$$p_{\theta 1}x_1 + p_{\theta 2}x_2 + m_\theta = g_\theta. \tag{2}$$

The political maximand is again a generalized Cobb–Douglas utility function. The parameters α_1 and α_2 are the dispensability parameters of the goods. The bordered determinant $|B|$ of the utility function is:

$$|B| = \begin{vmatrix} 0 & \dfrac{du_\theta}{dm_\theta} & \dfrac{du_\theta}{dx_1} & \dfrac{du_\theta}{dx_2} \\[2mm] \dfrac{du_\theta}{dm_\theta} & \dfrac{d^2u_\theta}{dm_\theta{}^2} & \dfrac{d^2u_\theta}{dm_\theta dx_1} & \dfrac{d^2u_\theta}{dm_\theta dx_2} \\[2mm] \dfrac{du_\theta}{dx_1} & \dfrac{d^2u_\theta}{dx_1 dm_\theta} & \dfrac{d^2u_\theta}{dx_1{}^2} & \dfrac{d^2u_\theta}{dx_1 dx_2} \\[2mm] \dfrac{du_\theta}{dx_2} & \dfrac{d^2u_\theta}{dx_2 dm_\theta} & \dfrac{d^2u_\theta}{dx_2 dx_1} & \dfrac{d^2u_\theta}{dx_2{}^2} \end{vmatrix}.$$

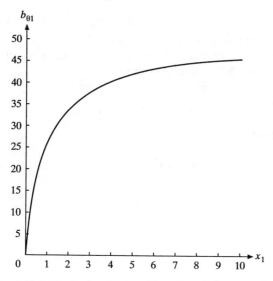

Figure MA.3 The Budget Output Function of the numerical example for model I

The principal minors of this determinant are:

$$|B_1| = \begin{vmatrix} 0 & (x_1 + \alpha_1)(x_2 + \alpha_2) \\ (x_1 + \alpha_1)(x_2 + \alpha_2) & 0 \end{vmatrix}$$

$$= -(x_1 + \alpha_1)^2(x_2 + \alpha_2)^2$$

$$|B_2| = \begin{vmatrix} 0 & (x_1 + \alpha_1)(x_2 + \alpha_2) & m_\theta(x_2 + \alpha_2) \\ (x_1 + \alpha_1)(x_2 + \alpha_2) & 0 & (x_2 + \alpha_2) \\ m_\theta(x_2 + \alpha_2) & (x_2 + \alpha_2) & 0 \end{vmatrix}$$

$$= 2m_\theta(x_1 + \alpha_1)(x_2 + \alpha_2)^3$$

$$|B_3| = \begin{vmatrix} 0 & (x_1 + \alpha_1)(x_2 + \alpha_2) & m_\theta(x_2 + \alpha_2) & m_\theta(x_1 + \alpha_1) \\ (x_1 + \alpha_1)(x_2 + \alpha_2) & 0 & (x_2 + \alpha_2) & (x_1 + \alpha_1) \\ m_\theta(x_2 + \alpha_2) & (x_2 + \alpha_2) & 0 & m_\theta \\ m_\theta(x_1 + \alpha_1) & (x_1 + \alpha_1) & m_\theta & 0 \end{vmatrix}$$

$$= 3m_\theta^2(x_1 + \alpha_1)^2(x_2 + \alpha_2)^2.$$

If m_θ, α_1, $\alpha_2 > 0$ and x_1, $x_2 \geq 0$, it follows that $|B_1| < 0$, $|B_2| > 0$ and $|B_3| < 0$ so that the utility function is quasi-concave.

The optimal output combination follows from maximization of the utility function subject to the income constraint.

The Langrangean maximand is:

$$Z = m_\theta(x_1 + \alpha_1)(x_2 + \alpha_2) + \lambda(p_{\theta 1}x_1 + p_{\theta 2}x_2 - g_\theta).$$

The first order condition is:

$$\frac{\delta Z}{\delta m_\theta} = (x_1 + \alpha_1)(x_2 + \alpha_2) + \lambda = 0 \tag{3a}$$

$$\frac{\delta Z}{\delta x_1} = m_\theta(x_1 + \alpha_1) + \lambda p_{\theta 1} = 0 \tag{3b}$$

$$\frac{\delta Z}{\delta x_2} = m_\theta(x_2 + \alpha_2) + \lambda p_{\theta 2} = 0 \tag{3c}$$

$$\frac{\delta Z}{\delta \lambda} = p_{\theta 1}x_1 + p_{\theta 2}x_2 + m_\theta - g_\theta = 0. \tag{3d}$$

Inserting $\lambda = -(x_1 + \alpha_1)(x_2 + \alpha_2)$ – from (3a) – in (3b) and (3c), and rearranging yields:

$$p_{\theta 1}x_1 = m_\theta - \alpha_1 p_{\theta 1} \tag{4a}$$

$$p_{\theta 2}x_2 = m_\theta - \alpha_2 p_{\theta 2}. \tag{4b}$$

Inserting (4a) and (4b) in (3d) yields:

$$3m_\theta - \alpha_1 p_{\theta 1} - \alpha_2 p_{\theta 2} - g_\theta = 0.$$

So:

$$m_\theta = \frac{g_\theta + \alpha_1 p_{\theta 1} + \alpha_2 p_{\theta 2}}{3}. \tag{5}$$

Inserting (5) in (4a) and (4b) yields:

$$x_1 = \frac{g_\theta - 2\alpha_1 p_{\theta 1} + \alpha_2 p_{\theta 2}}{3p_{\theta 1}} \tag{6}$$

$$x_2 = \frac{g_\theta + \alpha_1 p_{\theta 1} - 2\alpha_2 p_{\theta 2}}{3 p_{\theta 2}}. \tag{7}$$

The PF follows from inserting the income constraint in the political maximand:

$$u_\theta = (x_1 + \alpha_1)(x_2 + \alpha_2)(g_\theta - p_{\theta 1} x_1 - p_{\theta 2} x_2).$$

This is a function of the third degree which can be represented by a concave surface with a top at

$$\left(\frac{g_\theta - 2\alpha_1 p_{\theta 1} + \alpha_2 p_{\theta 2}}{3 p_{\theta 1}}, \frac{g_\theta + \alpha_1 p_{\theta 1} - 2\alpha_2 p_{\theta 2}}{3 p_{\theta 2}} \right)$$

and traces in the (x_1, u_θ) plane and (x_2, u_θ) plane, which are characterized by:

$$u_\theta = - p_{\theta 1} \alpha_2 x_1^2 + (\alpha_2 g_\theta - \alpha_1 \alpha_2 p_{\theta 1}) x_1 + \alpha_1 \alpha_2 g_\theta$$

and:

$$u_\theta = - p_{\theta 2} \alpha_1 x_2^2 + (\alpha_1 g_\theta - \alpha_1 \alpha_2 p_{\theta 2}) x_2 + \alpha_1 \alpha_2 g_\theta.$$

These traces are parabolas with vertex at:

$$\left(\frac{(g_\theta - \alpha_1 p_{\theta 1})}{2 p_{\theta 1}}, \frac{\alpha_2 (g_\theta + \alpha_1 p_{\theta 1})^2}{4 p_{\theta 1}} \right) \text{ and } \left(\frac{(g_\theta - \alpha_2 p_{\theta 2})}{2 p_{\theta 2}}, \frac{\alpha_1 (g_\theta + \alpha_2 p_{\theta 2})^2}{4 p_{\theta 2}} \right),$$

and u_θ intercept of $\alpha_1 \alpha_2 g_\theta$.

The TEF surface is a shifted mirror image of the indifference surface through the point $(0,0,g_\theta)$. The axis of symmetry is perpendicular to the m_θ axis and the shift takes place in the negative direction of that axis over a distance of g_θ.

The equation of the indifference surface through the point $(0,0,g_\theta)$ is:

$$m_\theta = \frac{u_\theta(0,0,g_\theta)}{(x_1 + \alpha_1)(x_2 + \alpha_2)}.$$

Hence, the general (bivariate) TEF is:

$$e_\theta = \frac{-u_\theta(0,0,g_\theta)}{(x_1 + \alpha_1)(x_2 + \alpha_2)} + g_\theta. \tag{8}$$

Furthermore, from (1):

$$u_\theta(x_1, x_2, m_\theta) = m_\theta(x_1 + \alpha_1)(x_2 + \alpha_2).$$

Hence:

$$u_\theta(0,0,g_\theta) = \alpha_1 \alpha_2 g_\theta. \tag{9}$$

Inserting (9) in (8) yields:

$$e_\theta = \frac{(x_1 x_2 + \alpha_2 x_1 + \alpha_1 x_2)g_\theta}{(x_1 + \alpha_1)(x_2 + \alpha_2)}. \tag{10}$$

The general (bivariate) BOF follows from division by the political agent's tax share:

$$b_\theta = \frac{(x_1 x_2 + \alpha_2 x_1 + \alpha_1 x_2)g_\theta}{\tau_\theta(x_1 + \alpha_1)(x_2 + \alpha_2)}. \tag{11}$$

Note that (10) and (11) cannot be used to derive a partial (monovariate) TEF or BOF because net private income at a given output of one good is affected by the output of the other good. Particularly, if the output of the second good is s_2, net private income available for the first good is $(g_\theta - p_{\theta 2} s_2)$. Similarly, if the output for the first good is s_1, net private income available for the second good is $(g_\theta - p_{\theta 1} s_1)$.
Hence:

$$e_{\theta 1} | (s_2) = \frac{-u_\theta(0, s_2, g_\theta - p_{\theta 2} s_2)}{(x_1 + \alpha_1)(s_2 + \alpha_2)} + g_\theta - p_{\theta 2} s_2 \tag{12}$$

$$e_{\theta 2} | (s_1) = \frac{-u_\theta(s_1, 0, g_\theta - p_{\theta 1} s_1)}{(s_1 + \alpha_1)(x_2 + \alpha_2)} + g_\theta - p_{\theta 1} s_1. \tag{13}$$

Furthermore, from (1):

$$u_\theta(x_1, x_2, m_\theta) = m_\theta(x_1 + \alpha_1)(x_2 + \alpha_2).$$

Hence:

$$u_\theta(0, s_2, g_\theta - p_{\theta 2} s_2) = \alpha_1(g_\theta - p_{\theta 2} s_2)(s_2 + \alpha_2) \tag{14}$$

$$u_\theta(s_1, 0, g_\theta - p_{\theta 1} s_1) = \alpha_2(g_\theta - p_{\theta 1} s_1)(s_1 + \alpha_1). \tag{15}$$

Inserting (14) in (12) and (15) in (13) yields:

$$e_{\theta1}|(s_2) = \frac{-\alpha_1(g_\theta - p_{\theta2}s_2)(s_2 + \alpha_2)}{(x_1 + \alpha_1)(s_2 + \alpha_2)} + g_\theta - p_{\theta2}s_2$$

$$= \frac{x_1(g_\theta - p_{\theta2}s_2)}{x_1 + \alpha_1} \tag{16}$$

$$e_{\theta2}|(s_1) = \frac{-\alpha_2(g_\theta - p_{\theta1}s_1)(s_1 + \alpha_1)}{(s_1 + \alpha_1)(x_2 + \alpha_2)} + g_\theta - p_{\theta1}s_1$$

$$= \frac{x_2(g_\theta - p_{\theta1}s_1)}{x_2 + \alpha_2}. \tag{17}$$

Division by the tax share yields the partial BOFs:

$$b_{\theta1}|(s_2) = \frac{x_1(g_\theta - p_{\theta2}s_2)}{\tau_\theta(x_1 + \alpha_1)} \tag{18}$$

$$b_{\theta2}|(s_1) = \frac{x_2(g_\theta - p_{\theta1}s_1)}{\tau_\theta(x_2 + \alpha_2)}. \tag{19}$$

Figure MA.4 shows the partial BOFs for a numerical example in which the parameters and exogenous variables take the following values:

$$\alpha = 1 \qquad p_{\theta2} = 5$$
$$\alpha = 1/5 \qquad \tau_\theta = 1/5$$
$$g_\theta = 15 \qquad s_1 = 0 \text{ or } 1$$
$$p_{\theta1} = 2 \qquad s_2 = 0 \text{ or } 1.$$

The corresponding functions are:

$$b_{\theta1}|(0) = \frac{75x_1}{x_1 + 1}; \quad b_{\theta2}|(0) = \frac{375x_2}{5x_2 + 1}$$

$$b_{\theta1}|(1) = \frac{50x_1}{x_1 + 1}; \quad b_{\theta2}|(1) = \frac{325x_2}{5x_2 + 1}.$$

Since for $s_2 = 1$ the budget constraint of the present example reduces to the budget constraint of the numerical example of model I, and since multiplication of a utility function with a constant factor does not affect the indifference field, it should not be surprising that the partial BOF for the first public good for that case equals the partial BOF in the example of model I (see p. 216).

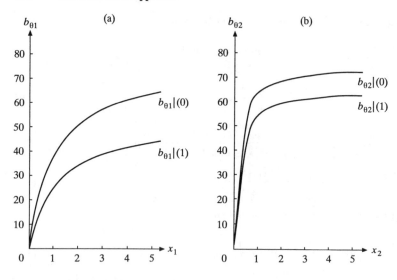

Figure MA.4 Partial Budget Output Functions of the numerical example for model II

The optimal values of m_θ, x_1 and x_2 follow from (5), (6) and (7). These values are $m_\theta = 6$, $x_1 = 2$ and $x_2 = 1$.

When the second good in the present example is a pure private good that does not benefit the politician, the utility function reduces to:

$$u_\theta = m_\theta(x_1 + \alpha_1).$$ (20)

In the case of the Cobb–Douglas utility function

$$u_\theta = m_\theta^{1-\beta_{\theta 1}-\beta_{\theta 2}}(x_1 + \alpha_1)^{\beta_{\theta 1}}(x_2 + \alpha_2)^{\beta_{\theta 2}},$$

this possibility comes down to inserting the parameter value $\beta_{\theta 2} = 0$, which would result in the function $u_\theta = u_\theta^{1-\beta_{\theta 1}}(x_1 + \alpha_1)^{\beta_{\theta 1}}$.

If the second good is a pure private good the determinant $|B|$ vanishes:

$$|B| = \begin{vmatrix} 0 & (x_1 + \alpha_1) & m_\theta & 0 \\ (x_1 + \alpha_1) & 0 & 1 & 0 \\ m_\theta & 1 & 0 & 0 \\ 0 & 0 & 0 & 0 \end{vmatrix} = 0.$$

Still, the utility function is quasi-concave (the criterion of the determinant $|B|$ is sufficient, not necessary). The quasi-concavity of the utility function follows from the convexity of the level sets $\{(m_\theta,x_1,x_2)\,|\,u_\theta(m_\theta,x_1,x_2) \geq l\}$ for every l in the range of the function. The indifference surfaces that form the boundaries of the level sets are characterized by:

$$m_\theta = \frac{l}{x_1 + \alpha_1} \text{ with } l \geq 0.$$

These indifference surfaces are cylinders with generatrix parallel to the x_2 axis (see figure 3.7, p. 59).

The directrix of each cylinder is a rectangular hyperbola with centre $(-\alpha,0)$, asymptotes $m_\theta = 0$ and $x_1 = -\alpha$ and m_θ intercept $\alpha_1^{-1}u_\theta$.

The equation of the indifference surface through the point $(0,0,g_\theta)$ is:

$$m_\theta = \frac{u_\theta(0,0,g_\theta)}{x_1 + \alpha_1}.$$

Hence, the general (bivariate) TEF is:

$$e_\theta = \frac{-u_\theta(0,0,g_\theta)}{x_1 + \alpha_1} + g_\theta. \tag{21}$$

Furthermore from (20):

$$u_\theta(x_1,x_2,m_\theta) = m_\theta(x_1 + \alpha_1).$$

Hence:

$$u_\theta(0,0,g_\theta) = \alpha_1 g_\theta. \tag{22}$$

Inserting (22) in (21) yields:

$$e_\theta = \frac{g_\theta x_1}{x_1 + \alpha_1}. \tag{23}$$

The BOF follows from division by the politician's tax share:

$$b_\theta = \frac{g_\theta x_1}{\tau_\theta(x_1 + \alpha)}. \tag{24}$$

Since the output of the second good does not figure in the TEF and the BOF, the surfaces characterized by these functions are also cylinders (in fact hyperbolic cylinders as well). The partial TEF and BOF for the first good is again dependent on the output of the second good:

$$e_{\theta 1}|(s_2) = \frac{x_1(g_\theta - p_{\theta 2}s_2)}{x_1 + \alpha_1} \tag{25}$$

$$b_{\theta 1}|(s_2) = \frac{x_1(g_\theta - p_{\theta 2}s_2)}{\tau_\theta x_1 + \alpha_1}. \tag{26}$$

However, since the output of the second good does not figure in the utility function of the politician, the value of the partial TEF and the partial BOF for the second good is zero throughout (the traces of the indifference surfaces in planes perpendicular to the x_1 axis are straight lines, perpendicular to the m_θ axis):

$$e_{\theta 2}|(0) = 0 \tag{27}$$

$$b_{\theta 2}|(0) = 0. \tag{28}$$

The unimodal Preference Function

Consider the following model:

$$\max u_\theta(\bar{x}, m_\theta) \tag{1}$$

$$\bar{p}_\theta.\bar{x} + m_\theta = g_\theta \tag{2}$$

$$a_i = a_i(x_i) \qquad \text{for } i = 1,2,\ldots,n. \tag{3}$$

$$p_{\theta i} \equiv \tau_\theta a_i(x_i)/x \tag{4}$$

Expression (1) is the utility function of politician θ. It is assumed to be monotonically increasing and quasi-concave in $\bar{x}$ and m_θ.

Expression (2) is the income constraint of politician θ.

Expression (3) is an Apparent Budgetary Cost Function (ABCF). It is assumed to be convex and monotonically increasing for $x_i > 0$. Note that $a_i(x_i)$ is also (weakly) convex if it is a linear function of output.

Expression (4) defines tax price as average apparent budgetary costs multiplied by tax share.

In order to show that the Preference Function (PF) is unimodal, it will first be shown that it is quasi-concave in $\bar{x}$. Subsequently, it will be shown that every quasi-concave function with a global maximum is unimodal.

The PF is strictly quasi-concave

Since (a) a function $g(\bar{x}) = g_1(\bar{x}) + g_2(\bar{x})$ is concave if $g_1(\bar{x})$ and $g_2(\bar{x})$ are concave, and (b) a function $-g(\bar{x})$ is monotonically decreasing and concave if $g(\bar{x})$ is monotonically increasing and convex,[2] it follows from (2), (3) and (4) that the politician's net private income is a monotonically decreasing and concave function of outputs:[3]

$$m_\theta = g_\theta - \bar{p}.\bar{x} = g_\theta - \sum_{i=1}^{n} p_{\theta i} x_i = g_\theta - \sum_{i=1}^{n} \tau_\theta a_i(x_i) \equiv m_\theta(\bar{x}).$$

Denote the PF by $u_\theta(\bar{x}, m_\theta(\bar{x}))$.

Consider now two combinations of outputs $\bar{q}$ and $\bar{r}$, such that:

$$u_\theta(\bar{q}, m_\theta(\bar{q})) \geq u_\theta(\bar{r}, m_\theta(\bar{r})) \tag{4}$$

$$m_\theta(\bar{q}) \geq 0 \tag{5}$$

$$m_\theta(\bar{r}) \geq 0. \tag{6}$$

From (5) and (6) it follows that $\bar{q}$ and $\bar{r}$ are feasible, given the income constraint.

By definition a function $g(\bar{x})$ is quasi-concave if and only if $g(\bar{q}) \geq g(\bar{r})$ implies:

$$g(\lambda \bar{q} + (1 - \lambda)\bar{r}) \geq g(\bar{r})$$

for every λ, $0 < \lambda < 1$.

Consequently, (4) implies:

$$u_\theta(\lambda \bar{q} + (1 - \lambda)\bar{r}, \lambda m_\theta(\bar{q}) + (1 - \lambda)m_\theta(\bar{r})) \geqslant u_\theta(\bar{r}, m_\theta(\bar{r})) \tag{7}$$

for every λ, $0 < \lambda < 1$.

Furthermore, by definition a function $g(\bar{x})$ is concave if and only if:

$$g(\lambda \bar{q} + (1 - \lambda)\bar{r}) \geq \lambda g(\bar{q}) + (1 - \lambda)g(\bar{r})$$

for every λ, $0 < \lambda < 1$.

Hence, since $m_\theta(\bar{x})$ is concave:

$$m_\theta(\lambda\bar{q} + (1 - \lambda)\bar{r}) \geq \lambda m_\theta(\bar{q}) + (1 - \lambda)m_\theta(\bar{r}) \tag{8}$$

for every λ, $0 < \lambda < 1$.

Since $u_\theta(\bar{x}, m_\theta)$ is monotonically increasing in m_θ, (8) implies:

$$u_\theta(\lambda\bar{q} + (1 - \lambda)\bar{r}, m_\theta(\lambda\bar{q} + (1 - \lambda)\bar{r})) \geq u_\theta(\lambda\bar{q} + (1 - \lambda)\bar{r} + $$
$$+ \lambda m_\theta(\bar{q}) + (1 - \lambda)m_\theta(\bar{r})) \tag{9}$$

for every λ, $0 < \lambda < 1$.

From (7) and (9):

$$u_\theta(\lambda\bar{q} + (1 - \lambda)\bar{r}, m_\theta(\lambda\bar{q} + (1 - \lambda)\bar{r})) \geq u_\theta(\bar{q}, m_\theta(\bar{r})) \tag{10}$$

for every λ, $0 < \lambda < 1$.

By the definition of quasi-concavity (4) and (10) imply that the PF $u_\theta(\bar{x}, m_\theta(\bar{x}))$ is quasi-concave in $\bar{x}$.

The preceding argument is illustrated in figure MA.5 for the case of a single publicly provided good.

Figure MA.5 shows the indifference field of politician θ, the transformation curve of the publicly provided good and two output combinations $(q_1, m_\theta(q_1))$ and $(r_1, m_\theta(r_1))$. Point $(q_1, m_\theta(q_1))$ is on a higher indifference curve than point $(r_1, m_\theta(r_1))$ so that condition (4) is satisfied. Both $(q_1, m_\theta(q_1))$ and $(r_1, m_\theta(r_1))$ are on the transformation curve so that (5) and (6) are satisfied.

Since $u_\theta(x_1, m_\theta)$ is quasi-concave in x_1 and m_θ, the indifference curves are convex. Consequently, every point on the straight line segment between $(q_1, m_\theta(q_1))$ and $(r_1, m_\theta(r_1))$ is on a higher indifference curve than $(r_1, m_\theta(r_1))$. Such a point is

$$(\lambda q_1 + (1 - \lambda)r_1, \lambda m_\theta(q_1) + (1 - \lambda)m_\theta(r_1)).$$

Furthermore, the transformation curve is concave so that:

$$m_\theta(\lambda q_1 + (1 - \lambda)r_1) \geq \lambda m_\theta(q_1) + (1 - \lambda)m_\theta(r_1).$$

Hence, since $u_\theta(x_1, m_\theta)$ is monotonically increasing in m_θ, point $(\lambda q_1 + (1 - \lambda)r_1, m_\theta(\lambda q_1 + (1 - \lambda)r_1))$ is on a higher indifference curve than point $(\lambda q_1 + (1 - \lambda)r_1, \lambda m_\theta(q_1) + (1 - \lambda)m_\theta(r_1))$, and *a fortiori* on a higher indifference curve than point $(r_1, m_\theta(r_1))$.

Hence: $u_\theta(\lambda q_1 + (1 - \lambda)r_1, m_\theta(\lambda q_1 + (1 - \lambda)r_1)) \geq u_\theta(r_1, m_\theta(r_1))$, so that $u_\theta(x_1, m_\theta(x_1))$ is quasi-concave in x_1.

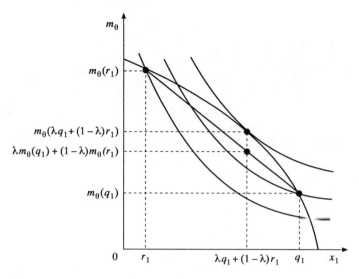

Figure MA.5 Constrained optimization of the political maximand

The PF is unimodal

By definition a function $f(\bar{x})$ is unimodal if it continually increases or remains constant along some continuous path from every point $\bar{x}$ in its domain to its global maximum. By definition a function $f(\bar{x})$ is strongly unimodal if it continually increases or remains constant along the straight line through every point $\bar{x}$ in its domain and its global maximum. Figure MA.6 shows examples of the boundaries of level sets of (a) a unimodal but not strongly unimodal function, (b) a strongly unmimodal but not quasi-concave function and (c) a quasi-concave function.

Now suppose that $f(\bar{x})$ is quasi-concave, that it has a global maximum at $\bar{q}$ and that $\bar{r}$, $\bar{r} \neq \bar{q}$, is some point in its domain.[4] Then $f(\bar{q}) \geq f(\bar{r})$.

Hence, since $f(\bar{x})$ is quasi-concave: $f(\lambda\bar{q} + (1-\lambda)\bar{r}) \geq f(\bar{r})$ for every λ, $0 < \lambda < 1$.

But for every point $\bar{t}$ upon the line segment between $\bar{r}$ and $\bar{q}$, there exists a λ, such that $\bar{t} = \lambda\bar{q} + (1-\lambda)\bar{r}$, so that $f(\bar{t}) \geq f(\bar{r})$.

Since it follows that $f(\bar{x})$ continually increases or remains constant along any line through a point in its domain and its global maximum, $f(\bar{x})$ is strongly unimodal and hence unimodal.

Note that quasi-concavity is sufficient for unimodality but not necessary. Therefore unimodality is not sufficient for quasi-concavity. Only in the case of a monovariate function, is unimodality sufficient for quasi-concavity.

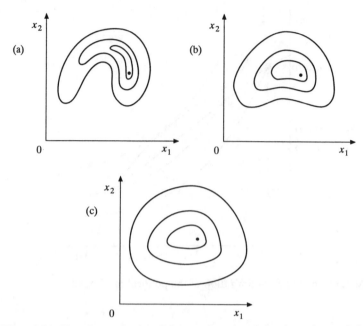

Figure MA.6 Level sets of unimodal, strongly unimodal and quasiconcave functions

This is the case because in a one-dimensional domain every r_i and t_i, $t_i \neq r_i$ are necessarily located upon the same straight line through the global maximum of the function. Therefore if a function $f(x_i)$ is unimodal and if r_i and t_i are at the same side of its global maximum with $f(t_i) \geq f(r_i)$, it must continually increase or remain constant between r_i and t_i, and if r_i and t_i are at different sides of its global maximum with $f(t_i) \geq f(r_i)$, it must continually increase or remain constant between r_i and the global maximum and it cannot decrease below $f(t_i)$, and hence not below $f(r_i)$, between the global maximum and t_i. Consequently $f(\lambda r_i + (1 - \lambda)t_i) \geq f(t_i)$ for every r_i and t_i, $r_i \neq t_i$ and every λ, $0 < \lambda < 1$, so that $f(x_i)$ is quasi-concave.

Numerical example for model IV

$$u_\theta = m_\theta(x_1 + \alpha_1) \tag{1}$$

$$u_1 = d_1 x_1 \tag{2}$$

$$m_\theta + p_{\theta 1} x_1 = g_\theta \tag{3}$$

$$c_1 = \gamma_1 x_1 \tag{4}$$

$$p_{\theta 1} \equiv \tau_\theta a_1 / x_1 \tag{5}$$

$$d_1 \equiv a_1 - c_1. \tag{6}$$

The political maximand and the income constraint in (1) and (3) are identical to those of the numerical example for model I, treated on p. 209.

The bureaucratic maximand in (2) is a generalized Cobb–Douglas utility function with output and Managerial Discretionary Surplus (MDP) as arguments. The principal minors of the determinant $|B|$, which consists of the Hessian determinant, bordered by the first derivatives are $|B_1| = -x_1{}^2$ and $|B_2| = 2d_1 x_1$. Consequently, for $d_1, x_1 > 0$, the bureaucratic maximand is quasi-concave.

The Total Cost Function (TCF) in (4) is linear and hence (weakly) convex. Since the TCF passes through the origin, there are no fixed costs.

In view of (14) on p. 216, the politician's Budget Output Function (BOF) is given by:

$$b_{\theta 1} = \frac{g_\theta x_1}{\tau_\theta (x_1 + \alpha_1)}.$$

Consequently, the Political Surplus Function (PSF) which describes the feasible combinations of output and MDP is:

$$f_{\theta 1} = b_{\theta 1} - c_1 = \frac{g_\theta x_1}{\tau_\theta (x_1 + \alpha_1)} - \gamma_1 x_1.$$

The optimal combination of output and MDP for the bureaucrat follows from maximizing the bureaucratic maximand subject to the constraint:

$$f_{\theta 1} - d_1 = \frac{g_\theta x_1}{\tau_\theta (x_1 + \alpha_1)} - \gamma_1 x_1 - d_1 = 0.$$

The Lagrangean maximand is:

$$Z = d_1 x_1 + \lambda \left[\frac{g_\theta x_1}{\tau_\theta (x_1 + \alpha_1)} - \gamma_1 x_1 - d_1 \right].$$

The first order condition is:

$$\frac{\delta Z}{\delta d_1} = x_1 - \lambda = 0 \tag{7a}$$

$$\frac{\delta Z}{\delta x_1} = d_1 + \lambda \left[\frac{\tau_\theta g_\theta (x_1 + \alpha_1) - \tau_\theta g_\theta x_1}{\tau_\theta^2 (x_1 + \alpha_1)^2} - \gamma_1 \right]$$

$$= d_1 + \lambda \left[\frac{\alpha_1 g_\theta}{\tau_\theta (x_1 + \alpha_1)} - \gamma_1 \right] = 0$$

(7b)

$$\frac{\delta Z}{\delta \lambda} = \frac{g_\theta x_1}{\tau_\theta (x_1 + \alpha_1)} - \gamma_1 x_1 - d_1 = 0. \tag{7c}$$

Inserting $\lambda = x_1$ – from (7a) – in (7b) yields:

$$d_1 + \frac{\alpha_1 g_\theta x_1}{\tau_\theta (x_1 + \alpha_1)^2} - \gamma_1 x_1 = 0$$

so that:

$$d_1 = \frac{-\alpha_1 g_\theta x_1}{\tau_\theta (x_1 + \alpha_1)^2} + \gamma_1 x_1. \tag{8}$$

Inserting (8) in (7c) and rearranging, yields the quadratic equation:

$$(2\gamma_1 \tau_\theta) x_1^2 + (4\alpha_1 \gamma_1 \tau_\theta - g_\theta) x_1 + (2\alpha_1^2 \gamma_1 \tau_\theta - 2\alpha_1 g_\theta) = 0$$

with roots:

$$x_1 = -\alpha_1 + \frac{g_\theta \pm \sqrt{g_\theta^2 + 8\alpha_1 \gamma_1 \tau_\theta g_\theta}}{4\gamma_1 \tau_\theta}.$$

Since $\sqrt{g_\theta^2 + 8\alpha_1 \gamma_1 \tau_\theta g_\theta} > g_\theta$ for $\alpha_1, \gamma_1, \tau_1, g_\theta > 0$, only one root is compatible with the restriction $x_1 \geq 0$. Consequently:

$$x_1 = -\alpha_1 + \frac{g_\theta \sqrt{g_\theta^2 + 8\alpha_1 \gamma_1 \tau_\theta g_\theta}}{4\gamma_1 \tau_\theta}. \tag{9}$$

The output given by (9) is the optimal output of the bureaucrat. If the bureaucrat is completely informed about political benefits (no uncertainty margin) she can attain this optimal output and the corresponding MDP through revelation of an appropriate kinked Apparent Budgetary Cost Function (ABCF) with the kink at the optimal output.

Figure MA.7 shows this ABCF for a numerical example in which the parameters and the exogenous variable take the following values:

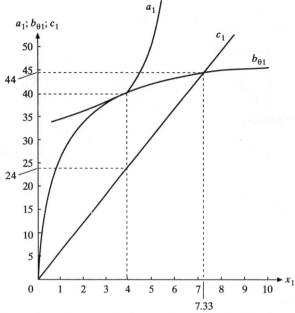

Figure MA.7 Apparent Budgetary Cost Function for the numerical example for model IV

$$\alpha_1 = 1$$
$$\gamma_1 = 6$$
$$g_\theta = 10$$
$$\tau_\theta = 1/5.$$

The corresponding optimal values for the bureaucrat are:

$$x_1 = 4$$
$$d_1 = 16$$
$$c_1 = 24$$
$$a_1 = 40.$$

If price discrimination is excluded, the bureaucrat has to reveal a linear ABCF through the origin. In that case the PSF, which describes the feasible combinations of output and MDP, is no longer dependent on the BOF, but rather on the politician's Individual Demand Function (IDF):

$$f_{\theta 1} = \frac{p_{\theta 1} x_1}{\tau_\theta} - c_1 = \frac{g_\theta x_1}{\tau_\theta (2x_1 + \alpha_1)} - \gamma_1 x_1.$$

The optimal combination of output and MDP for the bureaucrat follows from maximizing the bureaucratic maximand subject to the constraint:

$$f_{\theta 1} - d_1 = \frac{g_\theta x_1}{\tau_\theta(2x_1 + \alpha_1)} - \gamma_1 - d_1 = 0.$$

The Lagrangean maximand is:

$$Z = d_1 x_1 + \lambda \left[\frac{g_\theta x_1}{\tau_\theta(2x_1 + \alpha_1)} - \gamma_1 x_1 - d_1 \right].$$

The first order condition is:

$$\frac{\delta Z}{\delta d_1} = x_1 - \lambda = 0 \tag{10a}$$

$$\frac{dZ}{\delta x_1} = d_1 + \lambda \left[\frac{\tau_\theta g_\theta(2x_1 + \alpha_1) - 2\tau_\theta g_\theta x_1}{\tau_\theta^2(2x_1 + \alpha_1)^2} - \gamma_\theta \right]$$

$$= d_1 + \lambda \left[\frac{\alpha_1 g_\theta}{\tau_\theta(2x_1 + \alpha_1)^2} - \gamma_1 \right] = 0 \tag{10b}$$

$$\frac{\delta Z}{\delta \lambda} = \frac{g_\theta x_1}{\tau_\theta(2x_1 + \alpha_1)} - \gamma_1 x_1 - \alpha_1 = 0. \tag{10c}$$

Inserting $\lambda = x_1$ – from (10a) – in (10b) yields:

$$d_1 + \frac{\alpha_1 g_\theta x_1}{\tau_\theta(2x_1 + \alpha_1)^2} - \gamma_1 x_1 = 0$$

so that:

$$d_1 = \frac{-\alpha_1 g_\theta x_1}{\tau_\theta(2x_1 + \alpha_1)^2} + \gamma_1 x_1. \tag{11}$$

Inserting (11) in (10c) and rearranging, yields the following quadratic equation:

$$(4\gamma_1 \tau_\theta)x_1^2 + (4\alpha_1 \gamma_1 \tau_\theta - g_\theta)x_1 + (\alpha_1^2 \gamma_1 \tau_\theta - \alpha_1 \gamma_\theta) = 0$$

with roots:

$$x_1 = -\frac{\alpha_1}{2} + \frac{g_\theta \pm \sqrt{g_\theta^2 + 8\alpha_1 \gamma_1 \tau_\theta g_\theta}}{8\gamma_1 \tau_\theta}.$$

Since $\sqrt{g_\theta^2 + 8\alpha_1 \gamma_1 \tau_\theta g_\theta} > g_\theta$ for $\alpha_1, \gamma_1, \tau_\theta$, $g_\theta > 0$, only one root is compatible with the restriction $x_1 \geq 0$. Consequently:

$$x_1 = -\frac{\alpha_1}{2} + \frac{g_\theta + \sqrt{g_\theta{}^2 + 8\alpha_1\gamma_1\tau_\theta g_\theta}}{8\gamma_1\tau_\theta}. \tag{12}$$

The output given by (12) is the optimal output of the bureaucrat if price discrimination is excluded. If the bureaucrat is completely informed about political benefits (no uncertainty margin), she can attain this optimal output and the corresponding MDP through revelation of an appropriate linear ABCF through the origin. The slope of this ABCF has to equal the optimal bureaucratic price. This price is the optimal tax price that follows from inserting (12) in the IDF, times the reciprocal of the tax share.
The optimal tax price is:

$$p_{\theta 1} = \frac{4\gamma_1\tau_\theta g_\theta}{g_\theta + \sqrt{g_\theta{}^2 + 8\alpha_1\gamma_1\tau_\theta g_\theta}}$$

so that the equation of the ABCF is:

$$a_1 = \frac{p_{\theta 1}x_1}{\tau_\theta} = \frac{4\gamma_1 g_\theta x_1}{g_\theta + \sqrt{g_\theta{}^2 + 8\alpha_1\gamma_1\tau_\theta g_\theta}}.$$

Figure MA.8 presents the price–output diagram for a numerical example in which the parameters and the exogenous variable take the same values as used in figure MA.7 (so $\alpha_1 = 1$, $\gamma_1 = 6$, $g_\theta = 10$ and $\tau_\theta = 1/5$).
Figure MA.8 shows the politician's Individual Demand Function (IDF), the Marginal Revenue Function (MRF) and the Average Evaluation Function (AEF) and the bureaucrat's Marginal Tax Cost Function (MCTF) and Average Tax Cost Function (ACTF).
Since there are no fixed costs and since marginal costs are constant

$$\left(\frac{dc}{dx_1} = \gamma_1\right),$$

the MCTF and ACTF coincide and characterize a horizontal straight line. The corresponding functions are:

$$\text{IDF} \qquad p_{\theta 1} = \frac{g_\theta}{2x_1 + \alpha_1} = \frac{10}{2x_1 + 1} \qquad \text{(from (5) on p. 211)}$$

$$\text{MRF} \qquad \frac{dp_{\theta 1}x_1}{dx_1} = \frac{d\left(\dfrac{g_\theta x_1}{2x_1 + \alpha_1}\right)}{dx_1} = \frac{\alpha_1 g_\theta}{(2x_1 + \alpha_1)^2} = \frac{10}{(2x_1 + 1)^2}$$

$$\text{AEF} \qquad \frac{e_{\theta 1}}{x_1} = \frac{g_\theta}{x_1 + \alpha_1} = \frac{10}{x_1 + 1} \qquad \text{(from (13) on p. 215)}$$

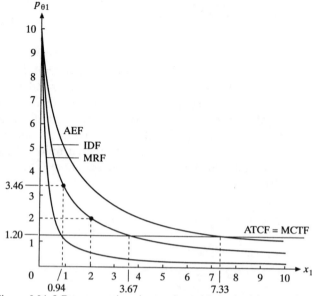

Figure MA.8 Bureaucratic price-setting with and without price discrimination

$$\text{ATCF} = \text{MCTF} \qquad \frac{\tau_\theta c_1}{x_1} = \tau_\theta \gamma_1 = 6/5 \qquad \text{(from (4)).}$$

The optimal values of output, MDP and tax price for the bureaucrat follow from (12) and from inserting the resulting optimal output in (11) and the IDF. These values are:

$$x_1 = 2$$
$$d_1 = 8$$
$$p_{\theta 1} = 2.$$

Note that if the bureaucrat was exclusively interested in MDP (so that the bureaucratic maximand would be $u_i = d_i$), the optimal output for the bureaucrat would result from equalling marginal revenue and marginal tax costs:

$$\frac{10}{(2x_1 + 1)^2} = \frac{6}{5},$$

so that $x_1 = \dfrac{5\sqrt{3}}{6} - \dfrac{1}{2} \approx 0.94$, $\quad d_1 = 28 - 10\sqrt{3} \approx 10.68$, and $p_{\theta 1} = 2\sqrt{3} \approx 3.46$.

If, on the other hand, the bureaucrat was exclusively interested in output (so that the bureaucratic maximand would be $u_1 = x_1$), the optimal output for the bureaucrat would result from equating tax price and average tax costs:

$$\frac{10}{2x_1 + 1} = \frac{6}{5}, \text{ so that } x_1 = \frac{11}{3} \approx 3.67, \ d_1 = 0 \text{ and } p_{\theta 1} = \frac{6}{5}.$$

Note that the optimal output according to the bureaucratic maximand given by (2) lies between these extreme values ($0.94 < 2 < 3.67$).

Since in this example marginal and average costs are constant and identical, the optimal output of the politician coincides with the optimal output of the output maximizing bureaucrat:

$$x_1 = \frac{11}{3}.$$

List of symbols

A. Variables

	Variable	Constant value of variable	Largest value of variable
1 Good	i		n
2 Output of good	x_i, y_i, z_i	o_i, q_i, r_i, s_i, t_i	
3 Set of goods	J		
4 Budgetary proposal (vector of outputs)	$\bar{x}, \bar{y}, \bar{z}$	$\bar{o}, \bar{q}, \bar{r}, \bar{s}, \bar{t}$	
5 Set of budgetary proposals	X	C, D, L, O, T	E
6 Politician	ξ	$\theta, \eta, \zeta, \psi, \chi, \phi$	v
7 Coalition (set of politicians)	S, T		N
8 Set of coalitions		$\mathcal{W}, \mathcal{L}, \mathcal{N}$	
9 Gross income of politician	g_ξ		
10 Net income of politician	m_ξ		
11 Tax price of good for politician	$p_{\xi i}$		
12 Managerial Discretionary Profit (MDP) of bureaucrat	d_i		

B. Functions	General function form
1 Apparent Budgetary Cost Function (ABCF)	$a_i(x_i)$
2 Budget Output Function (BOF)	$b_\xi(\bar{x})$
3 Total Cost Function (TCF)	$c_i(x_i)$
4 Total Evaluation Function (TEF)	$e_\xi(\bar{x})$
5 Marginal Evaluation Function (MEF)	$e'_\xi(\bar{x})$
6 Political Surplus Function (PSF)	$f_{\xi i}(x_i)$
7 Utility function of politician	$u_\xi(\bar{x},m_\xi)$
8 Preference function of politician	$u_\xi(\bar{x})$
9 Utility function of bureaucrat	$u_i(d_i,x_i)$
10 Characteristic function	$v(S)$
11 Preferred set	$P_\xi(\bar{x})$
12 Dominant set	$D(\bar{x})$
13 Pareto superior set	$S(\bar{x})$
14 Agenda function	$G(\bar{x})$

C. Parameters	
1 Dispensability of good	α_i
2 Preferred marginal expenditure share of good	$\beta_{\xi i}$
3 Marginal cost of good	γ_i
4 Tax share of politician	$\tau_{\xi i}$
5 Average apparent costs of good	π_i

Glossary

Agenda rule
Procedural rule that determines which proposals are admitted to the agenda of a committee for consideration and decision-making.
(See also: *procedural rule, committee*)

Appropriation law
Law that assigns regular budget authority for a specific fiscal year.
(See also: *budget authority*)

Attribute space
Geometrical space that has the outputs of the separate public and private goods of a budgetary game as coordinates.
(See also: *output, public good, private good, budgetary game*)

Authority
Actor or group of actors having competence to take collective decisions for a collective household.
(See also: *collective decision, collective household*)

Back-door expenditure
Expenditure which is effectively authorized by substantive law. The main forms of backdoor expenditure are expenditures flowing from contract authority and from entitlement law.
(See also: *expenditure, substantive law, contract authority, entitlement law*)

Budget authority
Competence assigned by law to commit expenditures other than guarantees. The main forms of budget authority are appropriations assigned by appropriation law and contract authority assigned by substantive law.
(See also: *expenditure, guarantee, appropriation law, contract authority, substantive law*)

Budget mechanism
The rule that relates the characteristics of demand or supply of a collective household to the preferences of its members.
(See also: *collective household*)

238

Budgetary decision
Collective decision by a competent authority of a government that authorizes expenditures from public funds or revenues to public funds.
(See also: *collective decision, authority, expenditure, revenue*)

Budgetary game
The *n*-person, cooperative, economic, simple majority game that has bundles of public and private goods as outcomes.
(See also: *cooperative game, economic game, simple game, public good, private good*)

Budgetary law
Appropriation law or annual authorization law with respect to revenues or borrowing.
(See also: *appropriation law*)

Bureaucrat
Actor who takes collective decisions for a public production household.
(See also: *collective decision, production household*)

Capacity of a good
Maximal number of persons that a local public good can benefit, apart from externalities.
(See also: *local public good, externality*)

Characteristic function
Function that indicates the value of an *n*-person, cooperative game to every possible coalition; value can be expressed by a real number (indicating 'joint pay-off') or by a set of vectors (indicating individual pay-offs).
(See also: *cooperative game*)

Charge
Contractual obligation based on public law to pay a sum of money to government in exchange for a specific service.
(See also: *money*)

Club good
Public good in supply or local public good from which potential consumers can be excluded.
(See also: *public good in supply, local public good, consumer*)

Collective decision
Decision that binds the members of a collective household.
(See also: *collective household*)

Collective household
Household that has more than one member.

Collectively beneficial set
The set of all proposals that every member of a coalition in a committee of politicians prefers to the proposal to forgo all services.
(See also: *politician, committee*)

Committee
Authority consisting of a group of actors.
(See also: *authority*)

Commodity
Any good but money.
(See also: *money*)

Competence rule
Decision rule that establishes the competences of an authority of a collective household.
(See also: *decision rule, authority, collective household*)

Consumer
Person who is a primary beneficiary of a good (as opposed to a beneficiary of an externality).
(See also: *externality*)

Consumption household
Household consisting of (a) consumer(s).
(See also: *consumer*)

Contract authority
Competence assigned by substantive law to enter into obligations that will result in immediate or future outlays and thus effectively authorizes expenditures.
(See also: *substantive law, outlay, expenditure*)

Contributory expenditure
Expenditure funded by fees, charges or earmarked tax.
(See also: *expenditure, fee, charge, earmarked tax*)

Cooperative game
N-person game that allows players to communicate freely among each other and to make binding agreements before choosing their strategies.
(See also: *strategy*)

Coordinated voting
Strategy of a politician in a budgetary game to the effect that she votes against her preferred alternative on the basis of a voting agreement with (an)other politician(s).
(See also: *strategy, politician, budgetary game*)

Core
The set of all proposals such that the dominant set with respect to every included proposal is empty.
(See also: *dominant set*)

Cost price
Minimal sum of money for which a commodity can be produced.
(See also: *money, commodity*)

Current law budget
The budget authorized by prevailing budgetary or substantive law.
(See also: *budgetary law, substantive law*)

Current services budget
The budget that follows from continuation of the output levels that are funded by prevailing budgetary or substantive law, accounting for future real and inflationary changes in costs and in the number of eligible consumers of the services.
(See also: *output, budgetary law, substantive law, consumer*)

Decision rule
Rule that determines how collective decisions are taken in a collective household.
(See also: *collective decision, collective household*)

Dominant set
The set of all proposals that an absolute majority of the politicians in a committee prefers to a given proposal.
(See also: *politician, committee*)

Earmarked tax
Tax that can exclusively be used to fund one or more specific services.
(See also: *tax*)

Economic constitution
The set of all decision rules of a collective household.
(See also: *decision rule, collective household*)

Economic game
N-person, cooperative game that has bundles of commodities as outcomes.
(See also: *cooperative game, commodity*)

Entitlement law
Substantive law that establishes an obligation of government to provide for one or more specific services, either on a permanent basis or for a number of fiscal years, and thus effectively authorizes expenditures for its term of operation.
(See also: *substantive law, expenditure*)

Expenditure
Action that establishes an obligation that will result in immediate or future outlays.
(See also: *outlay*)

Externality
External effect of production (consumption) that benefits or harms other persons than the producer (consumer).
(See also: *producer, consumer*)

Fee
Contractual obligation based on civil law to pay a sum of money to government in exchange for a specific service.
(See also: *money*)

General fund tax
Tax that can be used to fund any kind of service.
(See also: *tax*)

Group good
Public good in demand that benefits only a limited number of persons, apart from externalities.
(See also: *public good in demand, externality*)

Guarantee
Contract that establishes an obligation to redeem a loan in case of a debtor default.

Individually beneficial set
The set of all proposals that a politician prefers to the proposal to forgo all services.
(See also: *politician*)

Jurisdiction
Set of all dimensions of the attribute space of a budgetary game that according to the germaneness rule defines the admissible set against a given status quo proposal.
(See also: *attribute space, budgetary game, status quo*)

Lindahl tax price
Tax price of a good for a citizen that equals her marginal rate of substitution of the good for money.
(See also: *tax price, money*)

Local public good
Public good in supply that can benefit only a limited number of persons, apart from externalities.
(See also: *public good in supply, externality*)

Log-rolling
Form of coordinated voting on the basis of a voting agreement directed at larger outputs.
(See also: *coordinated voting, output*)

Market mechanism
The rule that relates the result of an exchange contract or a set of exchange contracts to the characteristics of demand and supply.

Market price
Maximal sum of money for which a commodity can be sold, or minimal sum of money for which a commodity can be purchased, in a relevant, not necessarily competitive, market.
(See also: *money, commodity*)

Money
Numeraire good that can be used as a measuring standard for the value of other goods and as a means of exchange.

Off-budget expenditure
Expenditure that is not authorized by budgetary law. The main forms of off-budget expenditure are tax expenditure, public loan and contributory expenditure.
(See also: *expenditure, budgetary law, tax expenditure, public loan, contributory expenditure*)

Outlay
Payment of a sum of money.
(See also: *money*)

Output
Number of units of a good provided by a public production unit to each consumer.
(See also: *consumer*)

Pareto optimal set
The set of all proposals such that the Pareto superior set with respect to every included proposal is empty.
(See also: *Pareto superior set*)

Pareto superior set
The set of all proposals that every politician in a committee prefers to a given proposal.
(See also: *politician, committee*)

Participation rule
Decision rule that establishes the composition of an authority of a collective household and determines who nominates or elects its members.
(See also: *decision rule, authority, collective household*)

Politician
Actor who takes collective decisions for a public consumption household.
(See also: *collective decision, consumption household*)

Preference set
The set of all proposals that a politician prefers to a given proposal.
(See also: *politician*)

Private contribution
Part of the apparent costs or market price of a commodity paid by the consumer in the form of a fee or charge.
(See also: *market price, commodity, fee, retribution*)

Private good (pure)
Good that can and does benefit only a single person.

Private good in demand (pure)
Good that benefits only a single person.

Private good in supply (pure)
Good that can benefit only a single person.

Private household
Household based on civil law, for instance family, association, business corporation, foundation.

Procedural rule
Decision rule that establishes how the collective decisions of an authority of a collective household are derived from the (individual) votes of their members.
(See also: *decision rule, collective decision, authority, collective household, vote*)

Producer
Actor who adds value to a good.

Production household
Household consisting of (a) producer(s).
(See also: *producer*)

Public contribution
Part of the apparent costs or market price of a commodity paid by the government. If the commodity is provided by the government itself, the contribution is a public contribution in narrow sense, otherwise it is a subsidy.
(See also: *market price, commodity, subsidy*)

Public good (pure)
Good that can and does benefit everybody.

Public good in demand (pure)
Good that does benefit everybody.

Public good in supply (pure)
Good that can benefit everybody.

Public household
Household based on public law, for instance government, incorporated public agency.

Public loan
Expenditure of government in order to lend a sum of money to another household.
(See also: *expenditure, money*)

Regulatory levy
Tax on the sale of a good in excess of the normal rate of the sales tax.
(See also: *tax*)

Revenue
Receipt of a sum of money.
(See also: *money*)

Simple game
N-person game that can be described by a characteristic function which distin-

guishes only winning and losing coalitions.
(See also: *characteristic function*)

Sincere voting
Strategy of a politician in a budgetary game to the effect that she votes for her preferred alternative.
(See also: *strategy, politician, budgetary game, collective decision*)

Sophisticated voting
Strategy of a politician in a budgetary game to the effect that she votes against her preferred alternative on the basis of her expectations about the votes of other politicians.
(See also: *strategy, politician, budgetary game, vote*)

Status quo proposal
The proposal to refrain from a new decision.

Strategic voting
Strategy of a politician in a budgetary game to the effect that she votes against her preferred alternative on the basis of a voting agreement with (an)other politician(s) (coordinated voting) or her expectations about the votes of other politicians (sophisticated voting).
(See also: *strategy, politician, budgetary game, coordinated voting, vote, sophisticated voting*)

Strategy
Potential course of action of a player in a game that affects the outcome of the game. In a budgetary game the strategies of the politicians consist of (individual) votes or series of (individual) votes.
(See also: *budgetary game, politician, vote*)

Subsidy
Expenditure by government in order to pay for a part of the market price of a commodity.
(See also: *expenditure, market price, commodity*)

Substantive law
Other law than budgetary law. Exceptionally, a substantive law assigns a permanent appropriation.
(See also: *budgetary law*)

Tax
Obligation based on public law to pay a sum of money to government in exchange for free access to an unspecified bundle of services.
(See also: *money*)

Tax expenditure
Expenditure by government in order to pay for a part of the market-price of a commodity in the form of a tax exemption.
(See also: *expenditure, market price, commodity*)

Tax price
Apparent costs of a commodity times the individual tax share of a citizen.
(See also: *cost price, commodity, tax share*)

Tax share
Total tax revenues of a government divided by the total individual tax burden of a citizen.
(See also: *tax, revenue*)

Top cycle
The set of all proposals such that every included proposal is in the dominant set with respect to every excluded proposal.
(See also: *dominant set*)

Transfer
Expenditure of government in order to change the distribution of net income.
(See also: *expenditure*)

Vote (individual)
Individual decision of a politician or elector from which a collective decision is derived by means of a voting rule.
(See also: *politician, collective decision, voting rule*)

Vote (round of voting)
Set of (individual) votes of all members of a committee or an electorate. The prevailing voting rule determines whether one or more rounds of voting are required in order to establish a collective decision.
(See also: *vote, committee, voting rule, collective decision*)

Vote trading
Form of coordinated voting on the basis of a voting agreement with respect to services in different jurisdictions.
(See also: *coordinated voting, jurisdiction*)

Voting rule
Procedural rule that determines how proposals are approved by voting in order to establish a collective decision.
(See also: *procedural rule, collective decision*)

Notes

1 Introduction

1 This question was asked in the paper, 'The lack of a budgetary theory' (Key, 1940). See also the reaction by Lewis, 'Toward a theory of budgeting' (1952).
2 This point is not entirely appreciated by Wildavsky in his well-known paper, 'Political implications of budget reform' (1961). Wildavsky seems to reason there that every change of procedure leads to a redistribution in the net benefits of outcomes and will thus be subject to political dispute. The same argument is made in his book, *The New Politics of the Budgetary Process* (1988). This argument neglects the opportunities for Pareto superior changes which not only exist at the level of budgetary decisions but also at that of constitutional decisions and that are probably larger at the latter level.
3 See for instance Berman (1975).

2 The structure of the budgetary process

1 A 'vote' in the sense of an individual decision should not be confused with a 'vote' in the sense of a 'round of voting'. Note also that in the latter sense the term is not synonymous with 'collective decision': often more than one round of voting is needed in order to establish a collective decision. More will be said about this matter in the section on procedural rules in this chapter.
2 In spite of its title, Buchanan's important work, *The Demand and Supply of Public Goods* (1968) is still representative of this tradition. According to current terminology it is devoted exclusively to the theory of public demand.
3 The value of capital originates in time preference or profitable investment opportunity: debts must be redeemed so that less taxation now means more taxation later. From a micro-economic point of view tax postponement is a public good like any other. People may like it mildly or strongly, but the fact that these preferences are often intertwined with beliefs of a theoretical nature about the consequences of public debt upon the economic system as a whole should not be considered as something special. Preferences for publicly provided services are in general dependent on theoretical beliefs as, for that matter, preferences for economic goods in general are. People demand vaccinations not because they like to be pricked, but because they believe it furthers their health.
4 Note that according to conventional terminology the 'secondary distribution of income' includes public but not private redistribution.
5 The average citizen is a member of many private households apart from his own family: sporting club, private business firm, labour union, etc.
6 In a strict sense, budgetary decisions are not external transactions themselves, but merely authorizations to conclude such transactions. Something more will be said about this distinction in the next section.
7 In the US federal government this phase is formalized in the 1974 Congressional Budget Act. According to this law, decisions about targets are taken in the form of a 'budget

resolution'.

8 The committee structure of the representative assembly may vary. Most assemblies have a standing committee for every executive department or agency, which investigates appropriations as well as substantive bills. In contrast, many American legislatures, including the US Congress, have separate committees for substantive legislation and appropriations.

9 Fenno and Wildavsky have described and illustrated with amusing examples the peculiar situation that may arise when an American Congressman attempts to gain information from an administrator that was initially concealed from him (Fenno, 1966, pp. 329–32; Wildavsky, 1964, pp. 80–90, 1988, pp. 179–81).

10 Annual authorization practices with respect to revenues and borrowing vary substantially between countries: in the UK, the term of operation of the main tax laws is limited to the current fiscal year, so that a large part of the revenues of central government must be authorized by an annual renewal Act (the so-called 'Finance Act'); in the USA, public borrowing is constrained by an annual Act that authorizes the debt ceiling; in the Netherlands, neither tax revenue nor the debt ceiling needs annual authorization.

11 In the US federal government, for instance, direct loans from unappropriated funds are common practice. For a survey see Wildavsky (1988, pp. 122–33).

12 Guarantees are sometimes authorized by substantive legislation. Of course, the settlement of loss declarations requires regular appropriations, regardless of how the loans or guarantees are authorized.

3 Demand in the public sector

1 The original formulation by Samuelson referred to goods 'which all enjoy in common in the sense that each individual's consumption of such a good leads to no subtraction from any other individual's consumption of that good' (Samuelson, 1954, 1955, 1958; in 1954, the definition was applied to the term 'collective consumption goods').

2 Note that a negative externality must be a 'non-optional good', a good from which one cannot exclude oneself.

3 See, for a survey of the Italian tradition, Buchanan (1960).

4 Analogous hypotheses could be formulated for multi-candidate elections (either in first-past-the-post systems under incomplete information or in systems of proportional representation). However, there is no analogous hypothesis for non-convergence (the first-mentioned hypothesis) because in multi-candidate elections there may be multiple equilibria. For the same reason, deviation from equilibrium positions is much harder to establish in such elections so that the other hypotheses are much harder to test. For a survey of electoral theory in multi-candidate elections see Shepsle and Cohen (1990).

5 The notion that in the absence of electoral equilibrium, politicians are free to pursue individual interests is also characteristic for the model of the revenue maximizing government ('Leviathan') as proposed by Brennan and Buchanan (1980).

6 This need not to imply that the politician resembles the citizens of which she is representative in all relevant economic characteristics, for instance, in gross private income. She can, for instance compensate a relatively large income, by relatively sober preferences, even when she is an elected politician.

7 The latter condition assures that it induces convex indifference curves in the output space.

8 The Budget Output Function was invented by Niskanen. Niskanen also coined its name (Niskanen, 1971).

9 For a survey of such procedures see Tulkens (1978). See also Mueller (1989, chapter 4).

10 Moreover, most of them are sensitive to individual strategic (non-sincere) voting. This is not the case with the so-called 'demand-revealing process' proposed by Tullock and Tideman (1976); see also the special issue of *Public Choice* on demand revelation (29(2), 1977).

11 For the difference between a subsidy and a public contribution in narrow sense recall chapter 2, p. 21.

12 Private goods in supply are always, and local public goods are often excludable (recall

p. 33–4), so that the number of consumers can to a certain extent be controlled by eligibility criteria. Excludable public goods are known as 'club goods'.

13 For some readers, it might be illuminating to note that in the literature on electoral demand, the factor h/k, which represents the number of units to be produced per unit provided to an eligible consumer, is often denoted as h^γ (Bergstrom and Goodman, 1973; Borcherding and Deacon, 1972). In this notation γ is a parameter of capacity, with $\gamma = 0$ for the case of a pure public good in supply (so that $h^\gamma = 1$), $0 < \gamma < 1$ for the case of a local public good (so that $1 < h^\gamma < h$) and $\gamma = 1$ for a pure private good in supply (so that $h^\gamma = h$).

14 This is an austere definition of a (relevant) consumption externality on the basis of a single characteristic. Some definitions that can be found in the literature mention additional characteristics, for instance, that the externality is non-optional (Head, 1962; Mishan, 1969, 1981), or that it leads to inefficient allocation (Buchanan and Stubblebine, 1962). For a survey of definitions see Baumol and Oates (1975).

15 Of course, externalities of type I are relevant from a normative point of view, for instance for the question whether subsidies are called for. A side remark in this connection is the following. The question whether subsidies are called for in specific cases because of externalities is one of the most frequently and arduously discussed questions in traditional public finance. It is curious that such discussions usually focus on attempts to 'prove' the existence of the externalities in dispute or to 'estimate' their size. This is scarcely a fruitful approach because the existence of externalities can usually not be proved in any direct way. A more pragmatic approach would be to start from the thesis that the presence of externalities implies that people who do not consume the good favour higher output levels, even if subsidization is required to bring such output levels about. This thesis is true for externalities of both types I and II. This thesis turns the traditional approach on its head: services must not be subsidized because they have externalities, but services must have externalities because people who are not consumers favour subsidization. In other words, there is no reason to worry about externalities until people start advocating subsidization of services that they do not consume!

4 Supply in the public sector

1 Some authors have described the dominant party as an 'agenda-setter' (for instance, Mackay and Weaver, 1978). This terminology is a little confusing, because it necessitates a distinction between two kinds of 'agenda-setting', namely by bureaucrats and by politicians. In the present discussion, the term 'agenda-setting' is reserved for agenda-setting by politicians (to be addressed in chapter 7).

2 The condition that the universe of alternatives can be reduced to two alternatives was explored in various papers by Romer and Rosenthal (1978, 1979; see also Ladha,Romer and Rosenthal, 1984). Note, however, that these authors never alleged that administrators of public agencies would possess this type of monopoly power vis-à-vis political authorities. In their empirical work, they applied the model to American school districts, where parents decide by referendum about school budget proposals.

3 Pigou distinguished (a) price discrimination between markets, or, in the extreme case, between clients, which he called discrimination of the third degree, (b) price discrimination between subsequent units sold to each client, which he called discrimination of the second degree, and (c) price discrimination between markets or clients as well as between subsequent units sold to each client, which he called discrimination of the first degree (Pigou, 1920).

4 The distinction that Breton and Wintrobe make in this connection between the 'supervision of the use of inefficient production techniques', directed at the control of productive efficiency, and the use of 'antidistortion devices that pertain to the flow of information', directed at the control of allocative efficiency, does not seem entirely adequate (Breton and Wintrobe, 1975). The latter type of monitoring reveals apparent costs at alternative output levels. This information may indeed enable the politician to choose an output with a larger political surplus, and thus improve allocation, but it is not

sufficient for that purpose. It is, on the contrary, highly probable that the bureaucrat has transformed her ABCF in such a way that there is no alternative output with a higher political surplus; otherwise the politician would not have chosen the current output in the first place. In that case, information on real rather than apparent costs of alternative output levels is necessary to improve allocation.

5 A different assumption has been made by Moene (1986). This author has described bureaucratic behaviour by a function of 'reported costs' which is assumed to be based on a probability distribution of political benefits.

6 Adam Smith said: 'It is not from the benevolence of the butcher, the brewer or the baker, that we expect our dinner, but from the regard to their own interest' (Smith, 1776, p.13).

7 In the corporate capitalism discussion the classical profit maximization assumption was challenged among others by Baumol, who proposed output-maximization, Marris, who proposed growth maximization and Alchian and Kessel as well as Williamson, who proposed 'managerial discretion': staff, amenities, etc. (Baumol, 1959; Marris, 1963, 1966; Alchian and Kessel, 1962; Williamson, 1963, 1964).

8 For a survey of this literature, see Young (1991).

9 See, for instance, Campbell and Naulls (1991); Dunleavy (1991); Lynn (1991); Peters (1989).

10 For a comparative perspective, see Campbell (1983) and Peters (1988, 1991).

11 See also Heclo (1977) for an interesting analysis of the role of 'amphibians' – whom the author calls 'public careerists' – in the US government.

12 It seems that Niskanen's view on the Migué and Bélanger paper had evolved a little since his original reaction, which was rather critical (Niskanen, 1974, cited under Migué and Bélanger, 1974).

13 If the budget (or output) is maximized, average benefit equals average costs, so that the cost elasticity of demand equals $(dx_1/d(b_{\theta 1}(x_1)/x_1)) \times ((b_{\theta 1}(x_1)/x_1)/x_1)$ or, after differentiation $-1 + (x_1 b_{\theta 1}{}'(x_1))/(x_1 b_{\theta 1}{}'(x_1) - b_{\theta 1}(x_1))$. This elasticity is less than -1 if the denominator of the last term is negative. This is the case if $b_{\theta 1}(x_1) > x_1 b_{\theta 1}{}'(x_1)$, that is if $b_{\theta 1}(x_1)/x_1 > b_{\theta 1}{}'(x_1)$, or if average benefit exceeds marginal benefit. This is the case if marginal benefits are monotonically decreasing.

14 Empirical studies on the basis of this approach focus on the effects of intergovernmental matching grants (which lower the costs of services) on the budget of the grant receiving governments. For a survey of this literature see Gramlich (1977). Wyckof (1990) has rightly observed that cost elastic demand not only follows from oversupply but also from productive inefficiency. It is possible, however, to distinguish between both causes of excessive budget by looking at the effects of lump-sum grants (as opposed to matching grants): whereas under bureaucratic budget maximization the budget of the grant receiving government will increase in reaction to both kinds of grants, under bureaucratic MDP maximization, it will increase in reaction to a matching grant, but remain constant in reaction to a lump-sum grant.

15 Surveys of studies based on this approach are provided in Mueller (1989) and Blankart (1978).

16 Some empirical studies based on this approach are Sjoquist (1982); Schneider (1989).

17 An empirical study based on this approach is Niskanen (1975).

18 Apparent budgetary costs could also have been inserted directly into the politician's budget constraint. This would have led to a non-linear budget constraint of the form $\tau_\theta a_1(x_1) + m_\theta = g_\theta$. In order to facilitate the comparison with the models of chapter 3, explicit presentation of the relation between tax price and apparent costs seems preferable.

19 The BOF is concave because the TEF is concave and because the BOF equals the TEF times a constant factor. The TEF is concave because it is the mirror image of a convex indifference curve (see, for instance, Chiang, 1967, p. 342).

20 Note that in Niskanen's original model the BOF was not derived from a utility function of the bureaucrat and could have a top. When the TCF intersects such a BOF at an output beyond the top, the budget is maximized at the top of the BOF rather than at the intersection of the TCF and the BOF. Niskanen called the resulting budget maximizing output an outcome in the 'demand constrained region' (Niskanen, 1971). In terms of figure 4.4,

marginal revenues as indicated by the IDF (in the absence of income effects) would then be zero at that outcome. In that case, output maximization and budget maximization would also lead to different outcomes with price discrimination.

21 Recall that in our models output of private or group goods is always defined in terms of units available to each consumer. This implies that the shape of the TCFs (expression (4) in models IV and V) is dependent on the number of consumers.

5 Political decision-making

1 Note that cardinal utility at the individual level does not imply 'interpersonal comparability' of utility; the latter property is even stronger than 'transferable utility'; for a discussion of this point, see Luce and Raiffa (1957, pp. 33–4).

2 For this reason, games that can be represented by real-valued characteristic functions are also called 'games with side payments'. Note, however, that in the older literature it was usual to consider the transferable utility case as a subcase of the side payments case alongside the subcase that side payments could be made but not in a commodity for which players held linear utility (see, for instance, Luce and Raiffa, 1957, pp. 169, 181; Aumann, 1967).

3 In some types of games there may be a difference between the outcomes a coalition can guarantee and the outcomes the players outside the coalition cannot prevent. Characteristic functions may be based on either notion of effectiveness (so-called 'alpha' and 'beta' theories of effectiveness). For our purpose, the former notion seems the most appropriate one (see, for instance, Shubik, 1982, pp. 136–7; Ordeshook, 1986, pp. 330–2).

4 Note that both the assumption of 'free disposal' and the present convention with respect to the pay-off-vectors in the characteristic set imply that if characteristic sets have any elements, they have by definition infinitely many elements. Free disposal implies that each individual pay-off of a member can be of any magnitude smaller than the specified maximum, the present convention implies that each individual pay-off of an excluded player can be of any magnitude. Note, also, that the present convention is compatible with the assumption that the value of the game to the empty coalition is the empty set: if the characteristic set of the empty coalition is empty in the 0-dimensional utility subspace (as opposed to containing one element), it is empty in the n-dimensional space as well.

5 In a general game in real-valued characteristic function form, the property of symmetry has a wider sense: such a game is symmetrical if its value to a coalition exclusively depends upon the number of the coalition members. In this wider sense, the property is not applicable to a game in set-valued characteristic function form, because in such a game individual pay-offs are not interpersonally comparable.

6 A majority group good in this sense may be a local public good that can benefit only a minority of the citizens. This is possible even if the good is not only consumed by a majority of the committee, but also by a majority of the citizenry. In that case more than a single good has to be produced per unit of ouput provided to each consumer (recall chapter 3, p. 56).

7 Note, however, that it is not permissible to say: 'a pay-off vector is feasible if it belongs to the characteristic set of any coalition', at least not if the convention concerning the structure of the characteristic set adopted in this study is adopted (recall that according to this convention the individual pay-off to players who are excluded from a coalition may be of any magnitude).

8 For a review of the literature about experimental research concerning the core and other solution concepts in spatial majority games, see McKelvey and Ordeshook (1990).

9 This is the case because the gradient direction at a point of an indifference curve is orthogonal to the direction of the indifference curve at that point.

10 The original Plott paper (1967) exclusively treated the case of an odd number of committee members with no more than one ideal point at the core point.

11 Note that since the cones are closed, a gradient pointing in the direction of a boundary of a cone is pointing into this cone in the sense of the stated condition.

12 The condition mentioned for core existence in the absence of pairwise symmetry refers to

games in a two-dimensional attribute space. Slutsky (1977) has stated similar conditions for games in attribute spaces of higher dimensionality.

13 Figure 5.15 is a variation on a figure in Enelow and Hinich (1984, p. 31).

14 Tullock has argued that a majority rule decision path that moves away from a central point or area in the distribution of voter ideal points is unlikely if the number of voter is large (Tullock, 1967a; formalized in Arrow, 1969). However, the number of voters in committees, in contrast to those in electorates is often not large.

6 Bureaucratic decision-making

1 See n. 3, pp. 249–50, in chapter 4.

7 Institutions

1 The notation has been adjusted to the conventions of this volume.

2 The expression 'vote trading' is often used in the literature as synonym for 'log-rolling'. The concept of log-rolling will be discussed further below. In the present discussion, 'vote trading' is used in the more literal sense specified here.

3 Note that if preferences of all politicians are separable, kinked median ridge lines cannot occur and sophisticated voting will lead to an equilibrium outcome (Kramer, 1972).

4 If $\bar{x}$ and $\bar{y}$ are vectors of dimensionality n, then $\bar{x} \geq \bar{y}$ is defined by: $x_i \geq y_i$ for all i, $i = 1,2,\ldots,n$.

5 Recall the definition of the contract set or collectively rational set of a given coalition, as mentioned in chapter 5, pp. 107–8. Note that the extended contract set includes the contract set which is indicated in the present example by the contract curve between the ideal points of θ and ψ.

6 An adequate treatment of explicit log-rolling in this sense requires the introduction of other solution concepts for cooperative n-person games than the core. In the context of this discussion, such a treatment is not necessary. As far as the budgetary process is concerned, vote coordination through coalitions seems more empirically relevant than the more sophisticated form of vote coordination through explicit log-rolling. For a game-theoretical treatment of explicit log-rolling see Ordeshook (1986, chapter 9).

7 The agenda function that induces this solution consists of the first part of the agenda function that induces the universalistic solution:

$$G(\bar{x}) = \{\bar{y}\,|\,\bar{y} \geq \bar{x}; \{\bar{z}\,|\,\bar{x} \leq \bar{z} \leq \bar{y}\} \cap S(\bar{y}) = \emptyset\}.$$

8 The empirical and theoretical justification of this assumption is very problematic. An even split of gains (in terms of outputs) cannot be deduced from any plausible solution concept.

9 One may wonder how a log-rolling equilibrium proposal that results in negative net social benefit (a social cost) can ever be approved. The (larger than minimal) winning coalition approving such a proposal in a single decision acts in a 'collectively irrational' way: every member of the coalition suffers. To explain this paradox, various complicated arguments – involving distinctions between different kinds of costs and benefits, 'political' versus 'economic' costs, etc. – have been advanced (Weingast, 1979; Shepsle and Weingast, 1981b). It seems, however, that these arguments are not necessary. A socially harmful log-rolling equilibrium can be attained by implicit log-rolling in a sequence of decisions.

10 Note that even if the log-rolling equilibrium yields a positive net social value, there will be better proposals in the Pareto optimal set. The 'best' proposal is neither the log-rolling equilibrium nor necessarily a proposal in the Pareto optimal set, but rather the Lindahl proposal. The Lindahl proposal has the effect that the tax price of each service for a politician equals her marginal rate of substitution of that service for money. Whether the Lindahl point is located below, in or above the Pareto optimal set depends upon the distribution of tax shares.

8 Ways to reform

1 This need not imply that in the absence of a line item veto, the President in the US federal government lacks influence upon appropriations laws. In particular, the President can influence members of Congress before decisions are taken.

2 For this reason, the deficiencies of the budget mechanism play an important role in the literature on the growth of government. They are known in this literature as 'institutional explanations', as opposed to 'demand side explanations', which focus on the need for public services or on the willingness to pay taxes for those services on the one hand, and as opposed to 'technological explanations', which focus on the real costs of public production on the other. For surveys of the growth of government literature see Aranson and Ordeshook (1981), Larkey, Stolp and Winer (1981); Tarschys (1975).

3 Note the terminology: information about the effectiveness of services in relation to the objectives that have been set for them enables the members of political authorities to judge the allocative efficiency (cost–benefit ratios) of public programmes.

4 Productive efficiency may be affected indirectly, if information about effects leads to a change in output.

5 The role of the public production sector with respect to subsidized services is limited to the administrative aspect: no value is added in the public production sector.

6 Of course, market structure is also important. If an agency, before incorporation, is subject to effective ministerial control of its production process, incorporation may lead to larger autonomy and abolition of the principal–agent relationship. However, we have assumed in chapter 2 that many executive agencies that are not incorporated can also be considered as independent suppliers of public services.

Mathematical appendix

1 See, for instance, Chiang (1967, p. 394).

2 See, for instance, Chiang (1967, p. 342).

3 Note that τ_θ is a constant factor so that $\tau_\theta f(x)$ is concave if $f(x)$ is concave.

4 A quasi-concave function either has a global maximum or is montonic. Since the PF is only defined for the output domain that is feasible within the income constraint, it must necessarily have a global maximum (possibly at a corner of the feasible output domain).

References

Aberman, J.D., R.D. Putman and B.H. Rockman, 1981. *Bureaucrats and Politicians in Western Democracies*, Cambridge, MA: Harvard University Press

Alchian, A.A. and A. Kessel, 1962. 'Competition, monopoly and the pursuit of money', in H.G. Lewis (ed.), *Aspects of Labour Economics*, Princeton: Princeton University Press

Aranson, P.H. and P.C. Ordeshook, 1981. 'Alternative theories of the growth of government and their implications for constitutional tax and spending limits', in H. Ladd and T.N. Tideman (eds.), *Tax and Expenditure Limitations*, Washington, DC: Urban Institute Press

Arrow, K.J., 1951. *Social Choice and Individual Values*, New Haven: John Wiley, 2nd edn, 1963
    1969. 'Tullock and an existence theorem', *Public Choice*, 6, pp. 105–11
    1983. 'The organization of economic activity: issues pertinent to the choice of market versus non-market allocation', in R.H. Haveman and J. Margolis, *Public Expenditure and Policy Analysis*, Boston: Houghton Mifflin

Aumann, R., 1967. 'A survey of cooperative games without side payments', in M. Shubik (ed.), *Essays in Mathematical Economics*, Princeton: Princeton University Press

Auten, G., B. Bozeman and R. Cline, 1984. 'A sequential model of Congressional appropriations', *American Journal of Political Science*, 28, pp. 503–23

Barr, J.C. and O.A. Davis, 1966. 'An elementary political and economic theory of the expenditures of local governments', *Southern Economic Journal*, 33, pp. 149–65

Barry, B., 1965. *Political Argument*, London: Routledge & Kegan Paul

Barzel, Y. and R.T. Deacon, 1975. 'Voting behavior, efficiency and equity', *Public Choice*, 21, pp. 1–14

Baumol, W.J., 1959. *Business Behaviour, Value and Growth*, London: Macmillan

Baumol, W.J. and W.E. Oates, 1975. *The Theory of Environmental Policy*, Cambridge: Cambridge University Press

Beesley, I., 1983. 'The Rayner scrutinies', in A. Gray and B. Jenkins (eds.), *Policy Analysis and Evaluation in British Government*, London: Royal Institute of Public Administration

Bendor, J., 1988. 'Formal models of bureaucracy', *British Journal of Political*

Science, 18, pp. 353–95

Bendor, J., S. Taylor and R. van Gaalen, 1985. 'Bureaucratic expertise versus legislative authority: a model of deception and monitoring in budgeting', *American Political Science Review*, 79, pp. 1041–60

1987. 'Politicians, bureaucrats and asymmetric information', *American Political Science Review*, 31, pp. 796–828

Benson, B.L., 1983. 'Logrolling and high demand committee review', *Public Choice*, 41, pp. 427–34

Bergstrom, T.C. and R.P. Goodman, 1973. 'Private demands for public goods', *American Economic Review*, 63, pp. 280–96

Berman, D.R., 1975. *State and Local Politics*, Boston: Holbrook Press

Berman, L., 1979. *The Office of Management and Budget and the Presidency 1921–1979*, Princeton: Princeton University Press

Bernholz, P., 1978. 'On the stability of logrolling outcomes in stochastic games', *Public Choice*, 33(3), pp. 65–82

Black, D., 1948. 'On the rationale of group decision making', *Journal of Political Economy*, 56, pp. 23–34

1958. *The Theory of Committees and Elections*, Cambridge: Cambridge University Press

Black, D. and R.A. Newing, 1951. *Committee Decisions with Complementary Valuation*, London: Chapel River Press

Blais, A. and S. Dion (eds.), 1991. *The Budget-maximizing Bureaucrat. Appraisals and Evidence*, Pittsburg: University of Pittsburg Press

Blankart, C.B., 1975. 'Zur ökonomische Theorie der Bureaucratie', *Public Finance*, 30, pp. 166–85

1978. 'Bureaucratic problems in public choice: why do public goods still remain public?', in K.W. Roskamp (ed.), *Public Choice and Public Finance. Proceedings of the 34th Congress of the IIPF*, Paris: Editions Cujas

Borcherding, Th.E. and R.T. Deacon, 1972. 'The demand for the services of non-federal governments: an econometric approach to collective choice', *American Economic Review*, 62, pp. 891–901

Bowen, H., 1943. 'The interpretation of voting in the allocation of economic resources', *Quarterly Journal of Economics*, 57, pp. 27–48

Boyne, G., 1985. 'Theory, methodology and results in political science: the case of output studies', *British Journal of Political Science*, 15, pp. 473–515

Brady, R., 1973. 'MBO goes to work in the public sector', *Harvard Business Review*, 51, pp. 65–75

Braybrooke, D. and C.E. Lindblom, 1963. *A Strategy of Decision: Policy Evaluation as a Social Process*, New York: Free Press

Brennan, G. and J.M. Buchanan, 1980. *The Power to Tax*, Cambridge: Cambridge University Press

Breton, A. and R. Wintrobe, 1975. 'The equilibrium size of a budget maximizing bureau', *Journal of Political Economy*, 83, pp. 195–207

1982. *The Logic of Bureaucratic Conduct*, Cambridge: Cambridge University Press

Browning, E.K., 1974. 'The diagrammatic analysis of multiple consumption externalities', *American Economic Review*, 64, pp. 704–17

1975. 'Collective choice and general fund financing', *Journal of Political Economy*, 83, pp. 377–90

Buchanan, J.M., 1959. 'Positive economics, welfare economics and political economy', *Journal of Law and Economics*, 2, pp. 124–38

1960. ' "La scienza delle finanze": the Italian tradition in fiscal theory', in J.M. Buchanan, *Fiscal Theory and Political Economy'*, Chapel Hill: University of North Carolina Press

1961. 'Simple majority voting, game theory and resource use', *Canadian Journal of Economics and Political Science*, 27, pp. 337–48

1962. 'Politics, policy and the Pigovian margins', *Economica*, 29, pp. 17–28

1966. 'Joint supply, externality and optimality', *Economica*, 33, pp. 404–15

1967. *Public Finance in Democratic Process*, Chapel Hill: University of North Carolina Press

1968. *The Demand and Supply of Public Goods*, Chicago: Rand McNally

1971. 'Principles of urban fiscal strategy', *Public Choice*, 11, pp. 1–16

1972. 'Toward analysis of closed behavioral systems', in J.M. Buchanan and R.D. Tollison (eds.), *Theory of Public Choice*, Ann Arbor: University of Michigan Press

1983. 'The achievements and limits of public choice in diagnosing government failure and offering bases for constructive reform', in H. Hanusch (ed.), *Anatomy of Government Deficiencies*, Berlin: Springer Verlag

1987. 'Constitutional economics', in J.M. Buchanan, *Explorations into Constitutional Economics*, College Station: Texas A&M University Press, 1989

Buchanan, J.M., 1989. *Explorations into Constitutional Economics*, College Station: Texas A&M University Press

Buchanan, J.M. and W.C. Stubblebine, 1962. 'Externality', *Economica*, 29, pp. 371–84

Buchanan, J.M. and G. Tullock, 1962. *The Calculus of Consent*, Ann Arbor: University of Michigan Press

Campbell, C.S.J., 1983. *Governments Under Stress: Political Executives and Key Bureaucrats in Washington, London and Ottawa*, Toronto: University of Toronto Press

1986. *Managing the Presidency: Carter, Reagan and the Search for Executive Harmony*, Pittsburg: Pittsburg University Press

Campbell, C.S.J. and D. Naulls, 1991. 'The limits of budget maximizing theory: some evidence from officials' views of their roles and careers', in A. Blais and S. Dion (eds.), *The Budget-Maximizing Bureaucrat*, Pittsburg: Pittsburg University Press

Chiang, A.C., 1967. *Fundamental Methods of Mathematical Economics*, Singapore: McGraw-Hill, 3rd edn, 1984

Chan, K.S. and S. Mestelman, 1988. 'Institutions, efficiency and the strategic behaviour of sponsors and bureaus', *Journal of Public Economics*, 37, pp. 91–102

Cohen, L., 1979. 'Cyclic sets in multidimensional voting models', *Journal of Economic Theory*, 20, pp. 1–12

Coleman, J.S., 1966. 'The possibility of a social welfare function', *American Economic Review*, 56, pp. 1105–22; comments by D.C. Mueller and R.E. Park, reply by J.S. Coleman, 1967, *American Economic Review*, 57, pp. 1301–17

Condorcet, M.J.A.N.C. de, 1785. *Essai sur l'application de l'analyse à la probabilité des decisions rendues à la pluralité des voix*, New York: Chelsea, 1972

Conybeare, J., 1984. 'Bureaucracy, monopoly and competition: a critical analysis of the budgetary maximizing model of bureaucracy', *American Journal of Political Science*, pp. 479–502

Cornes, R. and T. Sandler, 1986. *The Theory of Externalities, Public Goods and Club Goods*, Cambridge: Cambridge University Press

Crecine, J.P., M.S. Kamlet, D.C. Mowery and M. Winer, 1981. 'The role of the US Office of Management and Budget in executive branch budgetary decision-making', in J.P. Crecine (ed.), *Research in Public Policy Analysis and Management, Volume II*, Greenwich, CT: JAI Press

Cyert, R. and J.G. March, 1963. *Behavioral Theory of the Firm*, Englewood Cliffs, NJ: Prentice-Hall

Davis, M.D., 1970. *Game Theory. A Non-technical Introduction*, New York: Basic Books, 2nd edn, 1973

Davis, O.A., M. DeGroot and M.J. Hinich, 1972. 'Social preference orderings and majority rule', *Econometrica*, 40, pp. 147–57

Davis, O.A., M.A.H. Dempster and A. Wildavsky, 1966a. 'A theory of the budgetary process', *American Political Science Review* 60, pp. 529–47

1966b. 'On the process of budgeting: an empirical study of Congressional appropriations', *Papers on Non-market Decision Making I*, pp. 63–132

1971. 'On the process of budgeting II: an empirical study of Congressional appropriations', in R.F. Byrne, A. Charnes, W.W. Cooper, O.A. Davis and D. Gilford (eds.), *Studies in Budgeting*, Amsterdam: North-Holland

1974. 'Towards a predictive theory of government expenditure: US domestic appropriations', *British Journal of Political Science*, 4, pp. 419–52

Davis, O.A., M.J. Hinich and P.C. Ordeshook, 1970. 'An expository development of a mathematical model of the electoral process', *American Political Science Review*, 64, pp. 426–48

Deacon, R., 1979. 'The expenditure effects of alternative public supply institutions', *Public Choice*, 34, pp. 381–97

Dempster, M.A. and A. Wildavsky, 1979. 'On change: or, there is no magic size for an increment', *Political Studies*, 27, pp. 371–89

Denzau, A.T. and R.J. Mackay, 1976. 'Benefit shares and majority voting', *American Economic Review*, 66, pp. 69–76

1980. 'A model of benefit and tax share discrimination by a monopoly bureau', *Journal of Public Economics*, 13, pp. 341–68

1981. 'Structure induced equilibrium and perfect foresight expectations', *American Journal of Political Science*, 25, pp. 762–79

1985. 'Tax systems and tax shares', *Public Choice*, 45, pp. 35–47

Denzau, A.T. and R.P. Parks, 1977. 'A problem with public sector preferences', *Journal of Economic Theory*, pp. 454–7

1979. 'Deriving public sector preferences', *Journal of Public Economics*, 11, pp. 335–52

Domke, W.K., R.C. Eichenberg and C.M. Kelleher, 1983. 'The illusion of choice: defense and welfare in advanced industrial democracies', *American Political Science Review*, 77, pp. 19–35

Downs, A., 1957. *An Economic Theory of Democracy*, New York: Harper and Row

1967. *Inside Bureaucracy*, Boston: Little, Brown

Downs, G. and P. Larkey, 1979. 'Theorizing about public expenditure decision-making: (as) if wishes were horses', *Policy Sciences*, 11, pp. 143–56

Draper, F.D. and B.T. Pitsvada, 1980. 'Congress and executive branch budget reform: the House Appropriations Committee and Zero-Base-Budgeting', *International Journal of Public Administration*, 2, pp. 331–74

1981. 'ZBB. Looking back after ten years', *Public Administration Review*, 41, pp. 76–83

Drees, W., 1985. *Nederlandse Overheidsuitgaven*, Den Haag: VUGA

Drucker, P.F., 1954. *The Practice of Management*, New York: Harper & Row

1964. *Managing for Results*, New York: Harper & Row

1976. 'What results should you expect? A users' guide to MBO', *Public Administration Review*, 36, pp. 12–19

Dunleavy, P., 1991. *Democracy, Bureaucracy and Public Choice*, New York: Harvester Wheatsheaf

Dye, T.R., 1966. *Politics, Economics and the Public: Policy Outcomes in the American States*, Chicago: Rand McNally

Easton, D., 1953. *The Political System*, New York: Knopf, 2nd edn, 1971

Enelow, J., 1984. 'A generalized model of voting one issue at a time with applications to Congress', *American Journal of Political Science*, 28, pp. 587–97

1986. 'The stability of logrolling: an expectations approach', *Public Choice*, 51, pp. 285–94

Enelow, J.M. and M.J. Hinich, 1983a. 'On Plott's pairwise symmetry condition for majority rule equilibrium', *Public Choice*, 40, pp. 317–26

1983b. 'Voting one issue at a time: the question of voter forecasts', *American Political Science Review*, 77, pp. 435–46

1983c. 'Voter expectations in multi-stage voting systems: an equilibrium result', *American Journal of Political Science*, 28, pp. 820–7

1984. *The Spatial Theory of Voting*, Cambridge: Cambridge University Press

1987. 'Optimal decision-making when the shapes and locations of voter preference curves are unknown', *Economia della Scelte Pubbliche*, 3, pp. 161–70

Enelow, J.M. and M.J. Hinich (eds.), 1990. *Advances in the Spatial Theory of Voting*, Cambridge: Cambridge University Press

Feld, S.L. and B. Grofman, 1987. 'Necessary and sufficient conditions for a majority winner in *n*-dimensional spatial voting games: an intuitive geometrical approach', *Americal Journal of Political Science*, 31, pp. 709–28

Fenno, R.F., Jr., 1966. *The Power of the Purse: Appropriations Politics in Congress*, Boston: Little, Brown

Ferejohn, J.A., 1974. *Pork Barrel Politics. Rivers and Harbors Legislation 1947–1968*, Stanford: Stanford University Press

Ferejohn, J.A. and M.P. Fiorina, 1975. 'Purposive models of legislative behavior', *American Economic Review (Proceedings and Papers)*, 65, pp. 407–14

Ferejohn, J.A. and R. Krehbiel, 1987. 'The budget process and the size of the budget', *American Journal of Political Science*, 31, pp. 296–320

Ferejohn, J.A., M.P. Fiorina and H.F. Weisberg, 1978. 'Toward a theory of legislative decision', in P.C. Ordeshook (ed.), *Game Theory and Political Science*, New York: New York University Press

Fiorina, M.P., 1973. 'Electoral margins, constituency influence and policy moderation: a critical assessment', *American Politics*, 4, pp. 479–98

1977. *Congress: Keystone of the Washingtonian Establishment*, New Haven: Yale University Press, 2nd edn, 1989

Fiorina, M.P. and R.G. Noll, 1978. 'Voters, bureaucrats and legislators: a rational choice perspective on the growth of bureaucracy', *Journal of Public Economics*, 9, pp. 239–54

Fiorina, M.P. and K.A. Shepsle, 1982. 'Equilibrium, disequilibrium and the general possibility of a science of politics', in P.C. Ordeshook and K.A. Shepsle (eds.), *Political Equilibrium*, Boston: Kluwer

Fisher, G.W. and M.S. Kamlet, 1984. 'Explaining presidential priorities: the competing aspirations level of macro-budgetary decision-making', *American Political Science Review*, 78, pp. 356–71

Fisk, D.M., 1984. 'Public sector productivity and relative efficiency: the state of the art in the USA', in H. Hanusch (ed.), *Public Finance and the Quest for Efficiency, Proceedings of the 38th Congress of the International Institute of Public Finance*, Detroit: Wayne State University Press

Fletcher, S.M., 1972. 'From PPBS to PAR in the Empire State', in A.C. Hyde and J.M. Shafritz (eds.), *Government Budgeting. Theory, Process, Politics*, Oak Park, IL: Moore Publishing, 2nd edn, 1978

Friedman, M., 1953. 'The methodology of positive economics', in M. Friedman, *Essays in Positive Economics*, Chicago: The University of Chicago Press.

Ginsburg, B., 1976. 'Elections and public policy', *American Political Science Review*, 70, pp. 41–9

Goetz, C.J., 1977. 'Fiscal illusion in state and local finance', in T.E. Borcherding (ed.), *Budgets and Bureaucrats*, Durham: Duke University Press

Gramlich, E., 1977. 'Intergovernmental grants', in W.E. Oates (ed.), *The Political Economy of Federalism*, Lexington: Heath

Gray, A. and B. Jenkins, 1982. 'Policy analysis in British central government: the experience of Public Administration Review', *Public Administration*, 60, pp. 429–50

Greenberg, J., 1979. 'Consistent majority rules over compact sets of alternatives', *Econometrica*, 47, pp. 627–36

Hanusch, H., 1983. 'Inefficiencies in the public sector: aspects of demand and supply', in H. Hanusch (ed.), *Anatomy of Government Deficiencies*, Berlin: Springer Verlag

Harper, E.L., F.A. Kramer and A.M. Rouse, 1969. 'Implementation and use of PPB in sixteen federal agencies', *Public Administration Review*, 29, pp. 623–32

Hatry, H.P., 1980. 'Current state of the art of local government productivity improvement and potential federal roles', in Ch.H. Levine (ed.), *Managing Fiscal Stress*, Chatham: Chatham House

1981. 'The status of productivity measurement in the public sector', in Th. Lynch (ed.), *Contemporary Public Budgeting*, New Brunswick: The Bureaucrat Inc.

Head, J.G., 1962. 'Public goods and public policy', *Public Finance*, 17, pp. 197–221

1968. 'The theory of public goods', in J.G. Head, *Public Goods and Public Welfare*, Durham: Duke University Press, 2nd edn, 1974

1974. *Public Goods and Public Welfare*, Durham: Duke University Press

Heclo, H., 1977. *A Government of Strangers. Executive Politics in Washington*, Washington, DC: The Brookings Institution

Heclo, H. and A. Wildavsky, 1974. *The Private Government of Public Money: Community and Policy inside British Political Administration*, Berkeley: University of California Press

Hettich, W., 1975. 'Bureaucrats and public goods', *Public Choice*, 21, pp. 15–25

Hicks, J.R., 1943. 'The four consumer's surpluses', *Review of Economic Studies*, 11, pp. 31–41

1956. *A Revision of Demand Theory*, Oxford: Clarendon Press

Hinich, M.J., 1986. 'Discussion of "The positive theory of legislative institutions"', *Public Choice*, 50, pp. 179–83

Hitch, Ch.J. and R.N. McKean, 1960. *The Economics of Defense in the Nuclear Age*, Cambridge, MA: Harvard University Press

Holcombe, R.G. and E.O. Price III, 1978. 'Optimality and the institutional structure of bureaucracy', *Public Choice*, 33, pp. 55–60

Hotelling, H., 1929. 'Stability in competition', *Economic Journal*, 39, pp. 41–57

Hovey, H.P., 1968. *The Planning Programming Budgeting Approach to Government Decision Making*, New York: Praeger

Jackson, P.M., 1982. *The Political Economy of Bureaucracy*, Oxford: Philip Allan

Kamlet, M.S. and D.C. Mowery, 1987. 'Influences on executive and Congressional budgetary priorities *1955–1981*', *American Political Science Review*, 81, pp. 155–78

Kamlet, M.S., D.C. Mowery and T. Su, 1988. 'Upsetting national priorities: the Reagan Administration's budgetary strategy', *American Political Science Review*, 82, pp. 1293–308

Kenny, L.W., 1978. 'The collective allocation of commodities in a democratic society: a generalization', *Public Choice*, 33 (2), pp. 117–20

Key, V.O., Jr., 1940. 'The lack of a budgetary theory', *American Political Science Review*, 34, pp. 1137–40

Kiewiet, D.R., 1991. 'Bureaucrats and budgetary outcomes: quantitative analyses', in A. Blais and S. Dion (eds.), *The Budget-Maximizing Bureaucrat. Appraisals and Evidence*, Pittsburgh: Pittsburgh University Press

Kiewiet, D.R. and M.D. McCubbins, 1985a. 'Appropriations decisions as a bilateral bargaining game between President and Congress', *Legislative Studies Quarterly*, 10, pp. 181–201

1985b. 'Congressional appropriations and the electoral connection', *Journal of Politics*, 47, pp. 59–82

Koopmans, L. and A.H.E.M. Wellink, 1971. *Overheidsfinanciën*, Leiden: Stenfert Kroese, 5th edn, 1983

Kraan, D.J., 1984. 'Towards more flexibility of government expenditure: some recent developments in the Netherlands', *Policy Sciences*, 16, pp. 413–27

Kramer, G.H., 1972. 'Sophisticated voting over multidimensional choice spaces', *Journal of Mathematical Sociology*, 2, pp. 165–80

1977. 'A dynamical model of political equilibrium', *Journal of Economic Theory*, 16, pp. 310–34

Krehbiel, K., 1988. 'Spatial models of legislative choice', *Legislative Studies Quarterly*, 13, pp. 259–319

Ladha, K., Th. Romer and H. Rosenthal, 1984. 'If at first you don't succeed: budgeting by a sequence of referenda', in H. Hanusch (ed.), *Public Finance and the Quest for Efficiency, Proceedings of the 38th Congress of the International Institute of Public Finance*, Detroit: Wayne State University Press

Larkey, P.D., C. Stolp and M. Winer, 1981. 'Theorizing about the growth and decline of government: a research assignment', *Journal of Public Policy*, 1, pp. 157–220

Lauth, Th.P., 1978. 'Zero-Base Budgeting in Georgia State Government: myth and reality', *Public Administration Review*, 38, pp. 420–30

Leibenstein, H., 1966. 'Allocative efficiency vs. X-efficiency', *American Economic Review*, 56, pp. 392–415

1978. 'On the basic proposition of X-inefficiency theory', *American Economic Review, Proceedings and Papers*, 68, pp. 328–32

Leloup, L.T., 1980. *The Fiscal Congress: Legislative Control of the Budget*, Westport, CT: Greenwood Press

Lewis, V.B., 1952. 'Toward a theory of budgeting', *Public Administration Review*, 12, pp. 43–54

Lindblom, C.E., 1959. 'The science of muddling through', *Public Administration Review*, 19, pp. 79–88

1965. *The Intelligence of Democracy: Decision Making through Mutual Adjustment*, New York: Free Press

1968. *The Policy-making Process*, Englewood Cliffs, NJ: Prentice Hall

Lord, G., 1973. *The French Budgetary Process*, Berkeley: University of California Press

Lovell, M.C., 1975. 'The collective allocation of commodities in a democratic society', *Public Choice*, 24, pp. 71–92

Luce, R.D. and H. Raiffa, 1957. *Games and Decisions*, New York: John Wiley, 7th edn, 1967

262   **References**

Lukierman, A., 1988. *Public Expenditure. Who Really Controls it and How?*, Harmondsworth: Penguin

Lynch, Th.D., 1979. *Public Budgeting in America*, Englewood Cliffs, NJ: Prentice-Hall

Lynn, L.E., 1991, 'The budget-maximizing bureaucrat: is there a case?', in A. Blais and J. Dion (eds.), *The Budget-Maximizing Bureaucrat. Appraisals and Evidence*, Pittsburgh: University of Pittsburgh Press

MacKay, R.J. and C.L. Weaver, 1978. 'Monopoly bureaus and fiscal outcomes', in G. Tullock and R.E. Wagner (eds.), *Deductive Reasoning in the Analysis of Public Policy*, Lexington: Heath

1979. 'On the mutuality of interests between bureaus and high demand review committees: a perverse result', *Public Choice*, 34, pp. 481–92

1981. 'Agenda control by budget maximizers in a multi-bureau setting', *Public Choice*, 37, pp. 447–73

Malkin, J. and A. Wildavsky, 1991. 'Why the traditional distinction between public and private goods should be abandoned', *Journal of Theoretical Politics* 3, pp. 355–78

March, J.G. and H.A. Simon, 1958. *Organizations*, New York: John Wiley

Margolis, J., 1955. 'A comment on the pure theory of public expenditure', *Review of Economics and Statistics*, 37, pp. 347–49

1975. 'Review of "Bureaucracy and Representative Government" by W.A. Niskanen', *Journal of Law and Economics*, 18, pp. 645–59

Marris. R., 1963. 'A model of managerial enterprise', *Quarterly Journal of Economics*, 77, pp. 185–209

1966. *The Economic Theory of Managerial Capitalism*, London: Macmillan

McCaffery, J., 1976. 'MBO and the federal budgetary process', *Public Administration Review*, 36, pp. 33–9

McCubbins, M. and Th. Schwarz, 1984. 'Congressional oversight overlooked: policy patrols versus fire alarms', *American Journal of Political Science*, 28, pp. 165–79

1985. 'The politics of flatland', *Public Choice*, 46, pp. 45–60

McGuire, Th.G., 1981. 'Budget-maximizing agencies: an empirical test', *Public Choice*, 36, pp. 313–22

McGuire, T., M. Coiner and L. Spancake, 1979. 'Budget maximizing agencies and efficiency in government', *Public Choice*, 34, pp. 333–58

McKean, R.N., 1958. *Efficiency in Government through System Analysis, with Emphasis on Water Resource Development*, New York: John Wiley

McKelvey, R., 1976. 'Intransitivities in multidimensional voting models and some implications for agenda control', *Journal of Economic Theory*, 12, pp. 472–82

1979. 'General conditions for global intransitivities in formal voting models', *Econometrica*, 47, pp. 1085–111

McKelvey, R.D. and P.C. Ordeshook, 1990. 'A decade of experimental research on spatial models of elections and committees', in J.M. Enelow and M.J. Hinich, *Advances in the Spatial Theory of Voting*, Cambridge: Cambridge University Press

Meerman, J., 1980. 'Are public goods public goods?', *Public Choice*, 35, pp. 45–58
Merewitz, L. and S.H. Sosnick, 1971. *The Budget's New Clothes*, Chicago: Rand McNally
Migué, J.L. and G. Bélanger, 1974. 'Toward a general theory of managerial discretion', *Public Choice*, 17, pp. 27–43; comment by W.A. Niskanen, reply by J.L. Migué, G. Bélanger, 1974, *Public Choice*, 17, pp. 43–7
Miller, G.J., 1977. 'Bureaucratic compliance as a game on the unit square', *Public Choice*, 29, pp. 37–54
Miller, G.J. and T. Moe, 1983. 'Bureaucrats, legislators and the size of government', *American Political Science Review*, 77, pp. 297–322
1986. 'The positive theory of hierarchies', in H.F. Weisberg (ed.), *Political Science: The Science of Politics*, New York: Agathon Press
Miller, N.R., 1977. 'Logrolling, vote trading and the paradox of voting: a game theoretic overview', *Public Choice*, 30, pp. 51–75
Mills, G.B. and J.C. Palmer (eds.), 1984. *Federal Budget Policy in the 1980s*, Washington: Urban Institute Press
Mises, L. von, 1944. *Bureaucracy*, New York: Arlington House, 3rd edn, 1978
Mishan, E.J., 1969. 'The relationship between joint products, collective goods and external effects', *Journal of Political Economy*, 77, pp. 329–48
1981. *Introduction to Normative Economics*, New York: Oxford University Press
Moe, T.M., 1984. 'The new economics of organization', *American Journal of Political Science*, 28, pp. 739–77
Moene, K.O., 1986. 'Types of bureaucratic interaction', *Journal of Public Economics*, 29, pp. 333–45
Mueller, D.C., 1989. *Public Choice II*, Cambridge: Cambridge University Press
Munger, M.C., 1984. 'On the mutuality of interest between bureaus and high demand review committees: the case of joint production', *Public Choice*, 43, pp. 211–17
Musgrave, R.A., 1959. *The Theory of Public Finance*, New York: McGraw-Hill
1969. 'Provision for social goods', in J. Margolis and H. Guitton (eds.), *Public Economics*, London: Macmillan
1981. 'Leviathan cometh – or does he?', in H.F. Ladd and T.N. Tideman (eds.), *Tax and Expenditure Limitations*, Washington, DC: Urban Institute Press
Musgrave, R.A. and R.B. Musgrave, 1973. *Public Finance in Theory and Practice*, Tokyo: McGraw-Hill
Musgrave, R.A. and A.T. Peacock (eds.), 1967. *Classics in the Theory of Public Finance*, London: Macmillan
National Audit Office, 1989. *The Next Steps Initiative. Report by the Controller General*, London: Her Majesty's Stationary Office
Neumann, J. von and O. Morgenstern, 1944. *Theory of Games and Economic Behavior*, Princeton: Princeton University Press, 2nd edn, 1947
Niemi, R.G., 1983. 'Why so much stability: another opinion', *Public Choice*, 41, pp. 261–70
Niskanen, W.A., 1968. 'The peculiar economics of bureaucracy', *American Economic Review*, 58, pp. 293–305

1971. *Bureaucracy and Representative Government*, Chicago: Aldine-Atherton

1975. 'Bureaucrats and politicians', *Journal of Law and Economics*, 18, pp. 617–43

1991. 'A reflection on bureaucracy and representative government', in A. Blais and S. Dion (eds.), *The Budget-Maximizing Bureaucrat*, Pittsburgh: Pittsburgh University Press

Nispen tot Pannerden, F.K.M. van, 1993. *Het Dossier Heroverweging*, Delft: Eburon

Novick, D. (ed.), 1965. *Program Budgeting*, Cambridge, MA: Harvard University Press

   1968. 'The origin and history of program budgeting', *California Management Review*, 11, pp. 7–12

Olson, M., 1965. *The Logic of Collective Action*, Cambridge, MA: Harvard University Press

Ordeshook, P.C., 1976. 'The spatial theory of elections: a review and critique', in I. Budge, I. Crewe and D. Farlie (eds.), *Party Identification and Beyond*, New York: Wiley

   1980. 'Political disequilibrium and scientific inquiry', *American Political Science Review*, 74, pp. 447–51

   1986. *Game Theory and Political Theory*, Cambridge: Cambridge University Press

Ordeshook, P.C. and K.A. Shepsle (eds.), 1982. *Political Equilibrium*, Boston: Kluwer Nijhoff

Orzechowkski, W., 1977. 'Economic models of bureaucracy: survey, extensions and evidence', in Th.E. Borcherding (ed.), *Budgets and Bureaucrats*, Durham: Duke University Press

Ostrom, E., 1986. 'An agenda for the study of institutions', *Public Choice*, 48, pp. 3–25

Owen, G., 1982. *Game Theory*, New York: Academic Press

Pack, J.R., 1990. 'The determinants of the choice between public and private production of a publicly funded service reconsidered', *Public Choice*, 66, pp. 183–8

Page, B., 1978. *Choice and Echoes in Presidential Elections: Rational Man in Electoral Democracy*, Chicago: Chicago University Press

Parkinson, C.N., 1957. *Parkinson's Law*, Boston: Houghton Mifflin

Peacock, A.T., 1972. 'New methods of appraising government expenditure: an economic analysis', *Public Finance*, 27, pp. 85–91

   1980. 'On the anatomy of collective failure', *Public Finance*, pp. 33–4

Pennock, J.R., 1970. 'The pork barrel and majority rule: a note', *Journal of Politics*, 32, pp. 709–16

Peters, B.G., 1978. *The Politics of Bureaucracy*, New York: Longman, 3rd edn, 1989

   1988. *Comparing Public Bureaucracies*, Tuscaloosa: University of Alabama Press

   1991. 'The European bureaucrat: the applicability of "Bureaucracy and Representative Government" to non-American settings', in A. Blais and S. Dion (eds.), *The Budget-Maximizing Bureaucrat*, Pittsburgh: Pittsburgh University Press

Pigou, A.C., 1920. *The Economics of Welfare*, London: Macmillan

Plott, Ch.R., 1967. 'A notion of equilibrium and its possibility under majority rule', *American Economic Review*, 57, pp. 787–806

Pyhrr, P.A., 1970. 'Zero-Base-Budgeting', *Harvard Business Review*, 48, pp. 111–21

    1973. *Zero-Base-Budgeting*, New York: John Wiley

    1977. 'The zero-base approach to government budgeting', *Public Administration Review*, 37, pp. 1–8

Rapoport, A., 1970. *N-person Game Theory*, Ann Arbor: University of Michigan Press

Recktenwald, H.C., 1983. 'Potential welfare losses in the public sector. Anatomy of the nature and causes', in H. Hanusch (ed.), *Anatomy of Government Deficiencies*, Berlin: Springer Verlag

    1984. 'The public waste syndrome: a comprehensive theory of government failures', in H. Hanusch (ed.), *Public Finance and the Quest for Efficiency. Proceedings of the 38th Congress of the International Institute of Public Finance*, Detroit: Wayne State University Press

Riker, W.H., 1980. 'Implications from the disequilibrium of majority rule for the study of institutions', *American Political Science Review*, 74, pp. 432–46

Riker, W.H. and S.J. Brams, 1973. 'The paradox of vote trading', *American Political Science Review*, 67, pp. 1235–47; comments by P. Bernholz and G. Tullock, reply by W.H. Riker, S.J. Brams, 1974, *American Political Science Review*, 68, pp. 1687–92

Riker, W.H. and P.C. Ordeshook, 1973. *An Introduction to Positive Political Theory*, Englewood Cliffs, NJ: Prentice-Hall

Robert, H.M., 1893. *Robert's Rules of Order*, New York: Berkeley Publishing Group, 1977

Robertson, D., 1976. *A Theory of Party Competition*, London: John Wiley

Robinson, A. 1980. *Parliament and Public Spending*, London: Heinemann

Romer, Th. and H. Rosenthal, 1978. 'Political resource allocation, controlled agendas and the status quo', *Public Choice*, 33, pp. 27–44

    1979. 'Bureaucrats versus voters: on the political economy of resource allocation by direct democracy', *Quarterly Journal of Economics*, 93, pp. 563–87

Rose, R., 1977. 'Implementation and evaporation: the record of MBO', *Public Administration Review*, 37, pp. 64–71

Rowley, Ch.K., 1978. 'Market "failure" and government "failure"', in J.M. Buchanan (ed.), *The Economics of Politics*, London: Institute of Economic Affairs

Russet, B.M., 1969. 'Who pays for defense?', *American Political Science Review*, 63, pp. 412–26

Samuelson, P.A., 1954. 'The pure theory of public expenditure', *Review of Economics and Statistics*, 36, pp. 387–9

    1955. 'Diagrammatic exposition of a theory of public expenditure', *Review of Economics and Statistics*, 37, pp. 350–6

    1958. 'Aspects of public expenditure theories', *Review of Economics and Statistics*, 40, pp. 332–8

1969a. 'Pure theory of public expenditure and taxation', in J. Margolis and H. Guitton (eds.), *Public Economics*, London: Macmillan.

1969b. 'Contrast between welfare conditions for joint supply and for public goods', *Review of Economics and Statistics*, 51, pp. 26–30

Savas, E.S., 1982. *Privatization of the Public Sector: How to Shrink Government?*, Chatham: Chatham House

1987. *Privatization: The Key to a Better Government*, Chatham: Chatham House

Schelling, Th.C., 1978. *Micromotives and Macrobehavior*, New York: Norton

Schick, A., 1966. 'The road to PPB: the stages of budget reform', *Public Administration Review*, 26, pp. 243–58

1969. 'Systems politics and systems budgeting', *Public Administration Review*, 29, pp. 137–51

1973. 'A death in the bureaucracy: the demise of federal PPB', *Public Administration Review*, 33, pp. 146–56

1978. 'The road from ZBB', *Public Administration Review*, 38, pp. 177–80

1980. *Money and Congress*, Washington, DC: Urban Institute Press

Schneider, M., 1989. 'Intergovernmental competition, budget maximizing bureaucrats and the level of suburban competition', *American Journal of Political Science*, 33, pp. 612–28

Schofield, N., 1978. 'Instability of simple dynamic games', *Review of Economic Studies*, 55, pp. 575–94

Schofield, N., B. Grofman and S.L. Feld, 1988. 'The core and the stability of group choice in spatial voting games', *American Political Science Review*, 82, pp. 195–212

Schultze, Ch.L., 1968. *The Politics and Economics of Public Spending*, Washington, DC: The Brookings Institution

Scott Fosler, R., 1980. 'Local government productivity: political and administrative potential', in Ch.H. Levine and I. Rubin (eds.), *Fiscal Stress and Public Policy*, Beverly Hills: Sage

Shapley, L.S., 1962. 'Simple games', *Behavioral Science*, 7, pp. 59–66

Sharkansky, I., 1968. *Spending in the American States*, Chicago: Rand McNally

1969. *The Politics of Taxing and Spending*, Indianapolis: Bobbs Merrill

Shepsle, K.A., 1979. 'Institutional arrangements and equilibrium in multidimensional voting models', *American Journal of Political Science*, 23, pp. 27–59

1986a. 'Institutional equilibrium and equilibrium institutions', in H.F. Weisberg (ed.), *Political Science: The Science of Politics*, New York: Agathon Press

1986b. 'The positive theory of legislative institutions: an enrichment of social choice and spatial models', *Public Choice*, 50, pp. 138–78.

Shepsle, K.A. and R.N. Cohen, 1990. 'Multiparty competition, entry, and deterrence in spatial models of elections', in J.M. Enelow and M.J. Hinich (eds.), *Advances in the Spatial Theory of Voting*, Cambridge: Cambridge University Press

Shepsle, K.A. and B.R. Weingast, 1981a. 'Structure induced equilibrium and legislative choice', *Public Choice*, 37, pp. 503–20

1981b. 'Political preferences for the pork barrel: a generalization', *American Journal of Political Science*, 25, pp. 97–111

Sherwood, F.P. and W.J. Page, 1976. 'MBO and public management', *Public Administration Review*, 36, pp. 5–12

Shubik, M., 1982. *Game Theory in the Social Sciences. Concepts and Solutions*, Cambridge, MA: MIT Press

Simon, H.A., 1945. *Administrative Behavior: A Study of Decision-making Processes in Administrative Organization*, New York: Free Press

1957. *Models of Man*, New York: Wiley

1959. 'Theories of decision making in economics and behavioral science', *American Economic Review*, 49, pp. 253–83

1960. *The New Science of Management Decision*, New York: Prentice-Hall, 2nd edn, 1977

Sjoquist, D., 1982. 'The effect of the number of local governments on central city expenditures', *National Tax Journal*, 35, pp. 79–88

Slutsky, S., 1979. 'Equilibrium under x-majority voting', *Econometrica*, 47, pp. 1113–25

Smith, A., 1776. *The Wealth of Nations*, London: Dent, 1975

Smithies, A., 1941. 'Optimum location in spatial competition', *Journal of Political Economy*, 49, pp. 584–99

Spann, R.M., 1974. 'Collective consumption of private goods', *Public Choice*, 20, pp. 63–82

Stockman, D.A., 1986. *The Triumph of Politics. Why the Reagan Revolution Failed*, New York: Harper & Row

Sullivan, J. and E. Uslaner, 1978. 'Congressional behavior and electoral marginality', *American Journal of Political Science*, 22, pp. 536–33

Tarschys, D., 1975. 'The growth of public expenditures: nine modes of explanation', *Scandinavian Political Studies*, 10, pp. 9–31

Taylor, G.M., 1977. 'Introduction to Zero-Base-Budgeting', *The Bureaucrat*, 6, pp. 33–5

Thompson, E.A., 1973. 'Review of "Bureaucracy and Representative Government" by W.A. Niskanen', *Journal of Economic Literature*, 11, pp. 950–3

Thompson, F. and R. Williams, 1979. 'A horse race around a Mobius strip: a review and a test of utility maximizing and organizational process models of public expenditure decisions', *Policy Sciences*, 22, pp. 119–42

Tiebout, Ch., 1956. 'The pure theory of local expenditure', *Journal of Political Economy*, 64, pp. 416–24

Toirkens, J., 1988. *Schijn en Werkelijkheid van het Bezuinigingsbeleid 1975–1986*, Deventer: Kluwer

Treasury, Efficiency Unit, 1988. *Improving Management in Government: the Next Steps*, London: Her Majesty's Stationary Office

1991. *Making the most of Next Steps*, London: Her Majesty's Stationery Office

Tulkens, H., 1978. 'Dynamic processes for allocating public goods: an institution oriented survey', *Journal of Public Economies*, 9, pp. 163–201

Tullock, G., 1959. 'Problems of majority voting', *Journal of Political Economy*, 67, pp. 571–9; comment by A. Downs, reply by G. Tullock, 1961, *Journal of Political Economy*, 69, pp. 200–3

1965. *The Politics of Bureaucracy*, Washington, DC: Public Affairs Press

1967a. 'The general irrelevance of the general impossibility theorem', *Quarterly Journal of Economics*, 81, pp. 256–70

1967b. *Towards a Mathematics of Politics*, Ann Arbor: University of Michigan Press

1970a. *Private Wants, Public Means. An Economic Analysis of the Desirable Scope of Government*, New York: Basic Books

1970b. 'Review of "Bureaucracy and Representative Government" by W.A. Niskanen', *Public Choice*, 12, pp. 119–24

1970c. 'A simple algebraic logrolling model', *American Economic Review*, 60, pp. 419–26

1981. 'Why so much stability?', *Public Choice*, 37, pp. 189–205

Tullock, G. and T. Tideman, 1976. 'A new and superior process for making social choices', *Journal of Political Economy*, 84, pp. 1145–60

Vickers, J. and G. Yarrow, 1988. *Privatization: An Economic Analysis*, Cambridge, MA: MIT Press

Wagner, R.E., 1976. 'Revenue structure, fiscal illusion and budgetary choice', *Public Choice*, 25, pp. 45–61

Wander, W.Th., F.T. Herbert and G.W. Copeland (eds.), 1984. *Congressional Budgeting*, Baltimore: Johns Hopkins University Press

Weber, M., 1921. *Wirtschaft und Gesellschaft, Erster Teil*, New York: Free Press, 1947

1948. *From Max Weber: Essays in Sociology*, New York: Routledge, 1991

Weingast, B.R., 1979. 'A rational choice perspective on Congressional norms', *American Journal of Political Science*, 23, pp. 245–62

1984. 'A principal–agent perspective on Congressional–bureaucratic relations', *Public Choice*, 44, pp. 147–91

White, J. and A. Wildavsky, 1989. *The Deficit and the Public Interest: The Search for Responsible Budgeting in the 1980s*, Berkeley: University of California Press

Wildavsky, A., 1961. 'Political implications of budget reform', *Public Administration Review*, 21, pp. 183–90

1964. *The Politics of the Budgetary Process*, Boston: Little, Brown

1966. 'The political economy of efficiency: cost–benefit analysis, systems-analysis and program-budgeting', *Public Administration Review*, 26, pp. 292–310

1975. *Budgeting: A Comparative Theory of Budgetary Processes*, Boston: Little, Brown

1980. *How to Limit Government Spending*, Berkeley: University of California Press

1988. *The New Politics of the Budgetary Process*, Glenview, IL: Scott, Foresman

Williamson, O.E., 1963. 'Managerial discretion and business behavior', *American Economic Review*, 53, pp. 1032–57

1964. *The Economics of Discretionary Behavior: Managerial Objectives in a Theory of the Firm*, Englewood Cliffs, NJ: Prentice-Hall

Wittman, D.A., 1973. 'Parties as utility maximizers', *American Political Science Review*, 67, pp. 490–8

1977. 'Candidates with policy preferences: a dynamic model', *Journal of Economic Theory*, 14, pp. 180–9

1983. 'Candidate motivation: a synthesis of alternative theories', *American Political Science Review*, 77, pp. 142–57

1990. 'Spatial strategies when candidates have policy preferences', in J.M. Enelow and M.J. Hinich (eds.), *Advances in the Spatial Theory of Voting*, Cambridge: Cambridge University Press

Wolf, Ch., Jr., 1979. 'A theory of non-market failure: framework for implementation analysis', *Journal of Law and Economics*, 22, pp. 107–39

1983. 'Non-market failure revisited: anatomy and physiology of government deficiencies', in H. Hanusch (ed.), *Anatomy of Government Deficiencies*, Berlin: Springer Verlag

1988. *Markets or Governments: Choosing Between Imperfect Alternatives*, Cambridge, MA: MIT Press

Wyckof, P.G., 1990. 'The simple analytics of slack-maximizing bureaucracy', *Public Choice*, 67, pp. 35–49

Young, R.A., 1991. 'Budget size and bureaucratic carreers', in A. Blais and S. Dion (eds.), *The Budget-Maximizing Bureaucrat*, Pittsburgh: University of Pittsburgh Press

Index

270